# The Cambridge Platonists
# A Brief Introduction

*With Eight Letters
of Dr. Antony Tuckney
and Dr. Benjamin Whichcote*

Edited by Tod E. Jones
Translations by Sara Elise Phang

University Press of America,® Inc.
Dallas · Lanham · Boulder · New York · Oxford

Copyright © 2005 by
University Press of America,® Inc.
4501 Forbes Boulevard
Suite 200
Lanham, Maryland 20706
UPA Acquisitions Department (301) 459-3366

PO Box 317
Oxford
OX2 9RU, UK

All rights reserved
Printed in the United States of America
British Library Cataloging in Publication Information Available

Library of Congress Control Number: 2004104335
ISBN 0-7618-2873-7 (hardcover : alk. ppr.)
ISBN 0-7618-2874-5 (paperback : alk. ppr.)

∞™ The paper used in this publication meets the minimum
requirements of American National Standard for Information
Sciences—Permanence of Paper for Printed Library Materials,
ANSI Z39.48—1984

# Contents

| | |
|---|---|
| Preface | v |
| Acknowledgments | ix |
| **The Cambridge Platonists: A Brief Introduction** | 1 |
|    I   From Pre-Reformation to Pre-Restoration: The Social-Historical and Theological Context | 3 |
|    II   Principle Persons and Representative Ideas | 15 |
|    III   Reception | 37 |
|    Notes | 43 |
| ***Eight Letters of Dr. Antony Tuckney and Dr. Benjamin Whichcote*** | 51 |
|    Editorial Notes and Abbreviations | 52 |
|    Translator's Note | 53 |
|    Title Page of the 1753 Edition | 54 |
|    Preface by Samuel Salter | 55 |
|    **Letter I** | 71 |
|    **Letter II** | 75 |
|    **Letter III** | 83 |
|    **Letter IV** | 97 |
|    **Letter V** | 115 |

*Contents*

| | |
|---|---|
| **Letter VI** | 133 |
| **Letter VII** | 153 |
| **Letter VIII** | 155 |
| Bibliography | 157 |
| Index | 161 |
| About the Author | 165 |

# Preface

The first part of this book, *The Cambridge Platonists: A Brief Introduction*, evolved out of my work on the Broad Church movement of the nineteenth century. One cannot get very far into liberal Anglican thought, even that of moderns, without coming across references to the thought and work of the liberal or latitudinarian divines of the seventeenth century. I soon realized that, if I was to understand the Broad Church, I would first have to explore the Anglican precursors to that movement. What I discovered was so vast a mine of precious ore that I could entertain no further doubts as to the origin of the jewels that gave the Church of England its brilliance. It seemed as though there was to be no end of my digging, and my colleagues began to wonder whether I was ever to emerge. I did, and I do still consider myself a Victorianist, but—like the Victorian churchmen that I have admired and written about—I find myself personally enriched whenever I return to the still depths of that now largely neglected mine.

I have attempted to write the sort of *Brief Introduction* to the Cambridge Platonists that I myself might have benefitted from when I first began my search. It is written with the amateur and the novice theologian in mind, and aims to provide context as well as description, while outlining the most representative ideas of the school with clarity and brevity. I expect that, for many of my readers, this Introduction will meet their immediate needs, and they may choose to read no further. However, for those who wish to press onward and to read a selection from the writings of the Cambridge Platonists, the *Eight Letters of Dr. Antony Tuckney and Dr. Benjamin Whichcote* is a good text with which to begin. Not only do these letters offer a logical starting point in that they present some of the most characteristic ideas of the founding member of the school—which are further illustrated in this edition by copious quotations from the printed works of Whichcote—but they also help to clarify what sets the Cambridge Platonists apart from the dominant contemporary strain of religious thought in England.

This book is not a collection of the writings of the Cambridge Platonists. Since Matthew Arnold, in 1876, observed the need for such an anthology, several have been published, each with its unique strengths. First, E. T. Campagnac, Assistant-Lecturer in Classics at University College, Cardiff, released *The Cambridge Platonists: Being Selections from the Writings of Benjamin Whichcote, John Smith, and Nathaniel Culverwel* (Oxford: Clarendon Press, 1901). In his Introduction, Campagnac argues that these three authors, in this order, best represent the philosophical development of the school, a contention that I plainly take issue with in my own Introduction. Nevertheless, this collection is of value in that it presents a good selection of the works of Whichcote and two of his students, who each took from their master and developed his ideas in different directions. Several decades passed before a second anthology appeared, *The Cambridge Platonists*, edited by Gerald R. Cragg (New York: Oxford University Press, 1968). Cragg not only selected readings from a broader range of authors, including major and minor figures from within the school, but organized the selections according to their subject matter. While one can learn much about the Cambridge Platonists from such a collection as this, the readings are only excerpts, with the spelling modernized, and with the Latin and Greek passages either excised, translated, or left untranslated, as the editor deemed appropriate. Cragg's anthology was released while a third was already in the hands of the printers. This last anthology is *The Cambridge Platonists*, edited by C. A. Patrides (Cambridge, Mass: Harvard University Press, 1969), a selection of complete texts from the most representative thinkers of the school. Patrides chose to neither modernize the English nor to excise any Latin or Greek passages, but rather to add English translations in places where they were most needed. Patrides's respect for the integrity of the texts, along with his copious and scholarly notes, makes this collection also the most valuable for serious students. In my *Brief Introduction*, where quotations from the Cambridge Platonists are given, I have, whenever possible, referred the reader to both the original publication and to the text as it appears in the Patrides anthology.

I am pleased to offer to the reader the first complete edition of the *Eight Letters of Dr. Antony Tuckney and Dr. Benjamin Whichcote*, since its original publication by Samuel Salter in 1753. The correspondence took place within a two-month period, between September 8 and November 3, 1651. The letters that remained in the hands of Whichcote were not all autographs. It is clear from the letters themselves that duplicates were made, and sometimes by the recipient rather than the sender. Moreover, when the literary remains of Whichcote came into the possession of John Jeffery, the Archdeacon carefully recopied by hand each of the letters, after which the originals disappeared. Upon the Archdeacon's death, his papers were recovered by his brother, who made an additional copy of the letters. Eventually, the literary remains of Jeffery fell into the capable hands of Samuel Salter, who discovered at least one copy of the letters and, recognizing their importance, published them in the condition that he found them, together with explanatory notes and a substantial Preface. Still, due to the manner in which the *Eight Letters* were published, they remained virtually unknown, for Salter had annexed them, with a separate title page, and almost as an afterthought, to *Moral and Religious Aphorisms, Collected from the Manuscript Papers of the Reverend and Learned Doctor Whichcote, and Published in MDCCIII by Dr. Jeffery; Now Republished, with Very Large Additions, from the Transcripts of the Latter, by Samuel Salter,*

*Preface*

D.D. (London: Printed for J. Payne, 1753). The first part of this book, the *Moral and Religious Aphorisms*, was republished in 1930 "*literatim* from that of 1753," with a new Intro-duction by W. R. Inge; however, neither in this Introduction nor in any other part of this book is there any mention of the *Eight Letters*. Once again, it seemed that the letters were doomed to obscurity. Finally, as noted above, G. R. Cragg, in 1968, published brief excerpts from the first three of Whichcote's letters (Letters II, IV, and VI), for which he wrote a Preface. The edition of the *Eight Letters* that you now hold in your hands is not only entire, including Salter's notes and Preface of 1753, but adds, for the first time, an English translation of every passage and word in Greek and Latin.

Tod E. Jones

College Park, Maryland
January 23, 2004

# Acknowledgments

This book would never have materialized without the encouragement and support of my wife, Karen. Her faith in the merit of my work, and her willingness to frequently place my professional interests above her own were essential factors in the completion of this work. I must also acknowledge the contributions of Professor William S. Peterson of the University of Maryland, College Park, and the late Reverend Dr. Charles P. Price, Professor Emeritus of Virginia Theological Seminary. Both read my manuscript on the Cambridge Platonists and added valuable suggestions for improvement. I also want to publicly thank Dr. Sara Elise Phang, a distinguished alumnus of Columbia University, for contributing her translating skills toward the production of this new edition of the *Eight Letters*.

# The Cambridge Platonists

## *A Brief Introduction*

Tod E. Jones

# I
# From Pre-Reformation to Pre-Restoration: The Social-Historical and Theological Context

The mid-seventeenth-century school of thought that goes by the name of Cambridge Platonism defies the simple definition, but we could do much worse than identify it as a renaissance movement within the early modern period, an effort to revive the culture of religious humanism that had been first introduced into Cambridge by John Fisher and Erasmus.[1] If we consider the social impact of these and other evangelical humanists and moralists of the sixteenth century, such as William Grocyn, Thomas Linacre, and Thomas More, it may seem odd that, after so brief a period, evangelical humanism would require resuscitation. But, then, we need only recollect that the 130-year interim that separates Erasmus from the Cambridge Platonists is largely dominated by the tumult of the Protestant Reformation, against which the mild Platonic disposition of calm reflection and critical detachment could hardly compete. Because the Erasmian spirit had not been passed down as an heirloom to the succeeding generation, the Cambridge Platonists had to reclaim the rights of rational thought and catholic moderation in relation to religion. Bishop Gilbert Burnet (1643-1715) notes that "this set of men at Cambridge studied to assert and examine the principles of religion and morality on clear grounds and in a philosophical method," and so were branded by "men of narrower thoughts and fiercer tempers" as latitudinarians, Socinians, and atheists.[2] Burnet's *History of My Own Times* underscores the importance of the Cambridge Platonists, particularly as their influence contributed to the forming of a policy of toleration within the Church of England.[3]

It is a tortuous route that the history of ideas must travel if it would connect the Florentine Renaissance with the Cambridge School of Platonists. During the period between Erasmus's departure from Cambridge and Cromwell's rise to power, England underwent a revolution, not just politically, but culturally in nearly every conceivable way, and—although we cannot hope to do justice to history in this brief introduction—we cannot understand the relevance of the Cambridge school unless we first have before us a broad outline of England's transformation.

When John Colet began his Oxford lectures on St. Paul's Epistles in 1496, he had just returned from Italy, where he had associated with the scholar most responsible for returning scriptural interpretation to a pre-Augustinian, Platonist foundation. The Italian humanist Marsilio Ficino, in *De Religione Christiana* (1477), had created a synthesis of Christianity and the third-century Greek mysticism of Plotinus (204-270). Both Plotinus and Origen had been students of Ammonius Saccas, but unlike Origen, Plotinus thought of himself as a loyal and undeviating Platonist, and the system that he expounded in the *Enneads* is recognized sometimes as "Platonism" in the sense that it is an interpretive elaboration of Plato. Indeed, what is generally referred to as "Christian Platonism" is the peculiar form of Platonism either adopted from the Alexandrian Church Fathers, Clement and Origen, or through a composite of St. Paul and Plotinus, as was most successfully elaborated by Ficino. Colet's Oxford lectures contained scattered references to Ficino, and perhaps the most significant difference between Colet and the Florentine Academy was the emphasis that Colet placed on the *imitatio Christi*. It is not merely that this emphasis makes Colet more Pauline than Platonic, but that it imbues Colet's work with a practical and moral purpose, as opposed to the prevalent intellectualism of the Academy.

To whatever extent the Florentine Academy had spread its influence over Colet, it was not as diffusive as the influence of Colet upon Erasmus. This is evident, of course, in Erasmus's subsequent labors on the Greek New Testament and in his adoption of Colet as a model of the humanist reformer. However, it might also be detected in the fact that, after his visits with Colet in 1505 and 1506, Erasmus chose to spend the following three years in Italy, where the spirit of Ficino and Pico della Mirandola still survived in the Florentine Academy, before he returned to England in 1509. What Colet had sought to do for Oxford, Erasmus and John Fisher were to do for Cambridge. Fisher, who had become in 1504 not only Bishop of Rochester but also Chancellor of Cambridge, had a reputation as a great preacher and, in fact, established the prominence of the pulpit in the tradition of the university. He founded a Greek lectureship at St. John's and gave Erasmus a standing appointment as a Lecturer. Together, Erasmus and Fisher brought Christian humanism, including a reverence for Plato, to Cambridge, and their work actually had a more lasting impact than Colet's, whose influence at Oxford was, sadly, overshadowed and smothered by the prevailing scholasticism.[4]

Even so, the Reformation in England and the combined force of Luther's *De Servo Arbitrio* (*Bondage of the Will*, 1525) and Calvin's *Christianæ Religionis Institutio* (popularly known as *The Institutes*, 1536-59) quickly gained ascendance over the Christian Platonist doctrine of self-determination. The influence of the Florentine Academy, throughout the greater part of the sixteenth century, was nearly lost to English theology. The imagination may even recognize a foreshadowing of this succession of ideas in two major events that transpired in the city of Basel in 1536. There the young Calvin and the aged Erasmus unwittingly came together, the one to publish the first edition of *The Institutes* in March, the other to die four months afterwards. Nevertheless, the Florentine school continued to survive, and vitally so, in Elizabethan poetry, most obviously in the poetry of

Cambridge graduate Sir Edmund Spenser, whose *Færie Queene* (1596) is, to some extent at least, Neo-Platonist allegory.[5]

Before Elizabeth came to power, during the counter-Reformation of Mary Tudor (1553-1558), the persecution of Protestants resulted in the voluntary exile of a considerable body of clergymen. Whether they settled with Miles Coverdale, Bishop of Exeter, in Geneva, or with John Knox, former Chaplain to Edward VI, in Frankfurt, the result was often the same. As a rule, these refugees did not return to England with anti-Puritan views; however, every rule has its exception. In this case, perhaps the most notable exception appears in John Jewel (1522-1571), who accompanied Edwin Sandys, Vice-Chancellor of Cambridge, during his exile in Frankfurt and was later appointed Bishop of Salisbury by Elizabeth. Even with such exceptions, the combined influence of Calvinism and Lutheranism was formidable on the continent, especially where Protestants had been persecuted, and—after Mary had done her best to reinstate Romanism in England—the pendulum was entitled to a full swing on the island as well.

Richard Hooker (1553/54-1600) was born during the first year of Mary's reign. Although the son of a laborer, he was fortunate in his relations. When his superior intellect and good character were brought to the attention of his uncle, John Hooker, Chamberlain of Exeter, that gentleman proved himself worthy of his rank and title by using them to secure the patronage of Bishop Jewel. Jewel arranged for the fifteen-year-old Hooker to be made clerk for William Cole, President of Corpus Christi, Oxford. In this capacity he remained for three years, during which time he "attained unto a perfection in all the learned languages; by the help of which, an excellent tutor, and his unintermitted studies, he had made the subtilty of all the arts easy and familiar to him, and useful for the discovery of such learning as lay hid from common searchers."[6] At the age of nineteen, Hooker was admitted to the college as a Scholar, and in 1577 he was elected as fellow. He retained his fellowship until he married at the end of 1584, and within a few months preferment came to him in the form of a life-time appointment as Master of the Temple, in London. It was here that Hooker was to enter into controversy with Walter Travers, Lecturer at the Temple, a close friend and follower of the leading Puritan divine and advocate of presbyterian government, Thomas Cartwright.

Izaak Walton suggests that Travers's opposition to Hooker stemmed as much from professional jealousy as from theological difference, for Travers had hoped that he would be promoted to the mastership when the position fell vacant. In any event, from the moment that Hooker began his morning sermons, Travers began to oppose his preaching, so that it came to be said, "The forenoon Sermon spake Canterbury, and the afternoon Geneva."[7] Finally, Archbishop Whitgift censured Travers, prohibiting him from entering the pulpit, but Travers—contumacious fellow that he was—responded by publishing a petition of grievance, which had the design to disgrace both Whitgift and Hooker. In 1586 the Master of the Temple recognized that duty directed him to make a definitive and public response, and so he wrote an Answer, which was to become the Preface to his *Of the Laws of Ecclesiastical Polity*.

Hooker declares that, after careful consideration of Cartwright's arguments and comparison of them with the statements of Scripture, he had arrived at this two-fold conclusion: first, "the present form of church-government which the laws of this land have established is such, as no law of God nor reason of man hath hitherto been alleged of force sufficient to prove they do ill, who to the uttermost of their power withstand the alteration thereof"; second, "the other, which instead of it we are required to accept, is only by error and misconceit named the ordinance of Jesus Christ."[8] In order to arrive at this determination, Hooker had to ascertain the distinctions that separate human and divine law and, more fundamentally, the providence of reason, not only as a guide in making such distinctions, but also in the very making of human laws. As Basil Willey observes, Hooker's "immediate polemical aim" is "to determine to which of these two spheres, the Natural or the Supernatural, the business of Church polity belongs."[9] According to Cartwright and Travers, it belongs to Revelation; according to Hooker, it belongs to Nature or Reason.

Hooker is willing to enter into controversy with the Puritans, not because this issue is of any importance to spiritual well-being, but because his antagonists, who evidently think it is, are willing to contradict established authorities and strengthen their resistance by uniting themselves into conventicles and secret leagues of association. Hooker prophetically foresaw that, if the dissenters would not "labour under the same yoke, as men that look for the same eternal reward," but would instead "spend our few and wretched days in a tedious prosecuting of wearisome contentions," the ultimate end of the feud "will be heavy even on both sides."[10] Of course, in order to persuade the Puritans to his understanding, Hooker would have to write no less than eight books, and—having obtained leave from Whitgift to do so—this was the occupation of the remainder of his life.

Book I of Hooker's *Polity*, published along with the Preface, and Books II, III, and IV in 1594, is essential prefatory reading to any study of the context of Cambridge Platonism. Although Hooker's epistemology and psychology are rooted in Aristotle and scholasticism, there is, nevertheless, substantial agreement in their theory of Reason once they move beyond its point of origin. For Hooker, human understanding operates on two levels, that of "sensible knowledge," which knowledge humanity shares with other animals, and "natural reason." Reason makes its first appearance with maturity, and—with "the right helps of true art and learning"—is capable of developing beyond our experience. Reason discerns between truth and error, good and evil. "Goodness," says Hooker, "is seen with the eye of the understanding. And the light of that eye, is reason."[11] Indeed, were Reason unfettered in its development, humans would quickly mature to perfection and "the greatest conformity with God."[12] However, there are two general impediments to perfection. First, while "the object of the Will is that good which Reason doth lead us to seek," Appetite or Passion responds only to sensible knowledge, so that

"Appetite is the Will's solicitor, and the Will is Appetite's controller," so that the two do often contend against each other. The Will is free to pursue the good only when Appetite is fully subordinate. Second, although the light of the understanding is Reason, "goodness is seen with the eye of the understanding," and so it is identified by appearance merely. Since "Goodness doth not move [the Will] by being, but by being apparent," it often happens that a greater good is neglected in favor of a lesser good.[13]

For Hooker, human reason is consubstantial with the divine Reason and is nothing less than a bond of communication between Creator and creation. Therefore, he can declare with assurance, "The general and perpetual voice of men is as the sentence of God himself. For that which all men have at all times learned, Nature herself must needs have taught; and God being the author of Nature, her voice is but his instrument."[14] The Laws of Reason are evident and irresistible to a good man, such a one who has not dimmed the light of Reason through bad habits. They are known without the aid of supernatural Revelation, and although Revelation may add its testimony "to the natural assent of reason concerning the certainty of them," it cannot reject them as unnecessary.[15] What, then, is the purpose of Revelation? It is given to teach humanity how the perfection that is naturally desired is to be supernaturally attained. The object of Revelation is to declare in plain words all that is necessary to salvation and that cannot be ascertained by means of Reason. "It sufficeth therefore," concludes Hooker, "that Nature and Scripture do serve in such full sort, that they both jointly, and not severally either of them, be so complete that unto everlasting felicity we need not the knowledge of any thing more than these two may easily furnish our minds with on all sides."[16] Clearly, if Church polity is not a matter necessary to salvation, then it is not the object of Revelation to define it and declare it as a law binding upon all generations, and, therefore, human understanding may determine a polity that is best suited for a people's needs.

Cartwright and Travers were both fellows of Trinity College, Cambridge. In fact, Cartwright had been for three years Lady Margaret Professor of Divinity until deprived of his fellowship by the staunch episcopalian John Whitgift, Master of Trinity, in 1570. The tension at Cambridge between the Puritans and the humanists during the time of Hooker—that "God-centered Humanist"[17]—is dramatically depicted by Christopher Marlowe, who after graduating with an M.A. from Corpus Christi College, Cambridge, in 1587, wrote several dramas, his most well known being *Dr. Faustus* (publ. 1604). Faustus is a humanist scholar and magician whose insatiable quest for power in the form of knowledge leads him to sell his soul to Mephistopheles, a devil. Marlowe is not, of course, condemning humanism outright, but is rather recognizing the inherent danger of humanism in its appeal to intellectual pride. There is even less evidence to recommend the idea that Marlowe was condemning Platonism, or even that Faustus is a Platonist; rather, as C. S. Lewis suggests, Faustus, as a magician, can more profitably be understood as a type of Baconian empiricist, divorcing God in order to subdue reality and extract "facts."[18]

It needs to be noted here that the typical English humanist of the early seventeenth century, if he embraced Platonism at all, did not likely endorse Plotinian self-determination. He was simply a classicist who did not consider religion and philosophy necessarily at odds with each other. Moreover, the English Puritan of that period was by no means an anti-intellectual, but his profound distrust of the human condition inclined him to look askance at mental labors that might distract from religious devotion or arouse religious doubts. In fact, the humanist and the Puritan "were often the same people, and nearly always the same sort of people: the young men 'in the Movement,' the impatient progressives demanding a 'clean sweep.'"[19] During this period they stood together in their common disapprobation of the old school, the scholasticism that the universities were slow to abandon. Even John Milton, who took his M.A. from Christ's College, Cambridge, in 1632, complained of the Aristotelian cobwebs that still cluttered the halls of divinity. It was not until the 1640s, the same years that Cambridge Platonism began as a distinct movement, that the modern thought of Francis Bacon and Descartes were introduced into Cambridge lecture halls.

Respect for the classics was insufficient, in itself, to ensure the survival of a theology that allowed for self-determination, and most of the English humanists during the late sixteenth and early seventeenth centuries were also Calvinists. John Hales, who graduated from Corpus Christi College in 1603, was typical of the Englishman in his Calvinist theology. He was, perhaps, "the most liberal-minded" of Anglicans who were sent as a deputation by King James to attend at the Synod of Dort,[20] yet even his sympathies lie entirely with the Calvinist ecclesiastics who presided over the Synod. The Arminian dissenters were represented by Episcopius, one of the probable authors of the *Apologia Remonstratium* (1610), a statement of Arminian doctrine.[21] They were introduced on December 6, 1618; however, their case was prejudged, and they had been called to the Synod to listen rather than to be heard. They were given the opportunity not to present their case but rather to conform, and because they would not, they were sharply dismissed on January 14, 1619, and subsequently expelled from the Reformed Church.

Although Hales was not in agreement with the Arminians, the reasonable and peaceful manner in which they had conducted themselves, and the *odium theologicum* that had dictated the spirit of the dominant party left a definite impression on his sensitive mind. Twenty years later, when Puritan dogmatism was regaining the field and beginning again to triumph, he opened his "Tract concerning Schism and Schismatics" with this sentence: "*Heresy* and *schism*, as they are in common use, are two theological *Mormos*, or scarecrows, which they who uphold a party in religion use to fright away such as, making inquiry into it, are ready to relinquish and oppose it if it appear either erroneous or suspicious."[22] The Dutch Arminians very soon came to represent to the English the spirit of rational inquiry in matters of religion, and—such as in the case of Hales—even when their appeal to Scripture and reason did not result in a conversion to their doctrine, their peaceful conduct nevertheless succeeded in touching the sympathetic imagination and awakening an attitude of toleration.

Although King James professed to be a strong Calvinist, he found that the same clergymen who adopted Arminianism also tended to favor his notions of royal prerogative as *parens patriæ*, the politic father of his people, as well as the head of the body, leading the body, both State and Church, in matters of judgment. The Puritans, however, who were more in accord with Calvin in recognizing the need for a distinct separation between spiritual and temporal kingdoms, were inclined to favor a presbyterian form of church government. Since recognition of his divine right as king was more important to James than conformity in theology, his favor shifted to the Arminians. Now, if the Arminians had been simply Protestant episcopalians, the Calvinist Puritans might have tolerated them indefinitely, but there was a more vital point of difference which separated them, of which Arminianism and episcopalianism were merely indicative. We should recall that the Reformation had returned theology to the Augustinian doctrine of the nature of fallen man in his relation to God, whereas Catholicism had, beginning in the thirteenth century, followed Thomas Aquinas in adopting an understanding of humanity that repudiated the idea of *total* depravity.[23] Bearing this in mind, we can understand why Arminianism was readily picked up by what has come to be called the "High Church"—those possessed of liturgical and ritualist sympathies more closely associated with the Roman communion. Once this alignment of ideas and predispositions had taken place, two rival parties—both in theology as well as in politics—were formed within the Church of England, each wanting to move the church in a different direction, each straining the politic cord which held the nation together.

Cambridge was, by no means, immune from the national controversy. Queen Elizabeth had been a humanist of the first order, and when, in 1584, Sir Walter Mildmay, her Chancellor of the Exchequer (1566-1589), decided to found a Puritan college at Cambridge, he was able to do so only by misrepresenting his motives to the queen. He purchased a private residence that, before the suppression of monasteries, had been a Dominican convent.[24] To this former convent, now college, he gave the name Emmanuel, and it is significant to our present study because, with the exception of Henry More, all of the more prominent Cambridge Platonists would come from its halls. Its first master was Laurence Chaderton, who was to serve on the Bible translation committee for the Authorized (or "King James") Version of 1611.[25] Chaderton was succeeded in 1622 by John Preston, chaplain to Prince Charles, who was in turn succeeded by Arminian sympathizer William Sandcroft in 1628.

It is improbable that a man with Sandcroft's views would ever have been appointed to Emmanuel during the Jacobean period, but Charles I (1625-1649) was of the High Church and, encouraged by his assertive Catholic wife, he quickly got into the habit of making appointments that were bound to aggravate Protestant sensibilities. The year following Sandcroft's appointment, William Laud was made

Chancellor of Oxford, and in 1633 he was appointed as Archbishop of Canterbury. From this position of power, Laud began an anti-Puritan campaign and, no longer confined in his labors to Oxford, appointed Arminians as Masters of Queen's, Corpus Christi, and St. John's Colleges at Cambridge.

Throughout the 1630s and into the '40s tensions between the Puritans and the Laudian High Church increased throughout the country. The Catholic sympathies of Charles and the methods of his bishops were too much for a largely Puritan House of Commons to bear, and an antagonism developed between the king and his Parliament. In 1641 Parliament, with Cromwell sitting as the Member for Cambridge, impeached Laud and had him imprisoned in the Tower; then, they passed a "Grand Remonstrance" stating their grievances against Charles. When the king responded, in January 1642, by attempting to arrest five of their leading members, the separation was irreparable. The Royalists and the Parliamentarians prepared for war, and by August the voice of brothers' blood was crying out to God from English soil. The Puritans at Cambridge, momentarily empowered, were in no mood for toleration. Richard Holdesworth, who upon Sandcroft's death in 1637, had followed him into the position of Master of Emmanuel, received the full force of Puritan resentment after publishing a Royalist oration that he had first presented in July 1641. In November 1643, when Cambridge received the Parliamentary visitation of the Earl of Manchester's troops, Holdesworth was deprived not merely of his mastership, but also of his freedom, being sent to the Tower "for executing his majesty's command in printing at Cambridge such his declarations as were formerly printed at York."[26] He was replaced as master in 1644 by the Puritan scholar Antony Tuckney.[27]

After the final outcome became apparent, the Commons forced a trial for Laud on charges of treason, and the Archbishop was executed on January 10, 1645. The last of the Royalist forces were defeated at the battle of Naseby in June of that year, and the king himself was taken into house arrest at the end of January 1647. But by this time the power had shifted from Parliament to the army, led by Oliver Cromwell. It was with Cromwell that the king had to come to terms, but after negotiations failed, Charles managed to escape to Scotland and raise an army for an invasion of England. The invading force was met and quickly defeated, and the king was once again taken prisoner. This time, Cromwell and the other army leaders determined to put Charles on trial for waging war against his own people. He was convicted of treason and executed on January 30, 1649.

From the beginning of the war, the episcopal government of the Church of England had been forced into dissolution and, in its place, a presbyterian government had been established. The transformation of the Church became complete with the passing of the Calvinist "Westminster Confession of Faith" in 1643. It is safe to say that, if the Commons had been able to maintain their power, the condition of the Christian Church in England would have been very much like that in Holland after the Synod of Dort. Milton observed this when, in "On the New Forcers of Conscience under the Long Parliament," he wrote, "Presbyter is but Old Priest writ large!"[28] However, the power had, instead, fallen into the hands of the army, and Cromwell, who was given the title of Lord Protector, professed himself to be an Independent, a separatist from the Established Church and a supporter of neither presbyter nor priest. During the Protectorship, the rigorous dogmatism of the Calvinists was curtailed in part by the Cromwellian experiment in a more tolerant approach to religious expression. There were no penal laws in force requiring compliance with an established church. Jews were, for the first time since 1253, allowed—without official permission—to settle and open a synagogue.[29] Moreover, the Society of Friends, or Quakers, became one of the most prominent sects to spring up within this soil, and the degree to which it was tolerated can be taken as a measure of the latitude that was extended to the individual's conscience in matters of religion.[30]

One of the greatest documents of religious toleration was written during this period, not by an Independent, but by a former chaplain in the Royalist army. Jeremy Taylor (1613-67) was a native of Cambridge, and at one time he was a fellow of Caius College. While preaching in London, his eloquence and learning attracted the favorable attention of Laud, who subsequently, in 1636, transferred Taylor to Oxford, granting him a fellowship at All Souls and enlisting him into the number of his chaplains. He served the king during the Civil War and was taken prisoner in 1644. Upon his release, he opened a private school in Wales, where, in 1647, after the king had been taken prisoner, Taylor wrote his famous *Discourse of the Liberty of Prophesying*. In this work, the author distinguishes between essentials and non-essentials in matters of faith. What is essential is easily understood in Scripture and clearly stated in the Apostle's Creed and has as its object holiness of life. In all other matters, what is dictated by reason, demonstrated by experience, and required by God, is toleration. In answer to the question, "What deportment they are to use towards persons that disagree from them, and by consequence are in error," Taylor sets down these ten guidelines:[31]

    1. No Christian is to be persecuted for an opinion that does not lead to immorality or sedition.

    2. Since we are easily deceived, Christian religion should be recognized as consisting in "a simple profession of the articles of beliefe, and a hearty prosecution of the rules of good life."

    3. Both the prediction of Christ and the experience of Christendom teaches that, more often than not, persecutors fight against God, "and that it is errour and heresie, that is, cruell and tyrannicall."

    4. Whoever abuses power in order to persecute his enemy cannot urge mercy for himself when his enemy comes into power. "And therefore it is better, if it should so happen, that we should spare the innocent person, and one that is actually deceiv'd, then that upon the turn of the wheele, the true believers should be destroyed."

    5. We should take note that, even in matters of greatest importance, "the best and ablest Doctors of Christendome have been actually deceived."

6. Even if the disagreeing person is truly in error, "what greater folly and stupidity then to give to error the glory of Martyrdome, and the advantages which are accidentally consequent to a persecution."

7. Persecution for errors in understanding is unnatural, "for Understanding being a thing wholly spirituall, cannot be restrained, and therefore neither punished by corporall afflictions."

8. The exercise of force upon a person in error "can doe no good, but is very apt to doe hurt," as it "may make him an hypocrite, but never to be a right beleever."

9. Christianity "came in upon its own piety and wisdome, with no other force but a torrent of arguments and demonstrations of the Spirit," and by meekness, mercy, and charity "should also preserve it selfe and pronounce its owne interest."

10. Even if persecution were neither unjust nor unreasonable, "yet there is nothing under God Almighty that hath power over the soule of man, so as to command a perswasion, or to judge a disagreeing."

With Socratic modesty, combined with a touch of Pyrrhonic skepticism, along with a gentle appeal to common sense, Taylor argued for the Anglican ideal of a comprehensive Church. Urging unity in practice and liberty in theory, the *Discourse* is in advance of its age. England's legislators did not then or soon thereafter have ears to hear, but Taylor found an audience at Cambridge and would ultimately come to exercise significant influence on the eighteenth-century latitudinarians. Taylor and Hooker's liberal message of toleration and unity in diversity is melded into aphoristic style by Cambridge Provost Benjamin Whichcote:

> No *Force* reachest the Mind of Man. No Man's Mind is changed, or better'd, but by his own particular Consideration. . . .
> 'Tis a thing very desirable, to have the World be as smooth and calm, as quiet and tolerable, as may be. Offenses amongst Men are apt enough to arise. Where we cannot yield *internal Assent*, for want of Evidence, and Assurance in things; *external Obedience* and Compliance with Sense of others, may be yielded, for the maintaining of Peace, Love, and Good-will.[32]

Whichcote can be distinguished from the other Cambridge Platonists, not only as the founding member, but also as the one who most clearly reveals an indebtedness to the rational theology of Hooker and Taylor. In Whichcote, we might say, Aristotle and Plato meet, sit down together, and agree to disagree. In the midst of dogmatic disputation, Whichcote refused to systematize his theology; in the aftermath of civil war, he personified civility without compromise of conviction.

Within ten years after the execution of Charles, Cromwell was dead and succeeded by his much weaker son, Richard. Seventeen years had passed since the outbreak of the civil war, and the new generation had learnt to be not only more tolerant toward religious diversity but also less concerned about it. The age of Christian dogmatism had passed, the pendulum had begun its swing in the opposite direction, and there were already indications that a period of religious indifference and skepticism was coming into vogue. Then England looked back with fond memories to the days when there was a king in the land and a crown over its Church. But England had no desire to re-establish the feuding church of the 1640s, and Burnet, speaking of the period of the Restoration, claims that, had not "a new set of men . . . of a different stamp"—men "generally of Cambridge" and formed under the instruction and example of the Platonists—made their appearance, "the church had quite lost her esteem over the nation."[33]

# II
# Principle Persons and Representative Ideas

## The Cambridge School

Benjamin Whichcote (1609-1683) was a Shropshire lad, only sixteen, when he first arrived at Emmanuel in 1626. He was there throughout the period in which Sandcroft was master, becoming a fellow of the college in 1633, just after receiving his M.A. For the following ten years he appears to have kept himself busy at Emmanuel, first as a tutor and, then, after taking orders in 1636, as a priest. He was there throughout the mastership of Holdesworth and, no doubt, heard his notorious sermon of 1641. In fact, Whichcote had been trained at and had served Emmanuel during the very years when the masters of the college were decidedly not Puritan, and there is little to suggest that Whichcote, in his rejection of Calvinism, was something of an anomaly at Emmanuel. "One imagines," suggests Frederick Powicke, "that in the little society for free talk and discussion, which seems to have met in the common-room of Emmanuel, the relation of philosophy to theology and the relation of Plato or Plotinus to both was a favourite topic."[34] Yet, our imagination must also allow us to think of Whichcote, in his early years at Cambridge, sitting at the feet of his tutors, Anthony Tuckney and Thomas Hill, and earnestly considering the relation of Luther and Calvin to St. Paul. The fact that Whichcote remained in undisputed favor with the Puritan party until, at least, the mid-forties is evidence not only of his diplomatic tact, but even more, of his intellectual caution, his inclination to measure and weigh each particular in the scale of truth repeatedly, doubting of his own ability to do so fairly. His later advice, that when in doubt, it is safer "to err with the generality, than to err alone,"[35] is wisdom derived from his own experience.

Beginning in the late thirties, there was a Puritan backlash at Cambridge, a reaction against the Arminianism that had infiltrated the university, and Whichcote would ultimately stand out as one who refused to be a part of it, one who would not be intimidated by the dominant party. And, if we begin to consider Whichcote only when he becomes truly noticeable—that is, after he succeeds Samuel Collins as Provost of King's College in 1644 and acquires a position of power and influence— then it may appear that he had departed from the mainstream of Cambridge culture.

However, we should recall that, from Whichcote's perspective, it was Cambridge that had altered, and not for the better. Unwilling to benefit from such changes, Whichcote arranged that half of his salary as Provost was to go directly to Collins.[36] Since Collins had also been Regius Professor of Divinity, his ejection allowed for the appointment of John Arrowsmith into the vacated chair, just as the ejection of Holdesworth from the mastership of Emmanuel allowed for the subsequent appointment of Tuckney. These changes were merely representative of the transition forced upon Cambridge.

Carrying on the early Cambridge tradition begun by Fisher, Whichcote, after his installation as Provost, regularly preached in the afternoons at Trinity Church, and his sermons were well attended by students and fellows alike. He was not one to write for publication; in fact, even his sermons were not published until 1698, when Shaftesbury compiled the *Select Sermons*. Nevertheless, there is a power in the word spoken with conviction that cannot be reproduced in the press, and Whichcote was gaining considerable influence upon his audience. As John Tulloch (1823-86) puts it, "He was a born teacher—one whose highest qualities were stimulated by contact with young minds, and that play of speech which seems to be necessary to the finest development of certain intellectual natures, from Socrates downward."[37] There was one man in Whichcote's audience, however, whose mind was no longer young and who did not care for a "play of speech." He was not favorably impressed; he was, rather, uncomfortable—even a bit nervous. He was, of course, Tuckney.

Tuckney, as a member of the Westminster Assembly, had contributed to the drafting of the Confession of Faith, and although he was not in favor of a forced subscription to the "National Covenant," he reserved the right to hold suspect those who evaded subscription. Since Cromwell, an Independent, had come to power, subscription to the Covenant could not be legally enforced, and Whichcote had the sympathetic ear of Cromwell's chaplain, Peter Sterry. Whichcote demanded the same liberty for others that he enjoyed himself and, therefore, boldly interceded on behalf of the fellows of King's, sparing those who did not care to subscribe from the indignity of having to do so. Tuckney's suspicions regarding Whichcote appeared to be substantiated by the sermons preached from Trinity pulpit, but he and Arrowsmith were men under political restraints. Finally, in 1650, Whichcote became Vice-Chancellor of the University under Cromwell, and that autumn, after Whichcote presented the commencement address, Tuckney found that he could bite his tongue no longer. There followed an interchange of eight letters between the two men, in which Tuckney protests that Whichcote, in discussing salvation, made too much of reason and too little of divine election. Whichcote's responses are, observes Geoffrey Pawson, "a model of what controversy should be."[38] He courteously but firmly held his ground, Tuckney backed off, and when the dust from this skirmish settled, Cambridge Platonism could be seen to have emerged as a distinct movement on the advance.

In order to consider Whichcote's characteristic ideas as the beginning of a movement, we must first be introduced to three other men, of whom two were, along with Whichcote, part of that "little society for free talk and discussion" at Emmanuel. Ralph Cudworth (1617-1688) was "the leading systematic thinker among the Cambridge Platonists,"[39] in whose works we find the early development of ideas that would later receive their more perfect elaboration through the efforts of such eminent philosophers as John Locke and Immanuel Kant. In 1629 the university of Cambridge dissolved as a result of an outbreak of plague in the town, which, according to Thomas Fuller, carried off 347souls.[40] Cudworth entered Emmanuel at the time of the return of scholars, in 1630, at the age of thirteen. Nine years later, he took his M.A. and was elected fellow of Emmanuel. In 1645, one year after Whichcote became Provost, Cudworth was appointed both Master of Clare Hall and Regius Professor of Hebrew. In 1651 he took a Doctorate in Divinity, and finally, three years later, became Master of Christ's College. After the Restoration, although Whichcote was compelled to vacate his post on the command of the king, Cudworth was allowed to retain his. The reason for the difference in their treatment probably lies in the fact that Whichcote had occupied a political post under Cromwell, although Tulloch might also be correct in suggesting that "Cudworth was protected by some special influence."[41] There is no question but that the two men were close friends for the greater part of their lives, and when Whichcote made visits to Cambridge during his later years, he sometimes resided with Cudworth, in whose home, ultimately, in 1683, he died. Cudworth followed him five years later.

"One of the freest spirits of the Platonists,"[42] indebted to both Whichcote's and Cudworth's influence, was John Smith (1618-1652). He entered Emmanuel at the age of eighteen in 1636 and was, apparently, tutored by both during the course of his undergraduate studies.[43] He obtained his B.A. in 1640 and his M.A. in 1644, and was in this latter year chosen a fellow of Queen's. According to Simon Patrick—Smith's close friend who had formerly been one of his students and would afterwards be Bishop, first of Chichester (1689) and then of Ely (1691)—"This indeed was the end of his life, the main design which he carried on, that he might become *like to God.*"[44] Unfortunately, Smith died young, shortly after Whichcote closed his correspondence with Tuckney, and all that remains of his are the *Select Discourses* compiled by John Worthington (1660). Tulloch suggests that these ten discourses are the highest literary accomplishment of the Cambridge School. "They carry us," he writes, "so directly into an atmosphere of divine philosophy, luminous with the richest lights of meditative genius."[45] So consistently eloquent is Smith in the *Discourses* that they have been singled out as "one of the highest achievements in English literature of the seventeenth century."[46]

The life of Henry More (1614-1687) was full, and it is the most interesting life of all the Platonists. From the start he is set apart from the others by his lack of association with Emmanuel. After spending three years at Eton, he was admitted into Christ's College in 1631, at the age of seventeen. By this time he was already well on his way toward a complete rejection of Calvinism, and it was his fortune to have at Christ's an Arminian tutor. He took his B.A. in 1635, and in the same year entered into a spiritual crisis, what we might now call *existential*. After his years of study he began to question whether studying satisfied the purpose of his life, while at the same time he felt himself deeply unsatisfied and troubled by religious doubts and confusion. Turning to Plato and Plotinus, he determined to seek his happiness in the purification of his soul. There followed several years of discipline and purgation, until the divine will gained ascendancy over him and he recovered his true self and freedom.

In 1639 More received his M.A., was elected fellow of Christ's, and in the same year wrote a poem in Greek, "Euporia" or "The Extrication of the Soul," in which he celebrates both a life of "Faith, Wisdom, Love, fix'd Joy, free-winged Might" and the coterminous deliverance from "Death and Decay."[47] Two years later he was ordained into the priesthood, but he refused to leave Cambridge. With the exception of the months he spent in Ragley, developing his Platonic friendship (in the most literal sense) with the highly intellectual Anne, Lady Conway,[48] the precincts of Christ's remained his home throughout his life. From there, from late 1648 to early 1650, he conducted his correspondence with Descartes;[49] from there he wrote his poems and philosophical treatises. There he was given the honorary degree of Doctor of Divinity in 1660, and there he died in 1687.

More was the most prolific of the Cambridge School, and his works were well-known and well-loved by many during his lifetime. He was an early type of a now common phenomenon, the best-selling religious writer whose popularity is short-lived. Nevertheless, Samuel Taylor Coleridge recognized that More's *Theological Works* (1708) "contain more original, enlarged and elevating views of the Christian Dispensation, than I have met with in any other single Volume."[50] Henry More may have lacked the homiletic felicity of expression that gave the strong moral sensibility of John Smith a poetic force, so much admired by Matthew Arnold,[51] but More was the philosopher-priest possessed of a creative Imagination. He was just the sort of writer that Coleridge could not but profoundly admire. F. D. Maurice, comparing Cudworth and More, suggests that, whereas the former "had the stronger moral basis for his mind and was less bewildered by fancies, . . . there are hints and divinations in More which can never be discovered in Cudworth."[52]

Another figure who is sometimes listed among the Cambridge Platonists is Nathaniel Culverwell (1618/19-1651). If he is, as Tulloch suggests,[53] the son of Ezekiel Culverwell, then Lawrence Chaderton, the former Master of Emmanuel, is his uncle, the brother-in-law of his father. Culverwell entered Emmanuel in 1633, the very year that Whichcote was elected as fellow. By 1636 he had obtained his B.A., and by 1640 his M.A. Two years later he was made fellow of Emmanuel. Beyond this, very little can be known with any certainty about Culverwell's life, which stretched only to thirty-one years. The evidence of his scholarship, including the eight sermons published as *Spiritual Opticks* (1652), suggests the probability that he was ordained, but we can only surmise whether, as an undergraduate, he was ever tutored by Whichcote. Certainly, as they were together at Emmanuel for eleven years, until the latter was appointed Provost, Culverwell could not have escaped his conversation, even if he did not attend his sermons.

The influence of the Cambridge Platonist school upon Culverwell's *Elegant and Learned Discourse of the Light of Nature* (presented in the college chapel in the school year of 1645-1646) is incontrovertible, but if Smith had diverted from Whichcote in the direction of Florence, Culverwell diverted in the direction of Geneva. The *Discourse* has upon it the imprint of the Calvinism represented by Tuckney, and yet, as Robert Greene and Hugh MacCallum observe, "Its essential spirit, expressed in the bright shoots of a fertile rhetoric, as well as in its predilection for philosophical discussion and its dedication to a traditional Christian humanism, is much more closely aligned with the attitudes, beliefs, and intellectual style of Benjamin Whichcote."[54] Culverwell's close friend and colleague at Emmanuel, William Dillingham, recognized the value of the *Discourse* as a compromise between the Calvinism of Tuckney and the rationalism of Whichcote and so published it with his Dedication to Tuckney in 1652. Apparently, Dillingham's intention was to use his friend's lectures as shears with which to sever the buds from the neo-Platonist plant that had sprouted out of the nurturing soil of Whichcote's teachings.[55]

Since Culverwell is even less of a Platonist than Whichcote, we cannot situate him in the company of Cudworth, More, and Smith, but neither can we deny him a legitimate place among the followers of Whichcote. For this reason, his contribution must be noted; yet, because it may be misleading, if not in fact confusing, to include him within the scope of a general and topical discussion of the Cambridge Platonists, I have included a brief comparative analysis of Culverwell's *Discourse* nearer to the end of this study. Therefore, leaving Culverwell for the time being, let us return to Whichcote, Cudworth, Smith, and More.

Within the sermons and conversational discourses of these seventeenth-century Christian philosophers we find a general agreement of sweetness and light both in the tone and content. But, their message is much more than pleasant and appealing; it is inspirational. As one critic remarks, "Anyone who reads the Platonists even casually cannot fail to be inspired."[56] On the other hand, the style of the essentially *philosophic* writings of the Platonists, particularly Cudworth and More, does not lend itself to praise. The mode of writing that they adopted for the purpose of philosophy was already outdated at the time of its production. Instead of using the modern *essay* form that had been used by Montaigne and Descartes on the continent or by Bacon and Hobbes in England, Cudworth and More relied heavily on the use of quotations from classical sources and, like the Florentine pilgrim in Hell, descended into a pit of digressions from which, without the literary assistance of a Vergil, there could be no return. The result is that their longer philosophical works were never read by any but serious scholars and are now to be found collecting dust in only the most well-stocked libraries. When William Hazlitt observed that Cudworth's *True Intellectual System of the Universe* (1678) was "unwieldy, enormous,"[57] he expressed what, perhaps, every reader feels who begins to read either this learned treatise or one of Henry More's digressive dissertations. Too soon these books are returned to their shelves, and their brilliant gems are allowed to remain unknown, hidden in darkness. I have endeavored, therefore—and not by the dim light of my solitary candle—to gather together a few observations in regard to the Cambridge Platonists' essential thought, that which makes them a School.

## The Candle of the Lord

According to humanist philosopher Ernst Cassirer, in his *Platonic Renaissance in England*, the "central motif" of the Cambridge Platonists is the self-determination of the soul.[58] Aharon Lichtenstein makes the observation that the Platonists are predominantly immersed in the idea of the deification of man.[59] These observations are not really disparate, for the two motifs are inextricably intertwined, and yet they are both derivative of a more essential teaching of the Platonist's—that religion exists as an internal and natural condition of human beings. God is an internal revelation, the knowledge of whom is part of our createdness. Whichcote asks, "For are we not *made* to know there is a God? If we were not *made* to know that he is; we could never know. For this we can never be taught." Rejecting all extrinsic proofs, Whichcote rests his argument for Deity—and for Christian faith, which is grounded on the knowledge of God—on the sole evidence of human experience.[60] The internal revelation is, according to Whichcote, independent of the will to believe: "This *natural Knowledge of God* is wrapt up in the Inward of Man's Mind and Soul; that Men, whether they will or no, whether they be pleased or disaffected, whensoever they look into themselves, and consult with their own Principles, and answer their very Make, so oft are they satisfy'd in this Knowledge, *that there is a God.*"[61]

We are made with the inherent knowledge of "Principles," a certainty of an eternal and immutable standard of good and evil, which is as certain as the principles of mathematics.[62] This revelation is received by "Reason" and forms the conscience, so that "There is something in every Man, upon which we may work, to which we may apply; to wit, *the Light of Reason and Conscience*; to which the Difference of Good and Evil may be made to appear."[63] Reason is, for Whichcote, not merely the ability to form conclusions, either deductively or inductively, but is the organ of divine sense. It is what connects humanity to God. Whereas it is true that "Reason *discovers*, what is Natural," it is also true that "Reason *receives*, what is Supernatural."[64] Therefore, "This will be the World's Condemnation: that where Men either *did* know, or *might* know, they go against their Light: that Men put out the Candle of God in them, that they may do Evil without Check or Controul."[65]

One of Tuckney's complaints to Whichcote is that he and his followers overused and misapplied the phrase "Candle of the Lord," derived from Prov. 20:27, "The spirit of man is the candle of the Lord, searching all the inward parts of the belly."[66] Culverwell's *Discourse of the Light of Nature*, for example, contains no less than seventy-seven instances of its usage. Protestant interpretation of the passage had traditionally understood the "candle" to be a reference to Scripture, such as in

Psa. 119:105, "Thy word is a lampe unto my feete: and a light unto my path," where *word* is generally taken to imply the *written word*. For Tuckney, the passage in question signified the inadequacy of natural revelation. It is Scripture internalized that illuminates and redeems. The light of natural knowledge, what St. Paul in Rom. 2:15 refers to as "the law written in the heart,"is dimmed by sin and incapable, without the additional light of Scripture, to lead corrupt humanity toward salvation.

According to Calvin, "All of us born of Adam are bereft of God, perverse, corrupt, and lacking every good." Even if we perform some seemingly good action, "still the mind stays in its inner state of filth and crooked perversity." Moreover, any actual good that we appear to do is, in fact, done by God through us rather than by means of any innate human power. Calvin does not deny the existence of a conscience, but declares that this law of God stamped upon our hearts has only the purpose of revealing to us our incapacity to do good or, in other words, our inherent depravity. The human condition, apart from grace, is such that we have no sure communication from God that could lead us to repentance; but, "Seeing our condition, the Lord has provided us with a written law to teach us what perfect righteousness is and how it is to be kept."[67]

In contravention to Calvinist interpretation, Whichcote refers his audience to Rom. 1:18-19, where we are told that those "who hold the truth in unrighteousness" are self-condemned "because *that which may be known of God is manifest in them.*" St. Paul, says Whichcote, places religion firmly on the basis of Reason, appealing to the inherent revelation of God, "*the candle of the Lord*; Lighted *by* God, and Lighting us *to* God."[68] Henry More explicitly associates this candle of the Lord with the law in the heart: "*Right Reason*," he tells us, "by how much it shines forth, by so much doth it oblige the Conscience, even as a Law Divine inscribed in our Hearts."[69] Joseph Hall's *Christ Mystical* (1652) refers to Prov. 20:27 as illustrative of the fact that the spirits of man and of Christ "agree in all their spiritual concernments." It is not the written word, but our own inner conviction (the candle of the Lord) that bears witness in agreement with the Spirit of Christ that we are the children of God.[70] Although Hall (1574-1656), Bishop, first of Exeter, then of Norwich, is not counted among the Cambridge Platonists, he is the graduate of Emmanuel who became Professor of Rhetoric at Cambridge and accompanied Hales at the Synod of Dort, and his religious writings and poems provide us with a link between Whichcote and an earlier school of Cambridge humanists.

## Practical Reason

Reason is, for the Cambridge Platonists, essentially practical. Its function is primarily moral, guiding us in our behavior. Whichcote, adopting the voice of experience, declares, "Any Man that hath obtain'd any Degree of the Perfection of Reason; that doth follow the Divine Governour of Man's Life, *Reason*; he doth find that there are *Suggestions* and *Inspirations*; and that, many times, when he was resolv'd another way, there comes a *Light* into his Mind, a *still Voice*; he hears, and he is better directed."[71] Therefore, "*do* but with Reason, and you *do* well."[72] For Smith, too, Reason is "a Beam of Divine light;"[73] however, following Calvin more closely, he is less confident than Whichcote in the apprehension of natural knowledge by sinful humans, for "*Innate notions* of Divine Truth . . . are too often smothered, or tainted with a deep dye of men's filthy lusts."[74]

Whereas all of the Cambridge Platonists strictly adhere to the Socratic equation, Reason equals Virtue, Smith and More closely follow Plotinus in that they place greater emphasis on the equation Virtue equals Reason. More writes, "The true Ground of our being able and free to chuse what is best, consists rather in the Purity of the Soul from Vice, than in Advertency and Attention to the Object, while the Mind is vitiated and obscured for want of due Purification."[75] This, Smith declares, was the message of Christ, that "true Piety, and a Godlike pattern of purity, [is] the best way to thrive in all spiritual understanding. His main scope was to promote an *Holy life*, as the best and most compendious way to a *right Belief*."[76] There is an obvious objection to this argument, and Smith anticipates it. If the knowledge of good and evil resides within the inherent property of Reason, but Reason is defiled by vice, then how might vicious humanity ever be persuaded to do good in order to restore their Reason to its natural clarity? Smith answers, "There are some *Radical Principles* of Knowledge that are so deeply sunk into the Souls of men, as that the Impression cannot easily be obliterated, though it may be much darkened."[77] The path toward redemption, therefore, invariably begins with Reason.

If this path is, on the one hand, beset with temptations that would becloud the divine faculty, it is, on the other hand, threatened with the vain conceits of *melancholy*, which is "the most *Religious* complexion" in that it "will be as naturally tampering with Divine matters (though in no better light then that of her own) as Apes and Monkies will be imitating the actions and manners of Men."[78] More's *Enthusiasmus Triumphatus* (1656) was the classic pin-prick that, with firm but gentle touch, let the hot air out of the falsely inspired prophets and visionaries of his day and, a century later, was put to use again as an antidote against Methodism. This work was greatly admired by Joseph Glanvill, who, in *The Vanity of Dogmatizing* (1661), praised both the author and his book.[79] For More, as it is through Reason that humanity is made a partaker of the divine image, so too it is through Imagination that the human ascent is frustrated. The Imagination is "the Soul's weaknesse or unwieldinesse, whereby she so farre sinks into Phantasmes that she cannot recover her self into the use of her more free Faculties of *Reason* and *Understanding*."[80] Following Descartes, More argues that the Imagination is closely connected with the body and, unlike the more ethereal Reason, is swayed or determined by the corporeal humours, but chiefly through melancholy.

## Gnosticism and Calvinism

Both Smith and Cudworth appeal to Plotinus's treatise "Against the Gnostics."[81] For Plotinus, Christianity appeared to be but a form of Gnosticism, since it agreed with Gnosticism in its radical dualism, its sharp division between matter and spirit. Undoubtedly, Gnostic thought played an extremely important role in the development of Christian theology. One of the more serious heresies encountered by St. Paul among his converts was directly related to the pernicious implications of Gnosticism. Apparently, some early Christians—either entirely deaf to their own consciences or laboring in vain under a vague suspicion that the conscience is a product of social conditioning—supposed that, since the body and the spirit were entirely separate, the body could engage in any behavior without affecting the condition of the spirit. Thus, the apostle's First Epistle to the Corinthians addresses the numerous sins that Gnostic "knowledge" had encouraged. Plotinus, like St. Paul, directly addressed the moral and spiritual consequences of Gnostic dualism:

> For to say "Look to God" is not helpful without some instruction as to what this looking imports: it might very well be said that one can "look" and still sacrifice no pleasure, still be the slave of impulse, repeating the word "God" but held in the grip of every passion and making no effort to master any. Virtue, advancing toward the Term and, linked with thought, occupying a soul, makes God manifest: "God" on the lips without a good conduct of life, is a word.[82]

The Cambridge Platonists, who were trained classicists, expert in recognizing ancient philosophy in every so-called "new" doctrine, saw a connection between the effects of Gnosticism and Calvinism. Calvinists, who regarded sanctification as the result of an imputed righteousness and holiness as the effect rather than the cause of sanctification, recognized a holy life as evidence of divine election by grace to eternal salvation. However, it could be reasoned that, since God's decrees were unchangeable, the assurance of salvation that one had yesterday, while living a holy life—*if it was a valid assurance*—guaranteed the assurance of salvation today, regardless of one's manner of life. Thus, although virtue led to the assurance of salvation, the assurance itself too often had the effect of leading to moral complacency and vice. For example, Oliver Cromwell, on his deathbed, is reported to have anxiously asked, "whether it were possible for the elect to fall finally; and being answered in the negative, replied, 'Then I am safe; for I am certain that I *was once* in a state of grace.'"[83]

Cudworth, in *A Sermon Preached before the Honourable House of Commons, at Westminster, March 31, 1647*, confronts this very problem in his learned audience with an admirable boldness: "If S. John's rule be good here in the Text [1 Jno. 2:3-4], that no man truly knows Christ, but he that keepeth his Commandments: it is much to be suspected, that many of us which pretend to light, have a thick and gloomy darknesse within over-spreading our souls."[84] For Cudworth, as for Smith, a knowledge of Divinity is not to be derived from books, but rather from a holy life:

> The Grossenesse of our apprehensions in *Spirituall things*, and our many mistakes, that we have about them, proceed from nothing, but those dull and foggy *Stemes*, which rise up from our *foul hearts* and becloud our Understandings. If we did but heartily comply with Christ's commandments, and purge our hearts, from all grosse and sensuall affections, . . . we should find the Great Eternall God, inwardly teaching our souls, and continually instructing us more and more, in the mysteries of his will: and *out of our bellies should flow rivers of living water*.[85]

For Cudworth—soon to be *Dr.* Cudworth—a degree from Cambridge is no token of training in divinity. Such training can only come from the experiential knowledge of God's teaching from within, which is a training that takes place only as one progresses from virtue to virtue.

## Deification

This ascent of the soul or progress in virtue is denominated by the Cambridge School as the path of "deification." Whichcote finds sanction for the use of the word in 2 Pet. 1:3-4, which assures us that, "through the knowledge of him that hath called us to glory and vertue," we "might bee partakers of the divine nature, having escaped the corruption that is in the world through lust." The concept of deification is scriptural, and it was emphasized by Tauler and the Friends of God (*Gottesfreunde*) in fourteenth-century Germany. It attests to a spiritual communion with Christ by which one is possessed of the very attributes of God.[86] The peculiar emphasis of the Cambridge Platonists upon this concept appears to have derived not so much from Germany as from the Alexandrian patristics of Clement and Origen, and from the Plotinian philosophy of the Florentine Academy.

The process that these latter Platonists call *deification* takes its origin from the doctrine of *participation*, which itself derives from the much larger pantheist context developed by the Neo-Platonists, particularly the doctrine of *emanations*. Since all being originates in the One, from whom, by a process of declensional emanations, the Many take form, it is possible for the Many, through knowledge and action, to ascend—or, more accurately, to re-ascend—in the hierarchical chain of being. In doing so the Many attain to a state of participation with the One.

This idea of "participation" is expressed by Plotinus as part of his philosophical system in the *Enneads*:

> Man, when he commands not merely the life of sensation but also Reason and Authentic Intellection, has realized the perfect life.
> . . . . . . . . . . . . . . . . . . . . . . . . . . . . . . . . . . . . . .
> To the man in this state, what is the Good?
> He himself by what he has and is.
> And the author and principle of what he is and holds is the Supreme, which within

Itself is the Good but manifests Itself within the human being after this other mode.[87]

For Plotinus, the goal of the philosopher is to cleanse himself from the corruptions of the material world and to move upward toward a state of "proficiency," in which state his soul is devoid of desire for anything without and is in perfect sympathy with the Good, from which comes Beauty:

> What else is Sophrosyny, rightly so-called, but to take no part in the pleasures of the body, to break away from them as unclean and unworthy of the clean? . . .
> The Soul thus cleansed is all Idea and Reason, wholly free of body, intellective, entirely of that divine order from which the wellspring of Beauty rises and all the race of Beauty.[88]

This was the way of Christ, that archetypal Beautiful Man, and Cudworth suggests that the divine life is, indeed, *"something of God in flesh,"* so that "all particular Christians, that are really possessed of it, [are] so many *Mysticall Christs*."[89] In the same vein, More writes, "But to be of one will completely with God, will make us, or doth argue us to be the Sons of God."[90] Smith explains that, for the Christian, "This indeed is such a *Deification* as is not transacted merely upon the Stage of *Fancy* by Arrogance and Presumption, but in the highest Powers of the Soul by a living and quickning Spirit of true Religion there uniting God and the Soul together in *the Unity of Affections, Will* and *End*."[91]

## Freedom

Deification leads to a unity of will between the Creator and his creation. For Smith, this perfect unity is salvation: "*Salvation* is nothing else but a true Participation of the Divine Nature."[92] For Cudworth it is "Glory" or "*Holinesse Triumphant*; Holinesse with a Palme of Victorie in her hand, and a Crown upon her head."[93] However, it is also Freedom. Reason grants humanity the power of self-determination, but the will is not *free* until it is in complete agreement with Reason, which is the expression or revelation of the will of God. This, again, is in agreement with Plotinus, who argues, "Self-disposal . . . belongs to those who, through the activities of the Intellectual-Principle, live above the states of the body. The spring of freedom is the activity of the Intellectual-Principle, the highest in our being; the proposals emanating thence are freedom."[94] Thus, it is *only* through deification that humans escape from causal determination, which is a principle of matter, and attain freedom. As long as the soul is entwined with the body, it remains in bondage to the laws that govern matter.

The Cambridge Platonists' emphasis on freewill "is probably indebted to Erasmus,"[95] particularly to the *Diatribe de Libero Arbitrio* (1524), although it received further support from Arminianism. Cudworth, in *A Treatise of Freewill*, grants the truth of Democritian necessitarianism; all of the material universe moves by law of the causal nexus. Thus, "Bodies that cannot move themselves, can never act further than they suffer, and therefore if causes of motions or impulsions made upon them be of equal force or strength, they cannot move at all." In fact—and here Cudworth pointedly differs from Democritus—bodies cannot move. Matter has no inherent capability of moving itself; not even atoms within a void have the property of self-propulsion. As Aristotle argued, all things that move are moved by something else. Therefore, although all material movement is causally connected, there must be a *Prime Mover* in which movement is self-generated; that is, an eternal source of free movement. Cudworth observes that the error of Democritus—and, thus, also of that modern Democritus, Hobbes—is that he allows no place within his philosophical system for a source of movement outside of matter. Whereas it is true that human beings that are governed by their physical motives or desires are driven by necessity, Reason directly connects the soul with the eternal and immutable, the *primum* and *perpetuum mobile*, and the souls that are moved by the inherent instigation of Reason move by self-determination:

> But rational beings and human souls standing in equipoise as to motive reasons, and having the scales equiponderent, from the weight of the objects themselves without them, will not perpetually of necessity always thus hang in suspense, but may themselves add or cast in some grains into one scale rather than the other.[96]

The self-determination that Cudworth is describing here is not, it should be observed, "freedom." It is, rather, the usual human condition, in which one moves occasionally by the guidance of God. For the Cambridge Platonists true *freedom* can only be said to exist when one habitually moves, not *by* God, but *with* God. When the soul stands aloof from the body and is perfectly attuned to Reason, then the will is truly free.

## Spinoza and Hobbes

We might pause to briefly note some similarity between the self-determination of Cudworth and Spinoza. For Spinoza, self-determination is a power attained through having clear and distinct ideas of oneself in relation to God or Nature and through being detached from the sway of uninformed emotions. The greatest possible deliverance from necessity is to be realized only through perceiving the world, not from the viewpoint of oneself, but rather from the viewpoint of God. There are, however, at least two crucial differences between Cudworth and Spinoza that, within the present context, should be noted. First, Cudworth is more practical, Spinoza more metaphysical. As with the Cambridge School in general, the emphasis in Cudworth is on doing rather than thinking. A second and related point is that Spinoza, like the Calvinists, holds out the promise of salvation only to the elect few.[97] On the other hand, Cudworth wrote volumes, not to prove that there is a greater salvation in store for those who can realize the world *sub specie æternitatis*, but rather to defend the intellectual right of the common man to trust in the elementary principles of Reason as the key to eternal and immutable morality.

Cudworth's foremost philosophical adversary was not Spinoza, but Hobbes. Hobbes and the Puritans were certainly opposed to one another, but their opposition was a sort of ideological tug-of-war; they were, after all, both pulling the same rope. Cudworth's object—the purpose which seems to have driven him in his sustained intellectual labors, particularly in *The True Intellectual System of the Universe* (1678)—was to cut that rope. Both the Puritans and Hobbes argued that faith must submit to an absolute decree in which an alleged *Reason* had no say. For the Puritans, that absolute decree was the arbitrary will of Deity; for Hobbes, it was the will of the Head of State, the Monarchy. To both, an argument suggesting the pre-eminence of Reason seemed to be nothing less than an argument for anarchy. Cudworth's aim, in both *The True Intellectual System* and in *A Treatise Concerning Eternal and Immutable Morality* (published posthumously in 1731), is to prove that thought has priority over matter, that an objective morality has priority over thought, and that not even God can make good into evil or evil into good. It was a brilliant and risky argument, and James Martineau rightly observes that Cudworth's thought is both original and independent, "and to readers exempt from prepossession, can hardly fail to appear the expression of the larger and the nobler mind."[98]

There are at least two references to Spinoza in *The True Intellectual System*;[99] however, not even Hobbes is ever mentioned by name, and the references that appear to point toward Spinoza make it clear that Cudworth regarded him as a strict necessitarian. It is hardly surprising that Cudworth had a less than thorough understanding of this contemporary Dutch philosopher. After all, the *Tractatus Theologico-Politicus* was published in 1670, and Cudworth would not have received his copy until much of the work on his own *System* had already been completed. He probably had no information regarding the manuscript of the *Ethics* until 1675, and then only fragmentary reports.

Spinoza and Cudworth never met, but when, in 1655, Cudworth was elected as part of the advisory committee established by Cromwell in regard to the diplomatic mission of Rabbi Menasseh ben Israel,[100] Cudworth did meet one of the leading rabbis of the synagogue from which Spinoza had been excommunicated. Menasseh remained in London with his son Samuel for two years and was fiercely opposed by William Prynne, the Puritan lawyer and antiquarian. The rabbi returned to Amsterdam a heartbroken man after an outbreak of plague led not only to the loss of his son's life, but also to the adjournment of a Parliament still deadlocked on the issue of Jewish immigration and settlement. There is no indication, however, that Menasseh and Cudworth became personally acquainted, and it is unlikely that the rabbi would have introduced, as a topic of conversation, a "problem" Jew.

Rather, it was through Cudworth's membership in the Royal Society that he probably had his first introduction to Spinoza's thought—if, indeed, it could be called an introduction—by means of the Society's secretary, Heinrich Oldenburg, who had met Spinoza in 1661. Spinoza and Oldenburg had occasionally corresponded, with the secretary always soliciting the philosopher's views and the philosopher consistently responding in a guarded manner. Spinoza's caution did not, apparently, prevent the serious misapprehensions of Oldenburg and Robert Boyle, one of the Society's founding and most prestigious members. Therefore, even if Oldenburg made the correspondence available to the members of the Society, we should not expect that Cudworth would have acquired from it a more accurate perspective. Even so, we might note that one Ehrenfried Walther von Tschirnhaus, after having had access to Spinoza and the manuscript *Ethics* in 1674, visited the Royal Society in June of the following year and attempted to correct the members in their prejudices. Although Tschirnhaus claims to have effected a real change of opinion in favor of Spinoza, it is—as Steven Nadler suggests—more probable, in light of subsequent statements by Oldenburg, that the Society representatives were simply being polite and tactful.[101] We can neither adequately determine what impact Tschirnhaus had upon the Society, nor what Cudworth might have thought of Spinoza had he the leisure to study his chief writings more thoroughly. However, in regard to the latter speculation, we might reasonably suspect that Cudworth, if he had been allowed the opportunity, would have found more that was agreeable to him in Spinoza than he had prematurely supposed.[102]

Perhaps it is impossible to discuss Cudworth without moving into a digression or two. He is, after all, a master of tangential discussion, and so, if I have followed his style somewhat, my subject must be my apology. But now, let us return to our consideration of the Cambridge School and the essentially practical nature of Reason.

## Reason and Scripture

Despite the fact that the Platonists were a very literary group, they agree in making any knowledge that is not *natural* or internally derived, such as learning from books, including the Bible itself, subservient to Reason. The only necessary text for moral living is that text which is written on the heart. Although Whichcote acknowledges "*Two Lights*," the Light of Reason *and* the Light of Scripture, Scripture is merely an "After-Revelation," one that "is to be taken in a rational sense"–that is, illuminated by the greater Light of Reason.[103] For Smith, so crucial is it that knowledge in divinity derive from a life rooted in the soil of Reason and virtue that, without such a life, even training in theology may lead to evil consequences.[104] Cudworth is quite clear in making virtue, not Scripture, the essence of religion: "It is but the *Flesh*, and *Body*, of Divine Truths, that is printed upon Paper.... But there is a *Soul*, and *Spirit* of divine Truths, that could never yet be congealed into Inke.... The *Life* of divine

Truths, is better expressed in Actions then in Words, because Actions are more *Living* things, then words."[105]

In recognizing the all-sufficiency of Reason as the key to virtue, and virtue alone as the way toward knowledge of the divine, the Cambridge School necessarily conceded to the logical concomitant–that the virtuous pagan stood in a condition acceptable by God. The principle acknowledged by Whichcote is, "Where more is not reveal'd, God will not require more."[106] Thus, "God accepts alike the Faith that results from the dark Mists of the Ignorant, and from the clearest Intelligence of the Learned."[107] In fact, what is pleasing to God is not a mind that is a reservoir of revelation, but a life that is the proper moral response to whatever revelation is given: "The *Good Nature* of an Heathen is more God-like, than the furious *Zeal* of a Christian."[108] This approaches the "Saint Socrates" of Erasmus, and Cudworth declared as much to the House of Commons: "He that endeavours really to mortifie his lusts, and to comply with that truth in his life, which his Conscience is convinced of; is neerer a Christian, though he never heard of Christ; then he that believes all the vulgar Articles of the Christian faith, and plainly denyeth Christ in his life."[109]

Reason is a universal aspect of the human condition, and the knowledge of God and of the natural relation of humanity to God through virtue is, as More argues, an "active and *actuall Knowledge*" in every person. In *An Antidote against Atheism* (1652) he explains in detail:

> I understand thereby an active sagacity in the Soul, or quick recollection as it were, whereby some small business being hinted unto her, she runs out presently into a more clear and larger conception. And I cannot better describe her condition then thus; Suppose a skilful *Musician* fallen asleep in the field upon the grasse, during which time he shall not so much as dream any thing concerning his musicall faculty, so that in one sense there is no *actuall skill* or Notion nor representation of any thing musicall in him, but his friend sitting by him that cannot sing at all himself, jogs him and awakes him, and desires him to sing this or the other song, telling him two or three words of the beginning of the song, he presently takes it out of his mouth, and sings the whole song upon so slight and slender intimation: So the *Mind* of *man* being jogg'd and awakened by the impulses of outward objects is stirred up into a more full and cleare conception of what was but imperfectly hinted to her from externall occasions.[110]

Knowledge of divinity and of eternal and immutable truths may lie sleeping, as it were, in the consciousness of a person whose external circumstances have provided little occasion for the awakening of it. However, it remains nevertheless an "*actuall Knowledge*," the realization of which requires but a stimulus to be made *active*.

In reference to this aspect of their teaching, Basil Willey correctly recognizes that the early English Romantics, particularly Coleridge and Wordsworth, provide the perfect illustration and literary theory to support what the Cambridge School had argued from a purely theological position.[111] In "Lines Written in Early Spring" and "Expostulation and Reply" Wordsworth expresses his felt experience that, when the soul is linked to Nature, the *heart* thinks, being impressed by Powers independent of human activity. It is, thus, through "a wise passiveness" that we gain wisdom, knowledge that is implicitly ours before being made active.

## The Primitive Theology of the Gentiles

Cudworth and More believed that Plato had reasoned more correctly than many would-be Christian theologians (or, more precisely, had been in closer converse with the Divine *Logos*) in regard to the nature of God. Cudworth argues in great depth that "the *Catholick Doctrine* of the Platonick School" is, in its formulation of a divine Trinity, a closer approximation to orthodox Christian teaching than is Arianism, and moreover, suggests that Plato had approached as near as possible to the truth of God's nature as any philosopher might who had not the benefit of that supernatural manifestation granted to the world in the fullness of time:

> A *Christian Platonist* or *Platonick Christian*, would in all probability, Apologize for *Plato* himself, and the ancient and most Genuine Platonists and Pythagoreans after this manner. First, That since they had no Scriptures, Councils, nor Creeds, to direct their steps in the *Darkness* of this *Mystery*, and to confine their Language to a Regular Uniformity; but Theologized all Freely and Boldly, and without any Scrupulosity, every one according to his own private apprehensions, it is no wonder at all if they did not only speak many times unadvisedly, and inconsistently with their own Principles, but also plainly wander out of the *Right Path*. And that it ought much rather to be wondred at, that living so long before Christianity, as some of them did, they should in so *Abstruse* a Point, and *Dark a Mystery*, make so near an approach to the *Christian Truth* afterwards revealed, than that they should any where fumble or fall short of the Accuracy thereof.[112]

So convincing is Cudworth's explication of Plato the young, still Unitarian Coleridge, after having read the *True Intellectual System*, became a Trinitarian "*ad norman Platonis*"—that is, after the manner of Plato.[113] Perhaps, however, the altogether different reaction of W. R. Inge, the Dean of St. Paul's (1911-1934) whose sympathies were with the Platonic tradition, should also be noted: "The equation of the Neoplatonic divine hypostases with the Christian Trinity not only fails, but involves the writer in formal heresy."[114]

Given Cudworth's Apology for Platonism, one might suppose that the Cambridge School would have embraced the independence of the ancient Greeks from the prophetic revelation of God in Scripture as evidence of the universality of innate ideas, beyond the objective moral code. Not only the saintliness of Socrates and Plato, but then, their notions as well, could be pointed to as a sort of testimony to the "After-Revelation" of Scripture. Instead, we find that the Platonists fully subscribed to the theory of "the primitive theology of the Gentiles," according to which Pythagoras, as a contemporary of Moses, had read the Hebrew Scriptures, had grafted their theological and moral principles into his own philosophy, and so had introduced into Greek philosophy the teachings of Moses. "The implications," observes Patrides, "were neatly summed up in the oft-quoted rhetorical question ventured by Numenius of Apamea in the second century A.D.: 'What is *Plato* but *Moses Atticus*?'"[115] Cudworth, on the evidence of one Posidonius the Stoic (referred to by Strabo and Sextus Empiricus), grants historical credence to the suggestion that the concept of atoms was first invented by a Phoenician named Moschus. Moreover, "what can be more certain than that . . . Moschus the Phoenician and philosopher was no other than Moses, the Jewish lawgiver?" Wherefore, "the atomical philosophy . . . ought to be called neither Epicurean nor Democritical, but Moschical or Mosaical."[116]

It is disappointing that minds of the caliber of Cudworth and More were persuaded to believe "the primitive theology" theory, but it cannot be said that this theory is more contrary than contributory to their philosophic interests. Although it may have precluded any postulation of the Holy Trinity as an innate idea, yet—at the same time—it brought Plato into the vestibule of the Christian Church, positioning him as a sort of surrogate prophet to the people of God. In fact, the Cambridge Platonists could argue, so important is Plato as an intermediary between Jewish and Christian religion that those Christian theologians that have dismissed him as a mere Pagan have done so to their own detriment.

Of course, it might be said that, in this matter, the Cambridge Platonists were only participating in the thought of their time, and as Matthew Arnold states in connection with Smith's belief in witchcraft, "That a man shares an error of the minds around him and of the times in which he lives, proves nothing against his being a man of veracity, judgment, and mental power."[117] Since the time of the revival of Platonism, theologians with an invested interest in defending the supernatural inspiration of Scripture had been at pains to demonstrate *why* this type of revelation was essential, when men such as Socrates appeared to be in possession of the ethics of Scripture without having Scripture. The rather ingenious but historically unsubstantiated hypothesis that Posidonius's Moschus was actually Moses was the answer arrived at centuries earlier, in a less critical age. The fact that this hypothesis regained popular academic support in the seventeenth century merely suggests the pressures put upon theologians in the wake of the Renaissance to prove the priority of Scripture over Plato. The leading exponent of this theory during the time of the Cambridge Platonists was a Puritan by the name of Theophilus Gale, who published in 1671 his two-volume *Court of the Gentiles*.

## Of Heaven and Hell

One looks in vain to find within the work of the Cambridge School the sort of textual criticism that had been put to use so fruitfully by Spinoza. The Cambridge men were predominantly religious philosophers; the age of biblical criticism had not yet fully arrived—and, in any event, when it did arrive, England would not take the lead.

Nevertheless, they knew how to read the Bible as a work of literature, and they correctly perceived poetic metaphor where the Puritans did not. This is nowhere so evident as in their treatment of "heaven" and "hell." With Whichcote—no less than with the Victorian theologian F. D. Maurice—these are primarily states of conscience:

> It is a most gross Mistake; and Men are of dull and stupid Spirits, who think that State which we call *Hell*, is *an incommodious place*, only; and that God, by his Sovereignty, throws Men therein. For Hell arises *out of a Man's self*: And Hell's Fewel is *the Guilt of a Man's Conscience*. . . . And on the other side, when they think that Heaven arises from any *Place*, or any nearness to God, or Angels: This is not principally so; but it lies in a *refin'd Temper*, in *an internal Reconciliation to the Nature of God, and to the Rule of Righteousness*.[118]

The other Cambridge Platonists are in agreement; however, both Smith and Cudworth insist that "heaven" and "hell" are *only* spiritual conditions. "*Hell* is *rather a Nature* then *a place*," says Smith, "and *Heaven* cannot be so truly defined by any thing *without* us, as by something that is *within* us."[119] Cudworth is even more emphatic: "Were our hearts sound within, were there not many thick and dark fumes, that did arise from thence, and cloud our understandings, we could not easily conceive the substance of Heaven it self, to be any thing else but *Holinesse*; . . . neither should we wish for any other Heaven, besides this."[120] It should be noted, however, that the Platonists are not original in this regard, and Cassirer is simply mistaken when he asserts, "That grand and audacious speech which Milton puts in the mouth of Satan:

> The mind is its own place, and in itself
> Can make a Heav'n of Hell, a Hell of Heav'n

was first enunciated by the modest thinkers of the Cambridge Circle."[121] Possibly, as Cassirer suggests, Milton did pick up the thought from Whichcote; but, it was a notion that Cambridge had been long familiar with, and Marlowe had given expression to it several decades earlier:

> *Faust* [speaking to Mephistopheles]: Where are you damn'd?
> *Meph.*: In hell.
> *Faust*: How comes it then that thou art out of hell?
> *Meph.*: Why this is hell, nor am I out of it.
> >Think'st thou that I who saw the face of God,
> >And tasted the eternal joys of Heaven,
> >Am not tormented with ten thousand hells,
> >In being depriv'd of everlasting bliss?[122]

In Mephistopheles's reply we find the implication that "hell" is not a positive infliction, but consists rather in the subjective experience of the loss of completion and reality, the denigration of being. Mephistopheles's torment, in other words, is a mere but insufferable deprivation, the intensity of which can be weighed in the balance of his prior experience of wholeness and real existence in the presence of God. But we cannot even allow Marlowe to be original in his conception of hell, for five centuries previous, there was an Archbishop of Canterbury who often declared, "It is certain that only the wicked are tormented in hell, and only the good are happy in the kingdom of heaven. Therefore it is clear that the good, if they could enter hell, could not be visited with the punishment due to the wicked; nor could the evil, even if they could get to heaven, enjoy there the blessedness of the good." Knowing that the pains associated with hell are neither greater nor less than the torments consequent to the violation of the conscience, Anselm's only fear was the horrors of sin.[123]

This is the hell recognized by the Cambridge Platonists, for whom evil itself is but the negation of the good, a falling away from God and Nature. And, moreover, if hell is recognized, it can be vanquished, for the recognition itself presupposes a knowledge of and preference for the good. What a far cry is this from the message of the Frankfurt pessimist of the nineteenth century, who inverted Augustine's thesis and posited the good as the mere negation of a positive evil! For Schopenhauer, "The world is Hell, and men are on the one hand the tormented souls and on the other the devils in it."[124]

## Culverwell

Better armed for comparative criticism, we might now return to our consideration of Culverwell. As indicated earlier, he had two audiences, whom we might identify as the schools of Tuckney and Whichcote. Culverwell himself took up the middle ground, but not as a mediator. His mission was to bring about neither a reconciliation nor a compromise. Although he affirms the strengths of both schools, his ultimate object is not to unite them on the ground of their truths, but rather to erect a third school on the basis of their errors.

There are those who have called the *Discourse of the Light of Nature* a panegyric on reason, but this is a simplification. There are indeed passages that extol reason highly, but these must be thrown into the scale with passages of a seemingly opposite import, and the challenge for any critic of Culverwell is to arrive at the balance. The *Discourse* justifies Dillingham's preparatory admonition to the reader: "If, standing in the midst between two adversaries of extreme perswasions, while he opposes the one, he seeme to favour the other more than is meet; when thou shalt observe him at another time to declare as much against the other, thou wilt then be of another minde."[125] The potency of Culverwell's indignant declaration, that "to blaspheme *Reason*, 'tis to reproach heaven it self, and to dishonour the God of

*Reason*," is quickly diluted by his own definition of Reason as a "faint and languishing light."[126] The Candle of our Reason is a spark of the Divine light, and so it is truly the Candle of the Lord; yet "A Candle has no such goodly light, as that it should pride and glory in it. 'Tis but a brief and compendious flame, shut up, and imprison'd in a narrow compasse."[127] The rationale behind this muted praise is what sets Culverwell apart from Platonists.

For Culverwell, as for the Cambridge Platonists, to obey Reason is to obey Nature, but Culverwell emphatically distinguishes between the two. The Law of Nature is but the eternal law imprinted "upon the breast of a Rational being,"[128] and Reason is the dim light by which we stumble our way toward that Law, which expresses itself through our Reason as Common Notions or first principles of morality. Rejecting Plato's epistemology, and favoring Aristotle, Aquinas, and Suarez, Culverwell declares that Reason is *merely* the Candle; it illuminates, but is not an illumination; it reveals, but is not a revelation: "*Reason* does not make or produce the law, but only discovers it, as a Candle does not produce an object, but only presents it to the eye, and makes it visible."[129] If we are not averse to the light that God has given to us, we will eventually, through the process of observation and experience, arrive at the moral laws of our nature; but these Common Notions, insists Culverwell, are not to be confused as dormant knowledge or the pre-existent ideas of the soul that await to be aroused from sleep.[130] Thus, although "the Platonists in this were commendable, that they lookt upon the spirit of a man as *the Candle of the Lord*, . . . they were deceived in the time when 'twas lighted."[131]

Consistent with its epistemology, the *Discourse* relegates Reason to the domain of creation. Neither our Nature nor our Reason are of the Divine essence. Because of them, we may truly claim to be created in the image of God, but it is pantheist heresy to suggest that we are created out of God. Thus, Culverwell finds the Cambridge Platonist doctrine of deification an intolerable error: "They must have very low and dishonourable thoughts of God that make any creature partner or sharer with him in its essence, and they must have high and swelling thoughts of the creature. How proud is that soul that aspires to be a God!"[132]

From Culverwell's point of view, trusting one's salvation to Reason alone is like trusting one's path to the light of a candle, instead of using the candle to illuminate an infallible and clearly marked map. We must trust the light of our own candle rather than depend upon another's candle, but not all the candle-light of the world can replace the counsel of our only sure Guide. Culverwell inclines to the determination of Aquinas, that revealed truths "were never against Reason, they were alwayes above Reason." Right Reason can never be contrary to Revelation, but our faltering Reason will not always lead us all the way to where Revelation would have us arrive. Therefore, "Reason, though she will not put out her eye, for that's unnatural, yet she will close her eye sometimes, that faith may aime the better, and that's commendable."[133]

The Cambridge Platonists would have protested against this policy of sometimes placing the Candle of the Lord under a table. One may wonder what John

Smith had to say about this *Discourse*. Culverwell and Smith were about the same age, both natives of Northamptonshire, both eloquent and learned young men when they died, and both were independent thinkers who had parted from Whichcote into different directions. We can only imagine what dialogues they might have entered into had they lived. Perhaps, Culverwell would have ultimately recognized his intermediate posture as untenable; yet, this is speculation, and we can do nothing other than place him in the position he occupied at the time of his death. If we dismiss the accidents of historical association, then we should have no difficulty in recognizing that, as a thinker, Culverwell occupies a position apart from the Cambridge Platonists.[134]

The dismissal of historical association is, however, a two-sided operation. Whereas it severs ties on the one hand, it creates them on the other. Joseph Glanvill (1636-1680) and John Norris (1657-1711) of Oxford would then, by our rule of operation, could legitimately be classified among the Cambridge Platonists. Verily, Glanvill follows the chilling caution of Culverwell as the revivifying breath of spring:

> I infer, [says Glanvill] *That Reason is*, in a sense, *the Word of God, viz.* That which he hath written upon our Minds and Hearts; as Scripture is that which is written in a Book. The former is the Word, whereby he hath spoken to all Mankind; the latter is that whereby he hath declared his Will to the Church, and his peculiar People. Reason is that *Candle of the Lord*, of which *Solomon* speaks, *Prov.* 20.27.[135]

Here, in Glanvill, we find the rational spirit of Whichcote and the philosophical spirit of Cudworth and More. Like the youthful More, Glanvill was an outspoken opponent of religious enthusiasm and an admirer and apologist for the principles of "the Grand Secretary of Nature, the miraculous *Des-Cartes*."[136] Like Whichcote and Jeremy Taylor, he set himself against the sectarian spirit: "The union of a Sect within it self, is a pitiful *charity*: it's no concord of *Christians*, but a conspiracy against *Christ*; and they that love one another, for their *opinionated concurrences*, love for their *own sakes*, not their *Lords*: not because they have his *image*, but because they bear one *anothers*."[137] Even so, it is sufficient for the purpose of this chapter to note that the influence of the Cambridge School of Platonists did not confine itself to Cambridge and, in doing so, to direct the intellectual sojourner toward Oxford for further study.

# III
# Reception

As essentialists in matters of dogma, the Platonists were, of course, thought well of neither by the Puritan presbyterians nor by the High Church episcopalians. When Edward Fowler, who received his M.A. from Trinity College in 1655, ventured to defend the Platonists' doctrines in two books, *Free Discourse* (1670) and *The Design of Christianity* (1672), John Bunyan ventured a rather fierce response. In 1672 Bunyan was in the last year of his twelve-year imprisonment for preaching the gospel without a license and refusal to comply with the Act of Conformity (introduced immediately after the Restoration of 1660). In this year he responded to Fowler with *A Defence of the Doctrine of Justification by Faith*. He perceived, with *some* reason, surely, that the Cambridge School reduced Christianity to a moral philosophy. Moreover, he attacked Fowler himself, who, *after* the Restoration, was in good stead with the Established Church. Bunyan's intent, as he himself declared to Fowler, was to publicly expose "the rotteness of your heart." Fowler, unfortunately, unleashed an equally vituperative response, and in doing so, clearly failed to uphold the Platonist's manner, regardless of how correct he may have been in regard to their doctrine.

We are reminded of Whichcote's aphorism, quoted earlier, "The *Good Nature* of an Heathen is more God-like, than the furious *Zeal* of a Christian." Whichcote was astute enough to recognize that differences of understanding are not an unfortunate problem requiring a necessary toleration; rather, they are an essential aspect of the life of the church, a natural—and, thus, God-ordained—stimulus toward the development of doctrine.[138] But, Fowler is not the only guilty party in this exchange. Bunyan never relented in his opposition to Fowler and, it has been suggested, made him the object of satire through casting him as Mr. Worldly-Wiseman in the First Part of *Pilgrim's Progress*.[139] By-ends is another of Bunyan's characters who might have been created with the intention of representing Fowler. When Mr. Money-Love asks in regard to Christian and Hopeful, "Why did they not stay that we might have had their good company, for they, and we, and you Sir, I hope, are all going on pilgrimage?", By-ends responds with a criticism characteristic of a Broad-Church stance against dissent:

> We are so indeed, but the men before us are so rigid, and love so much their own notions, and do also so lightly esteem the opinions of others, that let a man be never

so godly, yet if he jumps not with them in all things they thrust him quite out of their company.[140]

Bunyan has By-ends captivated by the enticement of Demas, who offers the easy-diggings of a silver mine. The suggestion is, perhaps, that Fowler's acceptance of the Prayer-Book in 1662 was motivated by greed for worldly honor and security. Likely enough, Bunyan perceived all latitudinarianism as doctrinal insincerity nurtured by worldly lusts.

As a passing note—of possibly satiric interest to the general reader—in 1678, the year of the publication of the First Part of *Pilgrim's Progress*, that other Puritan author of notoriety, Lemuel Gulliver, was completing his three years of study at Emmanuel College. It would be another eleven years before he began his famous adventures that would be chronicled in *Travels into Several Remote Nations of the World* (1726).[141]

The Puritans had not the only voice of opposition to the Platonists. John Dryden, in the Dedication for his translation of Vergil's *Aeneid*, notes that "Doctor Cudworth," in *The True Intellectual System*, "has rais'd such strong objections against the being of a God, and Providence, that many think he has not answer'd them."[142] Dryden wrote this in 1697, decades after his conversion from the High Church *via-media* to Roman Catholicism. He was, of course, never sympathetic to the Cambridge Platonists, and Tulloch is correct in interpreting his remark as something less than an objective report. Adopting his indirect fashion of criticism, Tulloch says of Dryden, "There is never anybody so unthinkingly orthodox as the clever man of the world, when he thinks it necessary to interest himself in religion."[143]

Cudworth's work is, overall, a defense of Theism; however, there is some basis for Dryden's criticism, which must be extended to apply equally to the work of More. First, although they had both argued that the natural and innate revelation of good and evil is testimony to the human mind's affiliation with the mind of God, they had also effectively contradicted Descartes's and the Calvinists' claim that "good" and "evil" are determined by the arbitrary will of God. God could as well make the good into the evil, argued Cudworth, as he could make a round square. Thus, although human morality derived from God, ethics could exist as a science apart from God, since good and evil were absolutes. Second, both Cudworth and More fully accepted material determinism and argued that life forms acquired their shape through a "Plastick Nature" or "Spirit of Nature," which is "*Art it self, acting immediately on the Matter, as an Inward Principle,*" and by which "every thing comes to pass *Fortuitously*, and happens to be as it is, without the Guidance and Direction of any *Mind* or *Understanding*."[144] Martineau recognizes this theory as an anticipation of "a principle of Evolution,"[145] and more recent critics have noted the similarity between the idea of a "plastic nature" and Henri Bergson's theory of "vital impetus." Just as it used to be supposed that evolution was necessarily atheistic, so too did some of Cudworth's contemporaries believe that the doctrine of plastic nature was a form of atheism. Pierre Bayle took this stance against Arminian philosopher Jean Le Clerc, and their running argument appeared in nine volumes of the *Bibliotheque choisie* (1703-13). More accurately, Alain Petit defines the position of Cudworth as "a *via media* between mechanism and hyper-voluntarism, between a God who does nothing and a God who does everything."[146]

Only the most reactionary opponents of the Cambridge School would consider labeling them as atheists. More often, they were called "latitudinarians," a term invented specifically to describe their position and intended to be derogatory. They have also been regarded as contributors to the development and popularization of enlightenment Deism. There are undeniable similarities between the thought of the Cambridge School and that of Lord Herbert of Cherbury (1583-1648), popularly known as "the father of Deism." They both believe in innate ideas, what Herbert calls in *De Veritate* (1624) "Common Notions," as revelation from God and the proof of God's existence. Both also argue that God is to be worshiped through virtuous living. However, their differences are at least as significant. The Platonists, while interpreting Scripture in the light of Reason, are nevertheless deeply rooted in the Christian tradition, whereas Herbert believes that the method of finding pure religion, uncorrupted by speculative and political additions, is through a comparative study of world religions. Herbert's ideas may be thought of as having ultimately led to the development of the idea of a philosophy of religion and of an anthropology of myth. One can find something of the spirit of Herbert in the work of Joseph Campbell, inspired by Jungian psychology and in search of the ideal of which the "collective unconscious" speaks. Moreover, whereas Herbert plainly says that he disbelieves in miracles, the Platonists do not. In the tradition of the Alexandrian Church Fathers, they sometimes allegorize the miracles of Christ in order to find their deeper meaning; nowhere do they state a disbelief in them.[147]

In the debates that ensued between Christians and Deists during the latter seventeenth and early eighteenth centuries, both parties held firmly to the idea of the reasonableness of religion. The Age of Reason had passed on its legacy to the Enlightenment. In 1695 John Locke, who was on familiar terms with Cudworth's daughter, Lady Masham, published his *Reasonableness of Christianity*. Locke agreed with the Deists that reports of miracles were not generally credible; however, since reason endorsed the understanding of Scripture as a revelation *unique in kind*, the accounts of miracles therein were not contrary to reason. A sensible person who, in all other cases, maintained a strictly empiricist approach to understanding nature could, without compromise to conviction, believe in the miracles of Christ. Locke did not have to wait for David Hume's devastating essay "Of Miracles" (1748); John Toland, a tutor at Oxford, responded almost immediately to Locke in his classic exposition of Christian Deism, *Christianity Not Mysterious* (1696). Toland agrees with the Cambridge Platonists in arguing that Nature approves of all that is vital to Christianity, but he goes onward, adding his voice to Herbert in contending that all elements of supernaturalism in Scripture are the unwarranted additions of paganism and priestcraft. Matthew Tindal joined the list of Deists against Locke in 1730, with the publication of his highly influential *Christianity as Old as the Creation*. Six years later Joseph Butler published the classic defense of traditional Christianity against Deism, *The Analogy of Religion*. Both Nature and Scripture are the revelation of God, argued Butler, and both have their inconsistencies. Yet, such inconsistencies as they have do not present a barrier to logical acceptance, for all knowledge is ultimately grounded in the mere probability of truth. We do not lose faith in Nature when it behaves in ways that we cannot comprehend, and neither must we cease to trust the truth of Scripture.

Within this debate there is one figure who, more than all others, is the ideological descendant of the Cambridge School. That person is, of course, Anthony Ashley Cooper, the third Earl of Shaftesbury (1671-1713), who was both a Neo-Platonist and a Christian Deist. According to Shaftesbury, not only does the contemplation of Nature teach us virtue, but it also teaches us beauty. Moreover, in Plotinian fashion and anticipating Keats's famous dictum, Shaftesbury notes that "all beauty is truth."[148] There is no such thing as a *truth* that is not in accord with Nature; neither is there anything of Nature that is not *beautiful*. Truth is a property of the beautiful, as beauty is a property of truth, and both derive from Nature, which is not only the expression, but the emanation of God. Shaftesbury was a pantheist, not a dualist, and because aesthetics were more crucial to him than to his Platonist predecessors, he succeeded in giving aesthetic form to his own work. His *Characteristics*, more than any other English work, contributed to the development of humanism in Germany, exercising a profound influence on Herder, Schiller, and Goethe, and through them on Schelling.

Thus, through Shaftesbury, the doctrine of the Cambridge School "forms a sort of connecting-link between minds and epochs."[149] Although born in the unpoetic age of "clear and distinct ideas," their doctrine proved to have something of a plastic nature, conformable to the *Zeit-Geist*, and ultimately contributed to the development of literary aesthetics. Through Shaftesbury and the German humanists, Cambridge Platonism merged into the ideological melting-pot of the times and returned to England in the ever-shifting forms of Romanticism.

Largely through the influence of S. T. Coleridge, the acknowledged "father of the Broad Church movement," the thought of the Cambridge School began, in the second and third decades of the nineteenth century, to acquire a solid footing within the Church of England. Not only were the Cambridge Platonists similar in intellectual predisposition to the Victorian liberal churchmen, but as John Tulloch (1823-86) notes, the philosophical and theological questions that they discussed were "very much the questions still discussed under the name of Broad-Churchism."[150] An instance of this may be seen in the *Eight Letters* that follow this Introduction. One of Tuckney's arguments—that acceptance of Scripture expressions, apart from creedal interpretations and other forms of explication, is an insufficient basis for Christian unity—anticipates E. B. Pusey's and J. H. Newman's argument against R. D. Hampden in 1836.[151] This issue and others common to

Cambridge Platonists and Broad Churchmen are part of the heritage of liberal Anglicanism and have been absorbed into modernity. As one scholar recently observed, "The Cambridge Platonists were at the heart of the formation of modern thought, and many of their questions are still our own."[152] Possibly, some of their *answers* are our own as well.

# Notes

1. John Fisher (ca. 1470-1535), who had studied under William Grocyn at Oxford, was chaplain to Lady Margaret Beaufort, the mother of Henry VII, when he became Vice-Chancellor of Cambridge in 1501. Under the patronage of Lady Margaret, Fisher established a chair of divinity and introduced the study of Greek at Cambridge. Fisher offered the Lady Margaret Lectureship to Erasmus (ca. 1466-1536). When Erasmus left Cambridge in 1514, his influence there remained strong through such men as Richard Croke, the Greek scholar who became Cambridge's first Public Orator in 1522, and Henry Bullock, lecturer in divinity (*Vide* V. H. H. Green, *Religion at Oxford and Cambridge* [London: SCM Press, 1964], 83-5).

2. *Bishop Burnet's History of His Own Time: From the Restoration of King Charles II to the Conclusion of the Treaty of Peace at Utrecht, in the Reign of Queen Anne*, ed. Thomas Burnet, 4 vols. (London: Samuel Bagster, 1815), 1:240-41. Thomas Stackhouse, while abridging Burnet's *History* a decade after the author's death, could not refrain from adding his own indignant outburst at these "men of narrower thoughts": "So ungrateful a work it is to awaken a spirit of inquiry or to point out new lights to a people that is blinded with prejudice!" (Bishop Gilbert Burnet, *History of His Own Time*, ed. Thomas Stackhouse [ca. 1724; London: J. M. Dent and Sons Ltd, 1906], 45).

3. G. A. J. Rogers argues that the Cambridge Platonists were well aware of the political landscape that they inhabited and maintained "a position which they saw as advancing towards a political settlement in the troubled and dangerous years of mid-seventeenth century England" ("The Other-Worldly Philosophers and the Real World: The Cambridge Platonists, Theology, and Politics," *The Cambridge Platonists in Philosophical Context: Politics, Metaphysics, and Religion*, ed. G. A. J. Rogers, J. M. Vienne, and Y. C. Zarka [Boston: Kluwer Academic Publishers, 1997], 3-15, 4).

4. It cannot be said that Erasmus had no immediate impact upon Oxford studies, since Thomas Lupset, the first Professor of Greek at Oxford, received his initial training directly from Erasmus at Cambridge (H. Maynard Smith, *Pre-Reformation England* [London: Macmillan and Co., Ltd., 1963], 450).

5. Ernst Cassirer, *The Platonic Renaissance in England*, trans. James P. Pettegrove (Austin: Univ. Texas Press, 1953), 112. See also C. S. Lewis, "Neoplatonism in the Poetry of Spenser," *Studies in Medieval & Renaissance Literature* (New York: Cambridge University Press, 1966), 149-63. Spenser was a favorite poet of Alexander More, the father of Henry, who often read *The Færie Queene* with his son. W. R. Inge observes, "More's earlier poetry is full of echoes of Spenser" (*The Platonic Tradition in English Religious Thought* [London: Longmans, Green, and Co., 1926], 54).

6. Izaak Walton, "The Life of Mr. Richard Hooker: The Author of Those Learned Books of the Laws of Ecclesiastical Polity," 1665, rpt. in *The Lives of Dr. John Donne, Sir Henry Wotton, Mr. Richard Hooker, Mr. George Herbert, and Dr. Robert Sanderson* (London: Henry Washbourne, 1840), 161-254, 174.

7. Walton, 207-08.

8. Richard Hooker, *Of the Laws of Ecclesiastical Polity*, Preface i.2, in *The Works of That Learned and Judicious Divine Mr. Richard Hooker*, ed. John Keeble, 7th ed., rev. R. W. Church and F. Paget, 3 vols. (Oxford: Clarendon Press, 1888), 1:127.

9. Basil Willey, *The English Moralists* (London: Methuen and Co., Ltd., 1965), 104.

10. Hooker, Preface ix.3, 1:194-95.

11. Hooker, I.vi.3-vii.2, 1:217-20.

12. Hooker, I.v.3, 1:216.

13. Hooker, I.vii.3-7, 1:221-25.

14. Hooker, I.viii.3, 1:227-28.

15. Hooker, I.xii.1, 1:262.

16. Hooker, I..xiv.1-5, 1:267-71.

17. Willey, 102.

18. C. S. Lewis, *The Abolition of Man* (New York: Macmillan, 1947), 88.

19. C. S. Lewis, "Edmund Spenser, 1552-99," *Studies in Medieval & Renaissance Literature*, 121-45, 122.

20. John Tulloch, *Rational Theology and Christian Philosophy in England in the 17th Century*, 2nd ed., 2 vols. (Edinburgh: William Blackwood and Sons, 1874), 1:176.

21. F. L. Cross and E. A. Livingstone, eds., *The Oxford Dictionary of the Christian Church*, 2nd ed. (New York: Oxford University Press, 1974), 1173.

22. Tulloch, 1:231.

23. In response to the Counter-Reformation, Cornelius Otto Jansen (1585-38), author of the *Augustinus*, made an attempt to return Catholicism to an Augustinian foundation. His Catholic followers are called Jansenists.

24. Thomas Fuller, *The History of the University of Cambridge, from the Conquest to the Year 1634* (1655; eds. Marmaduke Prickett and Thomas Wright [Cambridge: Cambridge University Press, 1840], 277-78).

25. Frederick J. Powicke, *The Cambridge Platonists: A Study* (Cambridge, MA: Harvard University Press, 1926), 2.

26. Fuller, 319.

27. Powicke, 4-5. Fuller, proceeding in his account with confessed uncertainty, states that Holdesworth was also Vice-Chancellor of the University at the time of his arrest, and was succeeded in this capacity by Ralph Brownrig, a strict Calvinist, then Bishop of Exeter and Master of Catherine Hall (321). Brownrig's election was not unconditional, and he was deposed from office during the Protectorship.

28. For modern readers, this line of Milton's has a more obvious metaphorical meaning than it would have had for his contemporaries. Archbishop Richard Whately explains, "Originally, *Priest* was only a contraction (or shortening) of the word *Presbyter*; and it meant properly the same as Presbyter; that is *an Elder* of the Church. In this sense it is used in our Prayer-books, wherever our clergy are called *Priests*" (*Cautions for the Times* [London: John W. Parker and Son, 1853], 38).

29. This was thirty-seven years before, on 18 July 1290, the Jews were officially expelled from England (Cecil Roth, *A Short History of the Jewish People*, illustrated ed. [London: East and West Library, 1959], 224-25.

30. John Foxe notes that, although Quakers were not persecuted for their beliefs *per se*, they did fall foul of a number of laws during the Protectorate; for example, they were fined and

imprisoned for refusing to take oaths (*Fox's Book of Martyrs*, ed. William Byron Forbush [Grand Rapids: Zondervan Publishing House, 1967], 317).

31. Jeremy Taylor, *A Discourse on the Liberty of Prophesying, 1647* (Menston, Yorkshire: Scolar Press Ltd., 1971), Sect. XIII. Due to what is probably a printer's error, the number four is given twice, resulting in the appearance of nine rather than ten points.

32. Benjamin Whichcote, *Select Sermons of Dr. Whichcot* (Edinburgh: T. W. and T. Ruddimans, 1742), Part II, Sermon I, 186, 191-92.

33. *Bishop Burnet's History*, 1:238.

34. Powicke, 13.

35. Benjamin Whichcote, "The Unity of the Church Maintained by Sincere Christians," *Several Discourses*, ed. John Jeffrey, 3rd ed. (1703), Sermon XXX, 3:437-53; rpt. in *The Cambridge Platonists*, ed. C. A. Patrides, the Stratford-upon-Avon Library, Vol. 5 (London: Edward Arnold, 1969), 77-89, 82.

36. John Tillotson, *A Sermon Preached at the Funeral of the Reverend Benjamin Whichcot, D.D., and Minister of S. Lawrence Jewry, London, May 24th, 1683* (London: Printed by M. Flesher, 1683), 22-3.

37. Tulloch, 2:86.

38. G. P. H. Pawson, *The Cambridge Platonists and Their Place in Religious Thought* (London: SPCK, 1930), 19.

39. J. A. Passmore, *Ralph Cudworth: An Interpretation* (London: Cambridge University Press, 1951), 18.

40. Fuller, 314-15.

41. Tulloch 2:204.

42. Marjorie Hope Nicolson, *Conway Letters: The Correspondence of Anne, Viscountess Conway, Henry More, and Their Friends, 1642-1684* (New Haven: Yale University Press, 1930), 471.

43. Cf. Tulloch 2:123 and Passmore, 39n.

44. E. T. Campagnac, Introduction to *The Cambridge Platonists: Being Selections from the Writings of Benjamin Whichcote, John Smith, and Nathaniel Culverwell* (Oxford: Clarendon Press, 1901), i-xxxvi, xxviii.

45. Tulloch 2:186.

46. C. A. Patrides, Introduction to *Select Discourses* by John Smith (Delmar, NY: Scholars' Facsimiles and Reprints, 1979), v-xii, v.

47. Henry More, "Euporia," lines 7-8, in *An Addition of some few smaller Poems* (Cambridge, Roger Daniel, 1647), rpt. in *The Complete Poems*, ed. Alexander B. Grosart (Edinburgh: Edinburgh University Press, 1878), 182. Translation by Tulloch, 2:311-12.

48. *Vide* Anne Conway, *The Principles of the Most Ancient and Modern Philosophy*, 1692, ed. T. Corse and A. Coudert (Cambridge: Cambridge University Press, 1996).

49. More was, for a time, the foremost advocate in England of the Cartesian philosophy. His correspondence with Descartes, however, not only reveals admiration for Descartes's method and system, but also shows the lack of agreement that was to become for More the crucial point. The correspondence was broken off by Descartes's death in 1650, and by 1667 More had come to regard Cartesianism as a form of atheism, since it withheld extension to thought, and so essentially gave no *place* to spirit or space.

50. Brinkley, Roberta Florence, *Coleridge on the Seventeenth Century* (New York: Duke University Press, 1955), 316-17.

51. Matthew Arnold, "A Psychological Parallel," in *The Complete Prose Works of Matthew Arnold*, ed. R. H. Super, 11 vols. (Ann Arbor: University of Michigan Press, 1960-77), 8:136.

52. Frederick Denison Maurice, *Moral and Metaphysical Philosophy*, 2 vols. (London: Macmillan and Co., 1886), 2:349.

53. Tulloch 2:413.

54. Robert A. Greene and Hugh MacCallum, Introduction to *An Elegant and Learned Discourse of the Light of Nature* by Nathaniel Culverwell (Toronto: University of Toronto Press, 1971), ix-lv, xliii.

55. Green and MacCallum, xxxv-xxxvi.

56. Aharon Lichtenstein, *Henry More: The Rational Theology of a Cambridge Platonist* (Cambridge, MA: Harvard University Press, 1962), 25.

57. William Hazlitt, "Mr. Coleridge," *The Spirit of the Age; or, Contemporary Portraits* (1825), in *William Hazlitt: Selected Writings*, ed. Ronald Blythe (New York: Penguin Classics, 1982), 232-44, 237.

58. Cassirer, 27-8.

59. Lichtenstein, 45-7.

60. Benjamin Whichcote, *Select Sermons of Dr. Whichcot*, ed. William Wishart (Edinburgh: Printed by T. W. And T. Ruddimans, 1742), Part I, Sermon III, 52-78, 57. Patrides, who reprints the 1698 text, edited by Anthony Ashley Cooper, Lord Shaftesbury, also provides a title for this sermon: "The Use of Reason in Matters of Religion," 42-61, 47.

61. Whichcote, *Select Sermons*, Part I, Sermon III, 68; Patrides, 54.

62. Cudworth's *Treatise Concerning Eternal and Immutable Morality* presents, as an apology for the existence of God, the argument that there are truths known by reason, not by sense, that are yet independent of reason, such as mathematics and moral absolutes. In making this argument, it should be noted, Cudworth is partly indebted to Book II of Augustine's *De liberto arbitrio*.

63. Whichcote, *Select Sermons*, Part I, Sermon III, 63; Patrides, 51.

64. Benjamin Whichcote, *Moral and Religious Aphorisms*, §99, ed. John Jeffrey (1703), revised by Samuel Salter (1753); rpt., with Introduction by W. R. Inge (London: Elkin Mathews and Marrot, Ltd., 1930), §99, 13; Patrides, 327.

65. Whichcote, *Select Sermons*, Part I, Sermon III, 62; Patrides, 50.

66. All biblical quotations are from the King James (or "Authorised") Version (1611).

67. John Calvin, *Institutes of the Christian Religion*, 1536 ed., I.B.2-4, trans. Ford Lewis Battles (Grand Rapids: Wm. B. Eerdman's Publishing Co., 1986), 16-7.

68. Whichcote, *Moral and Religious Aphorisms*, §916; Patrides, 334.

69. Henry More, *Enchiridion Ethicum*, I.iii.5 (New York: The Facsimile Text Society, 1930), 15.

70. Joseph Hall, *Christ Mystical: Or, the Blessed Union of Christ and His Members*, ed. H. Carruthers Wilson (London: Hodder and Stoughton, 1908), 90.

71. Whichcote, *Select Sermons*, Part I, Sermon III, 73-4; Patrides 58.

72. Whichcote, *Select Sermons*, Part II, Sermon III, 216-36, 222; Patrides titles this sermon "The Manifestation of Christ and the Deification of Man," 62-76, 66.

73. John Smith, "The Excellency and Nobleness of True Religion," *Select Discourses*, ed. John Worthington (1660), Discourse IX, pp. 377-451, 389; Patrides, 155.

74. Smith, "The True Way or Method of Attaining to Divine Knowledge," *Select Discourses*, Discourse I, 1-21, 6; Patrides, 132.

75. John Norris, "Letters Philosophical and Moral between the Author and Dr. Henry More," in *The Theory and Regulation of Love, A Moral Essay in Two Parts* (London, 1688); qtd. in Lichtenstein, 43-4.

76. Smith, "The True Way or Method," 9; Patrides, 134.

77. Smith, "The True Way or Method," 13; Patrides, 137.

78. Henry More, *Enthusiasmus Triumphatus, or a Discourse of the Nature, Causes, Kinds, and Cure of Enthusiasme*, §XV (1662; Los Angeles: The Augustan Reprint Society, 1966), 10-11.

79. Joseph Glanvill, *The Vanity of Dogmatizing: Or Confidence in Opinions; Manifested in a Discourse of the Shortness and Uncertainty of our Knowledge, and Its Causes* (London: B.C., 1661), XI, 95-105; *Scepsis Scientifica: Or, Confest Ignorance, the Way to Science; in an Essay of the Vanity of Dogmatizing, and Confident Opinion* (London: E. Cotes, 1665), XIII, 70-7.

80. More, *Enthusiasmus Triumphatus*, §VI, 4.

81. Smith, "The True Way or Method," 9; Patrides, 134; Ralph Cudworth, *A Sermon Preached before the Honourable House of Commons at Westminster, March 31, 1647* (Cambridge: Printed by Roger Daniel, 1647), 17; Patrides, 90-127, 98. Cudworth's *Sermon* delivered to Parliament was later published as "The First Sermon" in *A Discourse concerning the True Notion of the Lord's Supper; to Which Are Added Two Sermons*, 2nd ed. (London: Printed by J. Fletcher for R. Royston, 1670), 103-87.

82. Plotinus, "Against the Gnostics," *The Enneads*, II.ix.15, trans. Stephen MacKenna (New York: Penguin, 1991), 127.

83. Richard Whately, *Essays on Some of the Difficulties in the Writings of the Apostle Paul*, 1828 (London: John W. Parker, 1849), 107n; cf. John Tulloch, *English Puritanism and Its Leaders* (London: Wm. Blackwood and Sons, 1861), 154.

84. Cudworth, *A Sermon*, 2; Patrides, 91.

85. Cudworth, *A Sermon*, 79-80; Patrides, 126.

86. For example, in the *Theologia Germanica* (a book that had exercised a significant influence on the development of Henry More's thought), the author writes of godly sorrow as "this divine attribute, which God will have man to possess," although "such a man feeleth in himself that he hath not made it to spring up in his heart, and that it is none of his, but belongeth to God alone" (trans. Susanna Winkworth, 2nd ed. [London: Longman, Brown, Green and Longmans, 1854], 121).

87. Plotinus, "Happiness," I.iv.4, 34-5.

88. Plotinus, "Beauty," I.vi.6, 51.

89. Cudworth, *A Sermon*, 33-4; Patrides, 105.

90. Henry More, "The Purification of a Christian Man's Soul," *Discourses on Several Texts of Scripture*, ed. John Worthington (1692), Discourse XIII, 394-418; rpt. in Patrides, 200-12, 207.

91. Smith, "The Excellency and Nobleness of True Religion," 418; Patrides, 176.

92. Smith, "The Excellency and Nobleness of True Religion," 410; Patrides, 170.

93. Cudworth, *A Sermon*, 48; Patrides, 112.

94. Plotinus, "On Free Will and the Will of the One," VI.viii.3, 515.

95. Sarah Hutton, Introduction to *A Treatise Concerning Eternal and Immutable Morality* with *A Treatise of Freewill*, by Ralph Cudworth, ed. Sarah Hutton (Cambridge: Cambridge University Press, 1996), ix-xxx, xvi.

96. Cudworth, *A Treatise of Freewill*, 164.

97. Although Spinoza and the Calvinists had different conceptions of the meaning of "salvation," similarities between the Spinozist and Calvinist systems has been repeatedly observed. Coleridge, for example, after reading Edward Williams's *Defence of Modern Calvinism* (1812), noted in a letter of March 1815 to R. H. Brabant, "If Dr. W's Opinions be indeed those of the Modern Calvinists collectively, I have taken my last Farewell of *Modern Calvinism*. It is in it's [sic] inevitable consequences Spinosism, . . . Spinosism with all it's Skeleton unfleshed, bare Bones and Eye-holes, as presented by Spinoza himself. In one thing only does it differ. It has not the noble honesty, that majesty of openness, so delightful in Spinoza, which made him scorn all attempts to varnish over fair consequences, or to deny in words what was affirmed in the reasoning" (Earl Leslie Griggs, ed., *Collected Letters of Samuel Taylor Coleridge*, 6 vols. [Oxford: Clarendon Press, 1956-71], 4:548-49). James Anthony Froude arrived at a similar conclusion: "If Calvinism be pressed to its logical consequences, it either becomes an intolerable falsehood, or it resolves itself into the philosophy of Spinoza" ("Spinoza," *Westminster Review* [1854], in *Short Studies on Great Subjects*, 4 vols. [London: Longmans, Green, and Co., 1894], 1:339-400, 364). However, Leo Strauss has argued that the apparent similarities between the thought of Spinoza and Calvin merely masks the fact that they "stand directly opposed to each other, without being able to arrive at agreement or even at mutual toleration" (*Spinoza's Critique of Religion* [1930], trans. E. M. Sinclair [New York: Schocken, 1965], 196).

98. James Martineau, *Type of Ethical Theory*, 2 vols., 3rd ed. (Oxford: Clarendon Press, 1901), 2:451.

99. Passmore, 5-6.

100. At the invitation of Cromwell, Menasseh ben Israel presented his "Humble Addresses" to the Lord Protector in October 1655. Menasseh's argument for the re-admission of the Jews into England were submitted to the Council of State and, afterwards, discussed in the Whitehall Conference which convened on the 4th of December (H. P. Stokes, *A Short History of the Jews in England* [London: SPCK, 1921], 67-72).

101. Steven Nadler, *Spinoza: A Life* (Cambridge: Cambridge University Press, 1999), 330-31.

102. Passmore argues that what at least one critic has taken to be the influence of Spinoza on Shaftesbury is actually the influence of Whichcote (97). The very fact that Whichcote's influence *can* be mistaken for that of Spinoza suggests some similarity in their ideas.

103. Whichcote, *Moral and Religious Aphorisms*, §109, §880; Patrides, 327, 334.

104. "When *the Tree of Knowledge* is not planted by *the Tree of Life*, and sucks not up sap from thence, it may be as well fruitful with *evil* and with *good*" (Smith, "The True Way or Method," 3-4; Patrides, 130).

105. Cudworth, *A Sermon*, 40-1; Patrides, 108.

106. Whichcote, *Select Sermons*, Part I, Sermon III, 70; Patrides, 55.

107. Whichcote, "The Unity of the Church," 81.

108. Whichcote, *Moral and Religious Aphorisms*, §114; Patrides, 327-28.

109. Cudworth, *A Sermon*, 14; Patrides, 96.

110. Henry More, *An Antidote against Atheism; or, An Appeal to the Naturall Faculties of the Minde of Man* (1655; Bristol: Thoemmes Press, 1997), I.v.2-3, 20-21; Patrides, 223.

111. Basil Willey, *The Seventeenth Century Background: Studies in the Thought of the Age in Relation to Poetry and Religion* (New York: Columbia University Press, 1967), 158f.

112. Ralph Cudworth, *The True Intellectual System of the Universe*, 2 vols. (London: Printed for Richard Royston, 1678), I.iv.36, 1:594-95. For Henry More's treatment of "the

*Platonists* Doctrine of the *Triunity of the Godhead*," see *An Explanation of the Grand Mystery of Godliness* (London: Printed by J. Flesher, 1660), I.iv, 7-11.

113. Samuel Taylor Coleridge, *Biographia Literaria: Or, Biographical Sketches of My Literary Life and Opinions*, 2 vols., ed. James Engell and W. Jackson Bate, vol. 7 of *The Collected Works of Samuel Taylor Coleridge* (Princeton: Princeton University Press, 1983), 1:204.

114. Inge, 58.

115. C. A. Patrides, "'The High and Aiery Hills of Platonisme': An Introduction to the Cambridge Platonists," in *The Cambridge Platonists*, ed. C. A. Patrides, 1-41, 6-7.

116. Cudworth, *A Treatise Concerning Eternal and Immutable Morality*, II.iv.1-2, 38-9. See also Henry More, *Enchiridion Ethicum*, III.x.21, 267. According to Joseph Glanvill, "the Atomical Hypothesis" of the Egyptians was conveyed to the Greeks by Democritus, but "the learning of the *Ægyptians* came from the *Chaldæans*, and was convey'd to *them*, as some learned Men affirm, by *Abraham*, who was of kin to *Zoroaster* the great *Chaldæan Legislatour* and *Philosopher*" (*The Author's Defence of "The Vanity of Dogmatizing"; against the Exceptions of the Learned Tho. Albius in his Late "Sciri"* [London: E.C., 1665], 89).

117. Arnold, "A Psychological Parallel," 128.

118. Whichcote, *Select Sermons*, Part I, Sermon III, 56-7; Patrides, 46. *Vide* Whichcote, *Moral and Religious Aphorisms* §100; Patrides, 327. Frederick Denison Maurice, in "Eternal Life and Eternal Death," observes, "The state of eternal life and eternal death is not one we can refer only to the future, or that we can in any wise identify with the future. Every man who knows what it is to have been in a state of sin, knows what it is to have been in a state of death. He cannot connect that death with time; he must say that Christ has brought him out of the bonds of *eternal* death. Throw that idea into the future and you deprive it of all its reality, of all its power" (*Theological Essays* [1853; New York: Harper and Brothers, 1957], 323).

119. Smith, "The Excellency and Nobleness of True Religion," 446-47; Patrides, 196.

120. Cudworth, *A Sermon*, 48; Patrides, 111.

121. Cassirer, 32; John Milton, *Paradise Lost* I.254-55.

122. Christopher Marlowe, *Dr. Faustus*, Act I, Scene 3.

123. Eadmer, *The Life of St. Anselm, Archbishop of Canterbury*, trans. R. W. Southern (Oxford: Clarendon Press, 1962), II.xv, 84.

124. Arthur Schopenhauer, "On the Suffering of the World," in *Essays and Aphorisms* (1851), trans. R. J. Hollingdale (New York: Penguin, 1970), 41-50, 48.

125. William Dillingham, "To the Reader," in Culverwell, 7.

126. Culverwell, Ch. I, 13-14.

127. Culverwell, Ch. XI, 79; Ch. XII, 104.

128. Culverwell, Ch. V, 34.

129. Culverwell, Ch. IX, 65.

130. Culverwell, Ch. XI, 80-2.

131. Culverwell, Ch. XI, 85.

132. Culverwell, Ch. XI, 90.

133. Culverwell, Ch. XVI, 142-44.

134. Although Campagnac correctly observes, "Smith and Culverwell did more than echo Whichcote's thoughts; they amplified them, and pursued them in directions which their master did not himself take," he overlooks the disparity in their thought and suggests that Culverwell had carried their "common principles on to a more purely philosophical development" (xxxiii-xxxvi).

135. Joseph Glanvill, "The Agreement of Reason and Religion," in *Essays on Several Important Subjects in Philosophy and Religion* (London: J.D., 1675), Essay No. 5, 20.

136. Glanvill, *Vanity of Dogmatizing*, XXI, 211; *Scepsis Scientifica*, XXV, 155.

137. Glanvill, *Vanity of Dogmatizing*, XXIII, 230; *Scepsis Scientifica* XXVII, 169.

138. Whichcote, *Moral and Religious Aphorisms*, §569, §712; "The Unity of the Church Maintained by Sincere Christians," in Patrides, 81.

139. Roger Sharrock notes in regard to Mr. Worldly-Wiseman, "This figure may be specially intended to satirize the Latitudinarian party in the Church of England.... [Bunyan] had conducted a bitter controversy with one particular Latitudinarian, Edward Fowler, vicar of Northill, near Bedford" (Notes to *The Pilgrim's Progress* by John Bunyan [New York: Penguin Classics, 1986], 280).

140. Bunyan, 89.

141. Jonathan Swift, *Gulliver's Travels* (1726, New York: Penguin Classics, 1985), 53-4.

142. John Dryden, Dedication to *Virgil's Aeneid*, trans. John Dryden, ed. Charles W. Eliot (Danbury, Conn: Grolier, 1909), 5-71, 30. Shaftesbury was amused by the fact that Cudworth was "accused of giving the upper hand to the atheists for having only stated their reasons and those of their adversaries fairly together" ("The Moralists, A Philosophical Rhapsody," Part II, Section III, in *Characteristics of Men, Manners, Opinions, Times*, ed. Lawrence E. Klein [New York: Cambridge University Press, 1999], 264-65).

143. Tulloch, 2:223.

144. Cudworth, *True Intellectual System of the Universe*, I.iii.37, 147, 155.

145. Martineau, *Types of Ethical Theory*, 2:433.

146. Jean Michel Vienne, Introduction to *The Cambridge Platonists in Philosophical Context: Politics, Metaphysics, and Religion*, xiii. The reference is to Chapter VII (101-10), "Ralph Cudworth, un platonism paradoxal: La Nature dans la *Digression concerning the Plastick Life of Nature*," by Alain Petit.

147. There were limits to Cudworth's toleration of the allegorical method, and he denounced "those high-flown *Spiritualists* of these latter times" who allegorize the death, resurrection, and ascension of Christ, whereby they "impudently slurre the Gospel according to the History and the Letter" (*A Sermon Preached to the Honourable Society of Lincolnes-Inne* [London: Printed by J. Fletcher for R. Royston, 1664], 10; reprinted as "The Second Sermon" in *A Discourse concerning the True Notion of the Lord's Supper*, 201).

148. Shaftesbury, "Sensus Communis: An Essay on the Freedom of Wit and Humour in a Letter to a Friend," *Characteristics*, 29-69, 65.

149. Cassirer, 198-201.

150. Tulloch, 1:x. Cassirer, writing in 1932, notes that "not even the most recent English publications have superseded Tulloch's results either in content or in principle" (4-5), and Ruth apRoberts, placing Tulloch's work beside Cassirer's and others, states that it "is still one of our best authorities on the subject" ("Arnold and the Cambridge Platonists," *CLIO* 17 [1988]: 139-50, 146). Five years following the publication of Tulloch's *Rational Theology and Christian Philosophy*, Matthew Arnold devised the plan, never realized, of editing an anthology entitled *Broad Church in the 17th Century* (Letter of M. Arnold to G. L. Craik; 9 January 1877, in *The Letters of Matthew Arnold*, 5 vols., ed. Cecil Y. Lang [Charlottesville: University Press of Virginia, 1996-2001], 4:353).

151. *Vide* Tod E. Jones, *The Broad Church: A Biography of a Movement* (Lanham: Lexington, 2003), 83-100.

152. Vienne, ix.

# Eight Letters

## *of Dr. Antony Tuckney*
## *and Dr. Benjamin Whichcote*

Edited by Tod E. Jones
Translations by Sara Elise Phang

# Editorial Notes and Abbreviations

The text is, throughout, very much the same as that published by Samuel Salter in 1753. I have introduced alterations only in such places where to omit them would impose an unnecessary hardship or inconvenience upon the reader. Whereas, on the one hand, the translator and I determined to transliterate (as well as translate) the Greek, on the other hand, I determined neither to modernize nor render consistent either the spelling or the punctuation, for to do so would deprive the text of part of its archaic quality and charm, and the spelling is not so unusual to modern readers that any person accustomed to reading student papers, for example, should find it troublesome. Where Salter used brackets (or, as he says, "hooks" and "crotchets") in order to place into the text Whichcote's marginal additions, I have used parentheses. This is appropriate, since these additions are part of the original text and are, generally, parenthetical in content. Moreover, this practice has allowed me to reserve the brackets for actual interpolations, which are of three sorts: first, there are those very few consisting of a word or two by which Salter appears to have attempted to clarify the sense of the passage; second, there are the English translations, which are introduced immediately following the Greek transliterations and Latin text and are placed within italicized brackets; third, there are the superscriptions added to Whichcote's Second Letter (Letter IV). These latter appear to have been added by Tuckney in order to indicate the text to which he responds (Letter V). Although these superscriptions are entirely irrelevant to Whichcote's content *in his Second Letter*, they are, nevertheless, essential markers for the reader of Letters V and VI who wishes to closely follow the argument. The only essential change I have made in the superscriptions is to substitute upper for lower case and a numbered letter (*e.g.*, [A2]) in instances where Tuckney had used the Greek alphabet.

The original footnotes by Salter are preserved at the end of each Letter and are designated by "SS." I have also sought to elucidate and illustrate Whichcote's teaching—the principle subject of the *Eight Letters*—by supplying quotations from his writings in print, designated by "BW." The abbreviations of these published works are as follows: *MRA* (*Moral and Religious Aphorisms*, ed. Samuel Salter [1753; London: Elkin Matthews and Marrot, 1930]); *SS* (*Select Sermons of Dr. Whichcot; in Two Parts*, ed. William Wishart [1742; facsimile, Delmar, NY: Scholar's Facsimiles and Reprints, 1977]); *SSN* (*Some Select Notions* [1685; facsimile, Menston, Yorkshire: Scolar Press, 1971]).

# Translator's Note

Tuckney and Whichcote provide many phrases and passages in Latin and Greek, which are translated into English in this edition. Precise quotations from classical sources have been noted. Frequently, however, the authors—in conformity with the contemporary practice of extemporizing in Latin—paraphrase or summarize a theological authority, such as St. Augustine. Many such passages have no precise source that can be located or cited. Perhaps, more theological passages in the *Eight Letters* can be traced to their sources, but this would be the work of a dissertation.

# EIGHT LETTERS

OF

# Dr. ANTONY TUCKNEY,

AND

# Dr. BENJAMIN WHICHCOTE:

CONCERNING

The Use of Reason in Religion.
The Differences of Opinion among Christians.
The Reconciliation of Sinners unto God.
The Studies and Learning of a Minister of the Gospel.

Written in SEPTEMBER and OCTOBER, MDCLI.

"It is better for us, that there shou'd be Difference of Judgement; if we keep Charity: but it is most unmanly to Quarrel, because we Differ."
Dr. WHICHCOTE's Aphorisms, No. 569.

"By the way, I will observe; how little there is in many Controversies: if Wise and Temperate men had the management of them. But when once there is Suspicion and Jealousy, these make and increase Differences."
Dr. WHICHCOTE's Discourses, Vol. II. Disc. vii. p. 152.

—— *Turpe putant parere Minoribus; et quae*
*Imbarbi didicere, Senes perdenda fateri.*
[—— *They hold it a shame to yield to their Juniors;*
*and to confess in old age that what they learned in*
*beardless youth should be destroyed.]*
HOR. *Ep.* 2.1.84-85.

MDCCLIII.

# Preface
## by Samuel Salter

The design of this second Preface[1] is to give some little account of the reverend Persons, whose letters it introduces; and of two or three others, who are occasionally mentioned in the letters: which account will render all farther discourse unnecessary and superfluous, on the part of the Editor.

ANTONY TUCKNEY was born in the last year of the sixteenth century, towards the end of the year; at *Kirton* near *Boston*, in *Lincolnshire*; where his Father was Minister. He was, at fourteen years of age, matriculated of the University of *Cambridge*; being admitted of *Emmanuel* College there: which shews, that he had been educated hitherto in a dislike to the church establishment; for that college, though it abounded for many years in most excellent scholars; and might therefore very justly be esteemed and flourish, on their account; yet was much resorted-to, for an other reason, about this time; *viz.* its being generally look'd-on, from it's first foundation, (which TUCKNEY himself acknowledges;) as a Seminary of Puritans.

Our young Scholar took his first degree, before he was seventeen years old; and was chosen Fellow of his college, three years after: in MDCXX he proceeded M.A. and was some time in the Earl of *Lincoln*'s family, before he resided on his fellowship. When he came back to live in college, he would not remain idle and unprofitable there; but soon became an eminent Tutor, and had many persons of rank and quality admitted under him: in this useful and honorable employment he continued, having taken his third degree of B.D. in MDCXXVII, about ten years; after which, tir'd probably of a college life, and wishing to settle in a family-way, he accepted the invitation of his countrymen; and went to *Boston*, as an Assistent to the famous Vicar of that town; Mr. JOHN COTTON: to whom he was probably very agreable on all accounts; and for whom, though a very zelous Non-conformist, his Diocesan Bishop WILLIAMS, when Lord Keeper, procured a Toleration under the Great Seal, for the free Exercise of his ministry, notwithstanding his dissenting in Cerimonies; so long as done without disturbance to the Church: But this was probably not very long; for Mr. COTTON quitted his native Country, before the civil wars; and withdrew, as many other resolute Non-Conformists did at that time, to *New-England*.[2] On his departure, the Corporation of *Boston* chose Mr. TUCKNEY, who was now married, into his place: and he kept this Vicarage, at their request, till the Restoration; or rather, his title to it; for he took no part of the Profit, when he no longer resided on it. Dr. How was his Successor, after the King's Return in MDCLX.

When the Parliament thought fit to convene an Assembly of Divines, Mr. TUCKNEY was one of the two nominated for the County of *Lincoln*; this summons he cheerfully attended, for divers reasons; and took his family up with him to town: nor did he any more return to *Boston*. He is said to have been much considered, in the Assembly; and obteined, as all the Favourites did, a parish in *London*: and when Lord MANCHESTER turn'd-out Dr. HOLDSWORTH, Master of *Emmanuel* College, and the Lady MARGARET's Professor of Divinity at *Cambridge*, from both those Preferments; Mr. TUCKNEY was put-in Master; and LOVE, the Master of *Bennet*, Professor; in MDCXLV. He did not go down to reside on this new Employment wholely; till he was chosen Vice-chancellor, three years after: when he removed all his Family to *Cambridge*, served that Office with credit, and commenced D.D. the year after; together with his friend ARROWSMITH, then master of St. *John*'s college; and his pupil WHICHCOTE, then provost of *King*'s. In MDCLIII Dr. HILL Master of *Trinity* college, dying, Dr. TUCKNEY preached his Funeral-sermon, which he printed; and with it an account of the deceased: this making a very important vacancy, Dr. ARROWSMITH was removed to *Trinity*-college; and Dr. TUCKNEY chosen by the Fellows, to be Master of St. *John*'s: and when the new master of *Trinity* resigned the Chair of Regius Professor of Divinity two years after on account of his health; which he had fill'd with honor for ten years, from Dr. COLLINS' ejection; the new master of St. *John*'s was, *invitó et pœné coäctus [compelled unwillingly and as a penalty]*, as he saith himself, chosen, by the unanimous vote of the regular electors, to succede him there also.

But although thus legally possessed of these two considerable preferments; although his behaviour in both was irreproachable and even highly commendable; though he ever consulted the interest both of the University and his College, and the honor of the Chair; yet he was civilly turn'd-out of both, at the Restoration: for Dr. GUNNING, a man of learning and character, and a great sufferer for his unshaken loyalty, was to have them both. Accordingly, duplicates of the following letter were sent to the Vice-chancellor, and to our Doctor; and that to the latter was accompanied by one from the same Lord MANCHESTER; who had brought him back to *Cambridge*, sixteen years before; and through whose hands, as now again Chancellor of the University, the Royal Orders regularly pass'd.

*C. R.*

> Whereas we are credibly informed; that Dr. *Anthony Tuckney*, Master of St. *John*'s college, and one of the Professors of Divinity, in our University of *Cambridge*, is well stricken in Years: and by reason of his Age, and some Infirmities of Body, may not hereafter be so well able to undergo the burthen of those two Places: We, out of our princely care both of that our University, and the said Dr. *Tuckney*, do judge it meet; that he, the said Dr. *Tuckney*, before the end of this Instant *June*, do

recede from the aforesaid Mastership and Professor's place; with the Rectory of *Somersham*, annexed thereunto by the grace and favour of our royal Grandfather. Which signification of our said pleasure if the said Dr. *Tuckney* shall submit unto, We shall be so well pleased with that his submission; that We shall graciously accept thereof: and will be ready to remember it, for his Good; upon any just occasion. And farther taking into our princely consideration the great pains and diligence of the said Doctor, in the discharge of the said Professor's place; without that benefit, which should have been received by him from the said rectory of *Somersham*; which, during the late unhappy and rapacious times, was unjustly detained from him: upon that his submission, Our will and pleasure is, and We do hereby order; that whatsoever persons during the natural life of the said Dr. *Tuckney* shall after his cession be elected or promoted to the said Professor's place, shall before their admission thereunto give sufficient assurance in Law to the said Dr. *Tuckney*, for the yearly payment of one hundred pounds out of the rectory of *Somersham* to the said Dr. *Tuckney*, for the reward of his former pains, by even and equal Portions, at the four usual feasts of the year; that is to say, at the Nativity of our Lord and Saviour, at the Annunciation of the blessed Virgin, the Birth of St. *John Baptist*, and the feast of *Michael* the Archangel; during the continuance of the said Professors, and the natural life of the said Dr. *Tuckney*: any Grant or Statute to the contrary nonwithstanding. Given at our Court at *Whitehall, June 1, MDCLXI.* By his Majesty's Command, EDWARD NICOLAS.

The Earl of *Manchester*'s Letter.

Sir,

You will find, by this inclosed, what the King's pleasure is; and how acceptable it will be to Him, that you make a speady quitting of your mastership of St. *John*'s college and the place of *Regius* professor. It is not out of any Dislike of your Person, or Distrust of your Ability; but for those reasons, which are expressed in His own Letters. One of them I send you; that you may keep it for your security: the other is deliver'd to the Vice-chancellor; to be kept in the Registry of the University: And I doubt not, but his Majesty will take care; that the conditions be performed. The Profits of both places You are to enjoy, till Midsummer next; and your Stay there with some convenient rooms, is allowed you, till *Sturbridge* Fair; a conveniency being allotted for Dr. *Gunning*'s use: and I hope, you will find all civilities from Him. I shall upon all occasions improve my interest for your advantage; with the reality of

Your assured Friend to serve you,<br>
E. MANCHESTER.

*Whitehall, June 3*
*MDCLXI.*

The poor infirm and aged man of LXII only, knew himself too weak however to contend with the Court; so he took his short warning, receded from *Cambridge*, and lived private and retir'd in *London*; till the Plague, the Fire, and the Five-mile Act drove him out of the great City; and obliged him to remove often from place to place. While he stay'd, he was nominated a Commissioner, on the Nonconformist side, at the Savoy conference; but never attended: alleging (as Mr. BAXTER with some indignation observes) his backwardness to speak; though he had been the Doctor in the Chair at *Cambridge*. But every one will see, whence this backwardness to speak arose; and will excuse his pleading it, though it were an *arguragschê [avarice]*[3] which occasioned it: for we may remember, he had only 100*l. per ann.* allowed; in compensation for all he was required to part-with. The Fire consumed all his Library. At length, after many removals and some troubles, he returnd to die in *London*; and was buried in the Church of St. *Andrew Undershaft*, in February MDCLXIX.

Dr. TUCKNEY printed some Sermons in his life time; and seven years after his death, Mr. JONATHAN TUCKNEY his Son, sometime Fellow of St. *John*'s and a young man of great hopes; till a deep melancholy deprived Him of himself, and the world of any benefit from his abilities; publish'd in a quarto volume, forty of his Father's Sermons: which he followed in MDCLXXIX by a collection of all his Latin pieces; consisting of Sermons *ad Clerum*, Positions, Determinations in the Chair and for his own degree, Lectures &c. To each book Mr. TUCKNEY prefixed a short preface, in the respective language of each: and to the latter is annexed a short account of the Doctor by *W. D.* who was very probably Dr. WILLIAM DILLINGHAM, TUCKNEY's successor in the headship of *Emmanuel* college.

From these his writings our Professor appears to have been a man of great reading, and much knowledge; a ready and elegant Latinist; but narrow, stiff and dogmatical: no enemy to the royal or episcopal power, as it shou'd seem; but above measure zelous for church power and ecclesiastical discipline: which such men as TUCKNEY, ARROWSMITH, &c. very sincerely wished and hoped to have established, by authority of the Parliament, following the repeted advice of the Assembly; and they sadly regretted their disappointment: their new masters constantly turning a deaf ear to all such admonitions. This the latter frankly owns, in his *Tactica sacra [Sacred Tactics]*, II.ii.10; where he reckons the loss of church discipline amongst the causes of the heterodoxy so rife then in *England*: tells, how often and earnestly the Assembly had labour'd to restore it; but adds pathetically and elegantly out of *Virgil*;

> *Ter conatus ibi collo dare brachia circum;*
> *Ter frustra comprensa manus effugit imago:*
> *Par levibus ventis, volucrique simillima somno.*
> *[Three times I tried to throw my arms around her neck;*
> *Three times the shade I grasped in vain escaped*
> *My hands—like fleet winds, most like a winged dream.]*[4]

and concludes thus, in a marginal note;—*Dicam aperte; quæ jamdudum eviluit*, (under the Bishops, I suppose;) *nuper evanuit* (under the Independents) *disciplina [I will speak openly: the discipline which already became worthless, now has vanished]*.⁵ In pursuance of these principles, we find Dr. TUCKNEY always fierce; when he mentions the freedom, which the new Government openly encouraged: in one of his determinations, on the subject of Divorce; he rails furiously at MILTON, whom he calls *infamis et non uno laqueo dignus [disgraceful and not worthy even of a rope]*; in most of them, the Papists Socinians and Arminians are fallen-upon, in the same breath; in one, upon the question of the *unaccountableness* of Princes, if I may so speak; he deplores, in very strong terms, the treatment and death of King *Charles*. He is said by CALAMY⁶ to have mainteined the dignity of his Posts, both of Vice-chancellor and Master; and to have been most resolutely disregardful of the arbitrary and irregular commands of those in authority; beyond any of his brethren: and he says of himself in these letters, when Dr. WHICHCOTE had given a hint of *imposing*; that "in the Assembly, he voted against subscribing or swearing-to the Confession, *&c.* set-out by authority": which was the more meritorious in Him; as he is affirmed to have had a great hand himself, in framing the Confession and Catechisms; and particularly, to have drawn the exposition of the Commandments in the larger Catechism. In his elections at St. *John*'s; when the President, according to the Cant of the times, wou'd call upon him have regard to the *Godly*; the Master answer'd, No one shou'd have a greater regard to the truely Godly, than himself; but he was determined to chose none but *Scholars*: adding, very wisely; They may deceive me, in their Godliness; they can not, in their Scholarship. This Story of Him, so much to his honor, is still upon record in the College; and was told me by the present worthy Master.

Upon the whole; he seems to have been a very honest and good man, a very industrious and learned scholar; his imperfections and weaknesses flow'd from his principles, rather than from his disposition; and he was worthy to have lived in better times, and a less prejudiced or bigoted age.

BENJAMIN WHICHCOTE was descended of an ancient and honorable family; which had been seated in the County of *Salop*, for many generations: he was the sixth son of CHRISTOPHER WHICHCOTE, *Esq*, by ELIZABETH his Wife, daughter of EDWARD FOX, *Esq*; of *Greet* in the same county; and was born at *Whichcote* Hall, in the parish of *Stoke*; *March* 11, MDCIX. He was admitted in *Emmanuel* college, *Cambridge*, under Mr. ANTONY TUCKNEY, MDCXXVI; upon whose leaving the college, Mr. THOMAS HILL became his Tutor: here he took his degrees regularly; going out Bachelor of Arts MDCXXIX, Master of Arts, MDCXXXIII, Bachelor of Divinity MDCXL. In the same year, that he took his second degree, he was elected Fellow of his college; and his tutor HILL leaving the University the year after, Mr. WHICHCOTE then took Pupils himself; and became very considerable for his Learning and Worth, his Prudence and Temper, his Wisdom and Moderation, in those times of trial: nor was less famous, for the number rank and character of his

Pupils; and the care he took of them: many of them becoming afterwards men of great figure themselves; as WALLIS, SMITH, WORTHINGTON, CRADOCK, &c.[7]

On the 5th of *March* MDCXXXVI, he was ordained both Deacon and Priest at *Buckden*, by WILLIAMS Bishop of *Lincoln*; which irregularity I know not how to account-for in a Prelate so obnoxious to the ruling Powers both in Church and State; as WILLIAMS is known to have been.[8] And I imagine, our young Divine immediately set-up the afternoon lecture on Sundays in *Trinity* church at *Cambridge*; which, Arch-bishop TILLOTSON says, he serv'd near twenty years.[9] He was also appointed one of the University Preachers: and in MDCXLIII was presented, by the Master and Fellows of his college, to the Living of *North-Cadbury* in *Somersetshire*. This vacated his Fellowship; and upon this, I presume, he married; and actually went down to his new Living: but was soon call'd back to *Cambridge*, being pitch'd-upon to succede the ejected Provost of *King*'s college, Dr. SAMUEL COLLINS; who had been in that post thirty years, and was also *Regius* Professor of Divinity. This choice was perfectly agreable to Dr. COLLINS himself, though not quite so to Mr. WHICHCOTE; who had scruples about accepting what was thus irregularly offer'd him: and there is still extant, in the hands of Sir FRANCIS WHICHCOTE Bart, the Doctor's great Nephew; which that Gentleman has done me the honour to shew me; a short Schedule, containing very imperfect heads of reasons *pro* and *con*, which occurr'd to Him in the course of this deliberation and debate with Himself. Happily for the College, for the University, and for the Church of *England*; he determined at last to accept the place: for somebody else wou'd certainly have been appointed, had He declined it; and so good a one, upon every account, cou'd very hardly at that time have been found. I mean, one; whose Capacity shou'd have been so indisputable, his Reputation for Piety Learning Prudence and Temper so established, his Interest and Credit with those in Authority so very considerable, and his Fortune so independent: by all which in conjunction our Author was enabled to do so much more Service than any other man; without stooping to any thing, unworthy of his Character. So he was admitted Provost, *March* 19, MDCXLIV. By the same authority, Mr. TUCKNEY was made Master of *Emmanuel*; Mr. ARROWSMITH, of St. *John*'s; and Mr. *Hill*, of *Trinity*: and thus four very intimate Friends, after a separation of some years; save that the three last met in the Assembly of Divines, as *Westminster*; saw each other again, in the several most honorable stations of the University: to which their Learning and Piety had deservedly recommended them.

This reunion of four men, so very dear to each other, must have been very satisfactory and delightful to each; if it had not soon appeared, that WHICHCOTE the youngest, but by far the most considerate of the four, was now become a very different man from what the rest had left him, a dozen years before; He had by this time disengaged himself, from the narrow and slavish principles of his Education; and not content to have emancipated himself, he employed all his Credit, Weight and Influence, which were justly great; in spreading and propagating a nobler freer and more generous sett of opinions: these the young Masters of Arts especially soon cordially embraced, to the no small dissatisfaction of the other three: who in vain opposed their authority, in the support of what wou'd not stand the test of Reason; nor cou'd, without violence and straining, be deduced from Scripture. After much smothering of their discontent in silence, or uttering it only to inward friends; it broke-out at length in the frank and honest expostulation from TUCKNEY, which opens the following Correspondence. Before this, TUCKNEY, ARROWSMITH, and WHICHCOTE went-out Doctors in Divinity; and were created together in *July* MDCXLIX: TUCKNEY had serv'd the office of Vice-chancellor, and WHICHCOTE was now in it; when his old tutor broke the Ice, in MDCLI; and fairly confess'd the displeasure, his friends and He had conceived.

To return to Dr. WHICHCOTE: he resigned his *Somersetshire* Living, and the College presented to it his friend the learned Mr. RALPH CUDWORTH, in MDCL; though this latter had left the college, in which he was brought-up; and was now master of *Clare-hall*: the next year, *King*'s college complemented their new Provost with the rectory *sine cura [without duties]* of *Milton* in *Cambridgeshire*; void by the death of Dr. COLLINS. This agreable piece of preferment he kept, as long as he lived; though after the Restoration, he was obliged, or advised, to take-out a Grant of it under the Great Seal, *ad corroborandum [in order to confirm it]*: and he thought proper to resign it, the year after; in order to resume it immediately, by a fresh presentation from the college.

Dr. WHICHCOTE was so zelous to preserve a spirit of sober Piety and rational Religion, in the University and town of *Cambridge*; in opposition to the fanatic Enthusiasm, and senseless Canting, then in vogue; that He set up an after-noon lecture for Sundays, at *Trinity* church; which (as has been observed before) he served for near 20 years: an other was set-up on Wednesdays, at the same Church, as Mr. BEARDMORE tells us, (in his account of his tutor TILLOTSON, lately printed by my learned friend Dr. BIRCH, with His life of that excellent Prelate;)[10] which was served by a sett of the very best preachers, fellows of divers colleges; friends it is probable and followers of WHICHCOTE. Dr. HILL set-up two other such sunday lectures; at St. *Michael*'s church, for the morning; and at *All-saints*, for the after-noon: at the former he constantly preached himself; of the latter he took a fourth part to himself: and this was so much the fashion of the time and place; that Mr. BEARDMORE observes his Tutor TILLOTSON, usually heard four sermons every Lord's-day; and Dr. TUCKNEY remarks, in his account of Dr. HILL; that the Gospel was nowhere so freely preached, and so absolutely without charge to any; as then at *Cambridge*.

The happy effect of Dr. WHICHCOTE's pains in this way appeared in the great talents and excellent performances of so many eminent Divines, after the Restoration: of whom most, of those who had received their education at *Cambridge*; were formed at least, if not actually brought-up, by Him. His truely Christian temper, and the worthy use He made of his great credit and interest with those in authority; at a time, when ARROWSMITH, LIGHTFOOT, and others, were apprehensive of a total destruction hanging-over and threatning these Seats of Learning; may be seen justly celebrated in the Sermon preached at his Funeral by TILLOTSON; and in the short character given of him by BURNET, in the History of his own times[11]: His generosity to his Predecessor COLLINS, and other ejected members of the Society; fully confutes the *injurious* inference, which the *Oxford* Historian draws *malignantly*, from a false Fact: See the passage in *Athenae Oxon.* Vol. II. where TUCKNEY is mentioned p. 576. Our Provost had too great and noble a spirit, to follow a party servilely; and was never so attach'd to any, as not to see and own and wish to serve real merit; where-ever it was to be found: of which we have one remarkable proof, in Mr. ABRAHAM HILL's account of Dr. BARROW; prefixed to the works of that excellent Philosopher and Divine.[12] BARROW was thrown-out, at his first application for the Greek Professorship; merely on account of his being a Royalist: yet he ever acknowledged with gratitude Dr. WHICHCOTE's good offices and readiness to serve him in it. And notwithstanding the differences between Dr. WHICHCOTE and his old Tutor, which make the subject of these letters; and which, the reader will see, were irreconcileable; He joined with the other six electors, a very few years after, in raising Dr. TUCKNEY to the Divinity Chair.

His Predecessor COLLINS had now been long dead; and Dr. WHICHCOTE's conduct was too moderate and obliging, to disgust any: yet at the Restoration he was removed from the Provostship, by especial order from the King; and Dr. JAMES FLEETWOOD was put into it. But though removed, he was not disgraced or frowned-on; so far from it, that he was on the contrary only called-up, from the comparative obscurity of a University life, to a higher and more conspicuous station; from a place, where he had already done much real service; to one, where there was still much to be done; by men like him. Accordingly, he was elected and licensed to the Cure of St. *Anne's Black-friars*, in *November* MDCLXII; and that Church being burned down in the dreadful Fire of MDCLXVI, he retired to *Milton*, for a while: but was again called-up, and presented by the Crown to the Vicarage of St. *Laurence Jewry*; vacant by the Promotion of Dr. WILKINS to the See of *Chester*.

This was his last stage; and here he continued in high and general esteem, preaching twice every Week; to his Death in MDCLXXXIII: the circumstances of which may be seen in the Sermon at his Funeral.[13] He was buried in the Chancel of his own Church; when Dr. TILLOTSON preach'd, who was the week-day Lecturer there.

He is reckoned by FULLER, who printed his History of *Cambridge* in MDCLV; among the Writers of *Emmanuel* college[14]: but I cannot find, that he published any thing before the Restoration; or in any part of his life.

He was married, but I cannot learn, to whom; when he was about thirty-four years of age: probably he never had any children; certainly he left none: but made three of his Nephews his Executors: one of whom, his name-sake, a merchant in *Bishops-gate Street*, to whom he bequeathed all his MSS, put them into the hands of Arch-deacon JEFFERY; and to Him we owe three volumes of discourses[15]: which for the excellent spirit, sound judgment, and sweet temper, most conspicuous throughout, will ever be admired by all men of sense: though totally void (as were also his Latin performances; of which one or two are preserved, and in my hands;) of all the graces and ornaments of style and composition. To many indeed, a greater proof can not well be given of the intrinsic merit of these Sermons; that the Lord SHAFTESBURY's having printed one volume of them in MDCXCVIII, with a large preface, highly in praise of the incomparable author.[16]

THOMAS HILL, born at *Knighton* in *Worcestershire*, admitted of *Emmanuel* college in *October* MDCXVIII, took his first Degree there in MDCXVIII, after which he went to the famous Mr. JOHN COTTON of *Boston*, as many other young men seem to have done: and "spent some good time with Him, (says Dr. TUCKNEY) for his farther perfecting; and the more happy seasoning of his spirit." Upon his return to college, he was chosen Fellow and proceded M.A. in MDCXXVI: not long after which he became an eminent Tutor; and so continued, till MDCXXXIV: when, being now B.D. he was presented to the Living of *Tichmersh* in *Northamptonshire*. Here he so greatly distinguished himself; that he was nominated a member of the Assembly for that County, in MDCXLIII; attended, and preach'd often before the House of Commons, on solemn occasions, as public Fast-days &c; and was chosen one of their morning week day preachers at the Abbey, as on the Lord's-day he officiated at St. *Martin*'s in the Fields. He was at first appointed, by the same authority of Parliament, Master of his own College; but this not seeming a sphere large or considerable enough for so active a man, that destination of him was changed; and he was put into Dr. COMBER's place, who was turn'd-out from the headship of *Trinity* college.

He was a celebrated and diligent Preacher; and did not slack his pains, on being thus promoted; but on the contrary set-up two lectures in the town of *Cambridge*, as above-mentioned; one of which he supplied himself altogether, and was much resorted-to; the other, in conjunction with three assistants. He printed only a few Sermons; which are now little known or inquired after: though Dr. TUCKNEY, who preached his Funeral Sermon at St. *Marie*'s on the 22d of *December*, MDCLIII, and printed with it a large account of Him, says; "he had made a fair progress, in a learned confutation of the great daring Champion of the *Arminian* Errors; whom the abusive Wits of the University with an impudent boldness wou'd say, none there durst adventure upon." By this adversary I take JOHN GOODWIN to be alluded-to; who two years before had dedicated his folio volume, called *Redemption redeemed*, to Dr. WHICHCOTE Vice-chancellor, and the rest of the heads of houses at *Cambridge*: and in that bold, but not (as Dr. TUCKNEY calls it) immodest or scurrilous, address, had challenged and required them to confute him; if he was in an error.

For the rest; Mr. HILL proceded D.D. in MDCXLVI; and died in MDCLIII: the University Orator, Mr. WIDRINGTON, at St. *Marie*'s; and Mr. TEMPLAR, one of the senior fellows of his college, in their Hall; making each a speech on the occasion: as did also Mr. JOHN RAY, then of the College; afterwards of the Royal Society: and well known by his learned and useful Writings.

JOHN ARROWSMITH was born at or near *Newcastle* upon *Tine*, in the county of *Northumberland*; the same year day and hour, that his collegue in the Assembly and University Dr. JOHN LIGHTFOOT was born at or near *Newcastle* under *Line*, in the country of *Stafford*; viz. *March* 29. MDCII. He was admitted of St. *John*'s college in *Cambridge* in MDCXVI; and took his first two degrees from thence, in the years MDCXIX and MDCXXIII: in this last year he was chosen Fellow of *Katherine* hall; where, as I suppose, he resided some years; and probably engaged in the Tuition of Youth: but in MDCXXXI he married, and removed to *Lynn* in *Norfolk*. He continued in this town, very much esteemed, some ten or twelve years; being first Assistent or Curate to another, afterwards Minister in his own right, of St. *Nicolas*' Chapel there. He was call'd-up to assist in the Assembly of Divines; for the county, in which he now lived; had a Parish in *London*, and is named with TUCKNEY HILL and others in the list of Triers, as they were call'd; *i.e.* persons appointed to examine and report the integrity and abilities of Candidates for the Eldership in *London*, and Ministry at large. When Dr. BEALE, Master of St. *John*'s college, was turn'd-out by the Earl of *Manchester*; Mr. ARROWSMITH, who had taken the degree of B.D. from *Katherine* Hall eleven years before, was put into his place; as also into the royal Divinity Chair, from which the old Professor COLLINS was removed: and after about nine years possession of these honors, to which he added that of a Doctor's degree in Divinity, in MDCXLIX; he was farther promoted, on Dr. HILL's death, to the mastership of *Trinity* college: with which he kept his professor's place only two years; his health being considerably impaired. He died in MDCLIX: and was succeded at *Trinity* college by Dr. WILKINS.

Dr. TUCKNEY, his successor in the Chair, speaks of his behaviour in it as very great and worthy; and of his own exceding unwillingness to come after him: but adds, he accepted it at last; to save the University the reproche and disgrace of having a Professor to seek *aliundè [from elsewhere]*; as none among themselves were disposed to undertake the province.

Dr. ARROWSMITH was, like his friends TUCKNEY and HILL; a very learned and able, but a stiff and narrow Divine; was, like them, offended with the popularity and credit of Dr. WHICHCOTE: for though they all respected and loved his person, they cou'd none of them bear-with his freedom. But ARROWSMITH's natural Temper was incomparably better than his Principles; and he is represented by both sides, as a man of a most sweet and engaging disposition. This even appears, through all the sourness and severity of his opinions, in his *Tactica sacra*; a book written in a clean style, and with a lively fancy; in which is display'd at once much weakness and stiffness, but withall great reading; and a very amiable candor towards the persons and characters of those, from whom he found himself obliged to differ: even towards JOHN GOODWIN above-mention'd; whom Dr. TUCKNEY (a very good man too, but *iracundior paullo [a little more prone to anger]*;) speaks-of with exceding sharpness: whereas with our gentler author, he is *doctus vir et diligens [a learned and studious man]*; (*absit enim ut ei quam meretur laudem invideam, ut ut aliter sentienti [may I not seem to envy the praise which he deserves, unlike that of a man of other temper]:*) p. 217. *doctus et disertus, sed judicii sequioris [a scholarly and learned man, should you seek judgment].* p. 147.

This book the Master dedicated to the Fellows and Students of his College, and printed it in MDCLVII; to supply, as he cou'd, the failure of Sermons; which his ill health wou'd not permit him to preach in the Chapel.[17] He had also printed three sermons, ten years before; and in MDCLIX, the year of his decease, his friends HORTON and DILLINGHAM, masters of *Queen*'s and *Emmanuel* college, printed a collection of his Theological Aphorisms in quarto; with the title of *Armilla Catechetica [Catechetical Bracelet]*.

These two last mention'd Doctors, HILL and ARROWSMITH, being spoken of with so much respect and affection by Dr. WHICHCOTE, in his first letter; and being with him in the places of highest rank in the University; and appearing to be so closely connected with TUCKNEY, as in other things; so also in the displeasure conceived against the Provost's new doctrines: I thought, the reader wou'd be pleased, to have some account of them all in this place: which has been collected with some care, from the best authorities I was able to procure.

A word or two has been said, by way of Note, concerning some others: where it was imagined of use to illustrate or explain the passages, in which their names occur. One only being forgotten, I will just add here concerning Him; that PAUL BAYNES was Fellow of *Christ*'s college, succeded Mr. PERKINS in the rectory of St. *Andrew*'s at *Cambridge*, and printed some notes on the Epistle to the *Ephesians*.

It remains only, that I acquaint the learned and curious, the candid and patient reader; (as I have by this time good reason to call and think him:) with the history of the Letters now presented to Him. The original transcripts of them, in Dr. WHICHCOTE's own hand; were, as I suppose, part of the treasure entrusted with Dr. JEFFERY: but I cannot learn, that they are now in being. For I have been very inquisitive after them; hoping, by means of them, however hastily or ill written, to satisfy my-self in the true reading of divers passages; which I cannot now be positive of. That Dr. WHICHCOTE wrote a bad hand, is pretty plainly hinted in the letters; more than once: that they were written at first, and transcribed by him after, in great haste; is also very certain: Dr. WHICHCOTE seems besides to have had in his temper a warmth eagerness and enthusiasm, but always under the command of his Reason; which made him, when handling a favorite argument, or inforcing a truth which he was *under the power of*, utterly neglect his style; and must have render'd him in a still greater degree impatient, under the cold restraint of writing accurately. From all these considerations I have reason to suspect, that Dr. WHICHCOTE might not always *write* exactly; nor Mr. JEFFERY always *read* exactly: for the copy in my hands was not taken by the Arch-deacon himself, but by his Brother; though it is corrected throughout by the former.

For my self: I have taken the least possible liberty; have followed, almost to a degree of affectation, the old mode of spelling; have copied my copy, with the utmost fidelity; and never varied from it, without absolute necessity. The passages, which the first writers wrote in the margins, are now taken into the text; but since they are quoted and referr'd-to, as being in the margin; I have taken care to keep them still separate, by inclosing them within crotchets.[18] And the references all through are made most precise and distinct; and free from all possible ambiguity.

If any shall be of opinion; that the letters are not of such consequence, as to deserve being made public; I am not disposed to dispute that point: yet, let me be permitted to say; the subjects, debated in them, are of unquestionable great concernment; and the men, who debated them, were excedingly capable of handling them acutely and judiciously: even consider'd in the lowest possible light, they are curious remains of the last century; and let us somewhat into the history and state of one of our Universities before the Restoration. And, to say no more; one advantage they may be of, to the very best and wisest of us all; to teach Us, by the example of these learned and good men, who, though they cou'd not either bring-over the other to his own way of thinking; yet preserved a respect and esteem for each other; and lived on in friendship and charity; if not in great intimacy and familiarity: teach Us, I say, by their example, how to "Differ without Quarrelling; to deal with each other in meekness calmness and reason; and so to represent the most high-God and Father of us all; who applies Himself constantly to Our faculties; and deals with Us in no other way, than by Reason and Argument."

SAMUEL SALTER.

*March* 8, MDCCLIII.
*Yarmouth* in *Norfolk*.

# Notes

1. Samuel Salter's first Preface immediately precedes Whichcote's *Moral and Religious Aphorisms*. See my Preface for further bibliographical information. *Ed.*

2. John Cotton (1584-1652), after receiving his M.A. from Trinity College, Cambridge, in 1606, obtained a fellowship at Emmanuel, at which college he rose to the position of dean before, in 1612, receiving his appointment as vicar of Boston, Lincolnshire. Thus, Cotton left Emmanuel College the year previous to Tuckney's matriculation. Although, under the reign of James I (as Salter observes) Cotton had procured some degree of toleration for his non-conformity, the high commission court of Charles I was less tolerant, and in 1633, Cotton resigned his living and immigrated to New England. Where Cotton settled, in Massachusetts Bay, thirty-three graduates of Emmanuel were to settle during the years from 1629 to 1640 (*Concise Dictionary of National Biography* [Oxford: Oxford University Press, 1939]; Samuel E. Morison, *The Founding of Harvard College* [Cambridge: Harvard University Press, 1935], Appendix B; qtd. by Gerald R. Cragg, Introduction to *The Cambridge Platonists*, ed. Cragg [New York: Oxford University Press, 1968], 8).

3. Literally, a "silver quinsy." The classical Greek orator Demosthenes "was said to have [this], when he held back from appearing in public on the plea of quinsy, though really (it was

alleged) because he was bribed" (Liddell and Scott's *Greek-English Lexicon* [1871; repr. 1989], 100). *Trans.*

4. Vergil, *Aeneid* 2.792-94; 6.700-02. In *Aen.* 2.792-94 Aeneas relates that he tried to embrace a vision of his wife Creusa, left behind in his flight from Troy; in *Aen.* 6.700-02, related in third person, he tries to embrace the ghost of his father Anchises in the underworld. Tr. Allen Mandelbaum (1971). *Trans.*

5. Salter here adds, by way of a footnote in Latin, several literary citations (xiii-xiv n). In my copy, this note is not sufficiently clear to allow for a trustworthy reproduction. *Ed.*

6. Edmund Calamy (1671-1732), D.D., presbyterian minister and biographer, published in 1702 an abridged version of Richard Baxter's *Reliquiae Baxterianae*, to which he appended *An Account of Many Others of Those Many Ministers Who Were Ejected after the Restauration of King Charles the Second.*

7. Of these "men of great figure," John SMITH requires no further introduction here (*v.* 15, 18-33). John WALLIS (1616-1703) received from Emmanuel his B.A. in 1632 and M.A. in 1640. Four years later he was admitted fellow of Queen's College, Cambridge. At various times, beginning in 1642, he served the government by deciphering intercepted despatches. From 1649 until his death, he occupied the chair of Savilian Professor of Geometry at Oxford. His ground-breaking *Arithmetica Infinitorum* was published in 1655. John WORTHINGTON (1618-1671) rapidly rose to eminence at Cambridge. After receiving his M.A. from Emmanuel College in 1639, he was appointed fellow in 1642, university preacher in 1649, and Master of Jesus College in 1650. In 1657, two years after obtaining his D.D., he was made Vice-chancellor of Cambridge, which position he held until the following year. In the year of the Restoration, he published the *Select Discourses* of John Smith, and was afterwards displaced from his mastership. Subsequently, he held diverse other livings. Samuel CRADOCK (ca. 1621-1706) was made fellow of Emmanuel College in 1645, a position he held for eleven years. He received his B.D. in 1651. After the passing of the Act of Toleration, he labored as a congregational preacher and publisher of theological treatises (*Concise DNB.*)

8. John Williams (1582-1650), a favorite of James I, was appointed Dean of Westminster in 1620 and, in the following year, both Bishop of Lincoln and Lord Keeper of the Great Seal. On the accession of Charles I, at Buckingham's instigation, he was deposed as Lord Keeper. In 1627 Bishop Williams determined, in opposition to the Vicar of Grantham, that the Holy Table, contrary to Roman tradition, should not be placed at the east end. In the year that he ordained Whichcote, he published his views regarding this issue in *Holy Table, Name and Thing*. This book placed him at odds with Archbishop Laud, who subsequently fined him and, in 1637, imprisoned him in the Tower. Subsequently, Williams regained his influence, and in 1642, while Laud himself was in the Tower awaiting his execution, King Charles appointed him Archbishop of York (S. L. Ollard, ed., *A Dictionary of English Church History*, 2nd ed. [London: A. R. Mowbray and Co., 1919]).

9. John Tillotson, *A Sermon Preached at the Funeral of the Reverend Benjamin Whichcot, D.D.* (London: Printed by M. Flesher for Brabazon Aylmer, 1683), 24.

10. Thomas Birch, *The Life of the Most Reverend John Tillotson, Lord Archbishop of Canterbury; Compiled Chiefly from His Original Papers and Letters; to which is added "Some Memorials of Dr. John Tillotson, Late Lord Archbishop of Canterbury," Written upon the News of His Death, by J[ohn]. B[eardmore]*. (London: Printed for J. and R. Tonson, and S. Draper, 1752).

11. Samuel Salter, in the "Testimonies" prefixed to Whichcote's *Moral and Religious Aphorisms*, gives the following account (xxxi-xxxii) from *Bishop Burnet's History of His*

*Own Times*, ed. Thomas Burnet, 4 vols. (London: Printed for A. Millar, 1753), 1:186:
> Whichcote was a man of a rare temper; very mild and obliging. He had great credit with some, that had been eminent in the late times; but made all the use he could of it, to protect good men of all persuasions. He was much for liberty of conscience: and being disgusted with the dry systematical way of those times, he studied to raise those who conversed him his to a nobler set of thoughts; and to consider RELIGION as a seed of a DEIFORM NATURE, (to use one of his own phrases.) In order to this, he set young students much on reading the ancient philosophers; chiefly Plato, Tully, and Plotin; and on considering the CHRISTIAN RELIGION as a doctrine sent from GOD, both to elevate and sweeten human nature; in which he was a great example, as well as a wise and kind instructor.

12. John Tillotson, ed., *The Works of the Learned Isaac Barrow*, 2nd ed., 3 vols., including "Some Account of the Life of Dr. Isaac Barrow" by Abraham Hill (London: Printed by J. Heptinstall for Brabazon Aylmer, 1700).

13. John Tillotson, in his funeral *Sermon* for Whichcote, has given the following account of his last days:
> Having given this account of his last Will, I come now to the sad part of all: sad, I mean, to us, but happiest to him. A little before *Easter* last he went down to *Cambridge*: where, upon taking a great Cold, he fell into a distemper which in a few days put a period to his life. He died in the house of his ancient and most learned Friend, Dr. *Cudworth*, Master of *Christ*'s College. During his sickness he had a constant calmness and serenity of mind: and under all his bodily weakness possest his soul in great patience. After the Prayers for the Visitation of the Sick (which he said were excellent prayers) had been used, he was put in mind of receiving the Sacrament; to which he answered, that he most readily embraced the proposal: And after he had received it, said to Dr. *Cudworth* I heartily thank you for this most Christian office; I thank you for putting me in mind of receiving this Sacrament: adding this pious ejaculation, *The Lord fulfill all his declarations and promises, and pardon all my weaknesses and imperfections*. He disclaimed all merit in himself; and declared that whatever he was, he was through the grace and goodness of God in *Jesus Christ*. He expressed likewise great dislike of the Principles of Separation: and said *he was the more desirous to receive the Sacrament that he might declare his full Communion with the Church of Christ all the world over*. He disclaimed *Popery*, and, as things of near affinity with it, or rather parts of it, *all superstition and usurpation upon the consciences of men*.
>
> He thanked God, *that he had no pain in his body, nor disquiet in his mind*.
>
> Towards his last he seemed rather unwilling to be detained any longer in this state; not for any pains he felt in himself, but for the trouble he gave his friends: saying to one of them who had with great care attended him all along in his sickness, *My dear friend, thou hast taken a great deal of pains to uphold a crazy body, but it will not do: I pray thee give me no more Cordials; for why shouldst thou keep me any longer out of that*

*happy state to which I am going. I thank God I hope in his mercy, that it shall be well with me.* (28-9)

14. "Amongst the learned writers of this college, I have omitted many still alive, as . . . Doctor Benjamin Whichcote, now Provost of King's" (Thomas Fuller, *The History of the University of Cambridge, from the Conquest to the Year 1632*, VII.17, Ed. Marmaduke Prickett and Thomas Wright [Cambridge: J. and J. J. Deighton and T. Stevenson, 1840], 280).

15. *Several Discourses, concerning the Shortness of Humane Charity, and the Perfection of the Mercy of God, by the Reverend and Learned Benjamin Whichcote, . . . Examined and Corrected by His Own Notes, and Published by John Jeffery*, 3 vols. (London: Printed for J. Knapton, 1702-1707). These volumes contain, respectively, sixteen, twenty, and thirty sermons.

16. According to Salter, the publication of the *Select Sermons of Dr. Whichcote; in Two Parts*, ed. Anthony Ashley Cooper, Third Earl of Shaftesbury (London: Printed for Awnsham and J. Churchill, 1698); was afterwards, in 1742, reprinted in Edinburgh with an additional preface by William Wishart. Shaftesbury's publication was apparently unknown to Archdeacon Jeffery, "or he wou'd hardly have reprinted, in their imperfect and inchoate state, though from the original notes of the preacher, those discourses; which compose the former part of that volume" (Preface to *Moral and Religious Aphorisms* by Benjamin Whichcote, xix-xx).

17. Salter, in a footnote, here supplies "a farther specimen of this work" to gratify "the curious reader"; however, since this lengthy Latin quotation in small print is, in places, difficult to make out, and since this work, "so little known or inquired after" in 1753 is not likely to be more inquired after today, I am omitting the specimen, but instead refer the curious and learned reader to the source of Salter's quotation, *Tactica sacre: sive De milite spirituali pugnante, vincente, and triumphante* (1657).

18. The only change that I have made to Salter's practice in this regard, is to substitute parentheses for brackets (or "crotchets"). *V.* Editorial Notes. *Ed.*

# Letter I

## Dr. TUCKNEY,
## Provost of Emmanuel College,
## to the
## Right Worshipfull
## Dr. WHICHCOT,
## Provost of King's College;
## and Vice-Chancelour
## of the University of Cambridge.

Sir,

Because I understand, that Mr. *Cradock*[1] was pleased, not long since, to say; (He knows, to whom;) that some of Us deal disingenuously with you: in speaking against some of your Tenents; without dealing with you in private: though I doe not fancy, as some others, this affected word *Ingenuous*;[2] and I wish, the thing itself were not idolized; to the prejudice of *Saving Grace*: yet, if I must use the word; truely, Sir, I desire to be so *ingenuous* with you; as, out of that ancient and still continued love and respect I bear you, to crave leave to tell you; that my heart hath bin much exercised about you: and that, especially since your being Vice-chancelour, I have seldom hear'd you preach; but that something hath bin delivered by you, and that so authoritatively, and with the big words, sometimes of "divinest reason," and sometimes of "more than mathematical demonstration;"[3] that hath very much grieved me; and, I beleive, others with me: and yesterday, as much as any time. I pass-by many things in your sermon; and crave leave to note three or foure.

I. Your second Position,—"that all those things, wherein good men differ, may not be determined from Scripture; and that itt in some places seems to be for the one part, and in some places for the other."—I take to be unsafe and unsound.

II. Your first advice,—"that we wou'd be confined to Scripture words and expressions; in which all parties agree; and not press other forms of words, which are from fallible men: and this wou'd be for the peace of Christendom."—I look-at, as more dangerous: and verily beleive; that Christ by his bloud never intended to purchase such a peace; in which the most Orthodox, (for that word I must use; though it be now-a-days stomached:) with Papists, Arians, Socinians, and all the worst of Hæretiques, must be all put into a bag together; and, let them hold and maintain their own, though never so damnable hæresies; yet, as long as they agree with Us in Scripture expressions, they must be accorded-with.—And yet,

III. Your second Advice gives your *ingenuous* man liberty to propound his own different conceptions; and, it may be, to brand the contrary opinion with the black mark of "Divinity taught in Hell": which will take-away as much peace; as the former Advice promised to give us. This *libertas prophetandi [freedom to prophesy]*, in most that ever hitherto pressed it, did *semper aliquid monstri alere [always nourish something monstrous]*: and when I discerne, whose footsteps appear in these two Advices; I am very sorry to see Dr. WHICHCOT, whom I so much love and honour, to tread in them. Of both these advices, what ground there was from the Text;[4] I leave indifferent men to judge. Sir, your heart, I beleive, was full of them; and that was the reason of that so *importune* propounding of them. And although you told us, You *cou'd not* pass them by; yet My dulness is such, as to think; many a good minister wou'd have made as profitable a sermon, from that text: and, having insisted on Christ's giving Repentance, which You omitted; wou'd never have thought of those notions: and, it may be, wou'd have as much smiled at Him, that shou'd have told him; that the text cou'd not be well handled, without them: as at Him, that shou'd have said; that a Commencement oration cou'd not have been made, without a large discourse of *Recta Ratio [Right Reason]*.[5]

IV. Your discourse about Reconciliation; that "it doth not operate on God, but on Us; that *e nobis nascitur [it is born from within ourselves]*, &c;" is Divinity, which my heart riseth against: and though, if you meant, that for God so to dissemble and overlook sin, as to be reconciled to them that continue in it; is an impossibility to the nature of God, and Divinity (as your deepe word had it,) taught in Hell; * * *[6] yet to say, that the ground of God's reconciliation is from any thing in Us; and not from His free grace, freely justifying the ungodly; is to deny one of the fundamental truths of the Gospel, that derives from Heaven; which, I bless God, lyeth neer to my heart: it is dearer to me, than my life: and therfore you will pardon me, in this my bolder *parrhêsia [frankness]* and freeness: in which if I have exceded, you will easily impute all oversights to the straytes of an hour; which I had, to write this letter; and a copy of it. And, Sir, altho' your Speech and Answers the last Commencement were, in the judgement of abler men than my self, against My Commencement Position the former year;[7] and your first yesterday Advice directly against My Commencement Sermon; and what You delivered yesterday about Reconciliation, if I mistake not, flatly against what I have preached for you in Trinity pulpit:[8] yet in holy reverence I call God to wittness, that all this I have laid aside; nor hath it putt any quickness into my pen. But Zeal for God's Glory and Truth; Desire, that young ones may not be tainted; and that Your name and repute may not be blemished; and that My self with other your friends may not be grieved, but comforted and edified by your ministry, and so may have more incouragement to attend upon it; have been the weights upon my Spirit, that thus sett the wheel a-going: which, if *upon the wheels*, in SOLOMON's phrase,[9] will have better access to you; and acceptance with you: which with my humble service I desire to present; and subscribe myself, Sir,

Your unfeigned Friend and Servant;<br>
A. TUCKNEY.

September 8, 1651.

# Notes

1. Samuel Salter: "*Samuel Cradock*, heretofore a pupil of Dr. *Whichcote*'s at *Emmanuel* college, and at this time fellow there; became University Preacher, in this year 1651; and was afterwards presented by the college to the living of *North-Cadbury* in *Somersetshire*, where *Whichcote* and *Cudworth* were his two next and immediate predecessors, and whence he was ejected for non-conformity in 1662. He wrote and published many books; and died in 1706, aged 85. His younger brother was *Zachary*; afterwards Chaplain in ordinary to King *Charles* II, and Provost of *Eton* college" (1 n).

2. This term, *ingenuous*, as used in these letters—although it embraces sincerity, honesty, straightforwardness, or candor in speech—signifies much more than current usage suggests, referring more generally to nobility of character and disposition. Tuckney, by contra-distinguishing *ingenuity* (or, the natural work of Reason in application to morality) and *saving grace* (or, the supernatural agency of the Holy Spirit, especially "imputed righteousness"), immediately arrives at the issue to be discussed. Whichcote argues, "Religion does not Operate, like a Charm of Spell; but ingenuously, by way of *Mind* and *Understanding*" (*Moral and Religious Aphorisms*, §343), and "The great Work of the Divine Spirit is to lead Men into right Apprehensions, and stay a Man's Thoughts in Consideration, till the Principles do receive Admittance, and become a Temper and Constitution, till they infuse and instill themselves, and make a lasting Impression" (*Select Sermons*, Part I, Sermon I, 29). *Ed.*

3. BW: "In *Morality*, we are sure as in Mathematics" (*MRA* §298; cf. *SS*, Part II, Sermon VI, 296; *Apostolical Apothegms* §29, in *SSN*, 124-25).

4. SS: "Probably, Luke xxiv.47" (3 n).

5. SS: "Dr. *Whichcote* had been very large on this subject; in his speech at the Commencement of this year" (4 n).

6. These asterisks are in the text published by Samuel Salter, and were probably added by Dr. Jeffery to indicate where the legibility of a word or phrase could not be made out. *Ed.*

7. SS: "Which his son *Jonathan Tuckney*, who printed it with the rest of his Latin pieces in 1679; calls *vindicatio Fidei a superbo Rarienis magisterio*. The sermon I have not seen, but I find one of his, on 2 Tim. i:13. on the usefulness of compendiarie systemes, commended and referr'd to, in the epistle to the reader before the second edition in 1658, of the Assemblie's Confession and Catechisms: which is most probably that here hinted at" (4-5 n).

8. SS: "Dr. *Whichcote* preached a lecture at *Trinity* church in *Cambridge*, (as Arch-bishop *Tillotson* saith) for near 20 years together; which was continued, after he left off, by a combination of learned fellows of colleges: as Mr. *Beardmore* seems to say, in his Paper on the Archbishop's death; just publish'd by the reverend Mr. *Birch*" (5 n).

9. SS: "See the marginal reading, Prov. xxv. 11. and the Commentator's on that text" (5 n).

# Letter II

## Dr. WHICHCOTE's First Letter; In Answer.

Sir,

I received your letter, last night; and my sleep since hath been mostly meditation thereon: and in the issue, my thoughts suggest; If I be faulty, "let the Righteous reprove me; it shall not break my head:"[1] and blessed be the man, that rids me of an Error!

Sir, I assure you, I have taken many things of late years, since your return to the University, very kindly from you; and have layd them up be me, as certain expressions of your faithfullness to me; but your plain dealings with me in this your last letter, I preferr before all the rest: and I do give you the advantage therein of a Messenger sent to me from Heaven. Onely I must *examine* the things that you say; for, saith the Apostle, "shou'd an angel from heaven bring, *&c.*"[2]

Sir, I do speak my heart to you, I do not dissemble, I have had you all along in very high esteem; and have borne you reverence, beyond what you do or can imagine; having in me a living and quick sense of my first relation to you: and, of all men alive, I have least affected to differ from You; or to call in quæstion either what You have done or said or thought: but your judgement I have regarded with reverence and respect. I do not, I can not, forgett my four first yeares' education in the University under you; and I think, I have principles by me, I then received from You.[3] In the next place I acknowledge DR. HILL[4] rising-up in the same place, as to Me; and continuing the relation of Tutor to me, for the next three years; and my inward hearty Friend, before and since. And give me leave to superadde Dr. ARROWSMITH,[5] though not in that relation to me; a later acquaintance indeed, but my friend of choice; a companion of my special delight: whom in my former years I have acquainted with all my heart, I have told him all my thoughts; and I have scarcely either spoken or thought better of a man; in respect of the sweetness of his spirit, and amiableness of his conversation.

Sir, to my great grief and trouble, I have been of late very sensible of an abatement of former familiarity and openness; and we have not conversed with that singleness and simplicity of heart, as heretofore: our Hearts have not seemed to be together, when our Persons have bin: but we have looked upon one another, rather with shieness and fear; than with former love and good-will. I have sometimes attempted to make a discovery of the matter; but I have mett with reservedness, and an endeavour to decline all discourse of that nature: whereupon I resolved, that time wou'd work-out all displicency and offence; and lead into a good understanding. Sir, your letter hath now given me the happiest advantage possible; by discovering to me the *cordolium [heartfelt grief]*: I am freely willing, heartily ready, to be accountable, to give satisfaction. If I have done prejudice to saving grace, by idolizing natural ingenuity; the Lord reprove itt in me, and discover to me this sin, by any hand whatsoëver. If I have given true cause of offense and grief, to the hearts of good men; I desire, I may know itt: I shall be ready to deprecate itt. If I have any way tainted the minds of young ones with errour and falshood; blessed be the man, whosoëver he be, that confutes that errour. I heartily pray, that no man may receive an Opinion from me; but onely abide in the Truth: I never hear with better acceptance, and greater delight; than when the speaker professeth to correct a mistake: I wou'd be, I am sure, a lover and pursuer of Truth.

Now, Sir, to deal clearly with you; the matter of your letter meets with no guilt in my conscience: I am not self-convinced; not self-condemned: either you have mistaken me; or, in my understanding, it is God's truth you do reprove. To make this appear to you, I will give you an account of particulars.

For the *matter* of my Commencement Speech; I must stand to it, as a manifest truth of God; of great importance: it was well considered by me; God was sought, for direction and assistance; and hath bin since acknowledged, by me. I shou'd sin against God, *stante hoc judicio [according to this judgment]*, to decline it, to disown it. And I assure you, Sir, preaching seven years since at Trinity lecture[6], on the first chapter of the *Romans*; and taking notice withall of somewhat in the second; these phrases of the Apostle, concerning men not under a gospel dispensation—*to gnôston tou Theou [knowledge of God]*, I. v. 19. leaving the natural use, *v*. 27. without natural affection, *v*. 31. holding truth in unrighteousness, *v*. 18. *ta aorata autou tois poiêmasi nooumena [the invisible things of him are clearly seen, understood by that which is made]*, *v*. 20. *gnontes ton Theon [those who know God]*, *v*. 28. *eis asuneton kardian, eis pathê atimias, eis adokimon noûn [to the stupid heart, to those afflicted with disbelief, to the uneducated mind]*, II. *v*. 14. and *ethnê ta tou nomou poiê phusei [they are a law unto themselves]*—have forced upon me all those notions I do entertain, or have publiquely delivered; concerning natural light, or the use of reason.[7] I now forbear many other parallel scriptures, to establish the truth; and instance onely in these: my sermon-notes upon which lying yet by me of seven year's date, being a good evidence for me; that the notion itself, was by me publiquely declared, long before your Commencement Quæstion.[8] And indeed I took not offense at your quæstion; but was well enough satisfied in your explication and defense of it: thinking, if we differed in some expression, yet we agreed in sense and meaning.[9] And, I assure you, that the primary intention of my Commencement speech was, *de certitudine et dignitate Christianae religionis [On the certainty and goodness of the Christian religion]*; thinking that a subject worthy such a meeting, and to edification: wherto whatsoëver I said, of its satisfactoriness to true Reason, the mind and understanding of man, came in as accessory; and primarily neither foreseen nor intended. What befell us in disputation, was sudden, occasional, unthought-of; it may be, before the answer, as little known to me, as the argument; wherof however I have no record by me: and therfore I referr that part to Conference; wherby the memory of the argument may call-back the memory of the answer.

Concerning your Commencement Sermon; truly I doe not think, it hath bin in my memory, of many months; till your letter yester-night caused me to recall it: sure I am, I had no consideration of it; in my late preparing or preaching of my sermon: neyther do I now know, whether there be any inconsistency; between what you then said, and I since. Concerning sermons you have preached for me at Trinity; (which truly is a great obligation upon me: and I hope, you will not impute such baseness to me; as indignly to reflect upon so great a respect and kindness to me:) as I was not present to hear, so to this hour I know no more, 'bate what is in your letter, concerning them; than onely that my wife still told me, how much she was revived by your excellent paines, as I think, upon "We, as ambassadours, beseech you to be reconciled."[10] But to call in quæstion or contradict you, in aught you had taught, was neyther in the sense of my mind; nor indeed, within the compass of my possibility: the things being wholely unknown to me.

In the last place, concerning my late sermons; I have betaken my self to my notes, my rule in speaking;[11] and I shall give you the Positions: as I find them written, and remember them spoken.

"I. I perswade myself; that all truly good men among us, do substantially agree; in all things saving."[12]

"II. That some things, wherein we differ, are not certainly determined in Scripture; but that which both parties say, seems to have countenance somewhere or other.[13] Yea, I think, God may have reserved somewhat from us, as not *huius temporis [of the time]*; or His secret, and that He wou'd not have us know. *Nolite altum sapere [Do not seek to know the deep things]*, in this case."

"III. The proposal for peace—That all be looked-upon as fallible, which is *ultra et citra scripturam [more and less than what is written]*."[14]—And, Sir, is there on earth power to adde, alter or change? is not the foundation of Protestancy, *Sacra scriptura est adaequata regula fidei [Holy scripture is the sufficient standard for the faith]*? are not scripture formes of words sufficient, yea aptest, to convey and carry all saving truth to the mindes and understandings of men?[15] Farther I argued thus for peace among good Christians.—"Good men, differing in *their own* expressions, yet agree in *Scripture* formes of words: acknowledging, the meaning of the holy Ghost in them is true; and they endeavour to understand and finde it out, as well as they can: therfore they shou'd continue friends; and think, they agree; rather than think, they do not agree; (because they *do* agree, in what is God's and infallible; though they differ, in what is their own and fallible:) and upon this consideration forbear one another; and not impose their own, either sense or phrase." And I think, all Protestants hold; that *Cuilibet Christiano conceditur judicium discretionis [Freedom of judgment is granted to any Christian whatever]*: against the Pope's usurpation of *Iudex infallibilis visibilis in rebus fidei [The Judge is clearly infallible in matters of faith]*.

And truly, Sir, I think; I shou'd give a great deal too little to the wisdom of God in Scripture: if I shou'd not think it, without any humane supplement, sufficient; to convince Popery, to assert the divinity of Christ, and to declare the notion of His death, and to secure the mindes of men from whatsoëver supposed hæresy or blasphemy. And I perswade my-self; that good men have light enough, and direction plain and full enough, from Scripture; to enable them to discover and decline such wicked company, as your letter supposeth. And, Sir, wheras you say; you discerne, in whose footsteppes I tread: if you meane any late author, I can assure you; I can shew you all these matters in a Position in EMANUEL college chappel, at Problemes[16] made by me, fourteene yeares agoe, *de potestate et regimine ecclesiae [On the powers and rule of the Church]*: which I wonder that *those* times shou'd beare, and not *these*. So that it is true, that you saye; my heart was full: for indeed, my head hath bin possessed with this truth, these manie yeares; and I have long since freely reasoned and disputed it, with some of the ancientest and in chiefe place in the university: so that I am not late or newe in that persuasion; concerning scripture sufficiency and non-imposing.

"IV. The proposal for progress and growth in knowledge—That an ingenuous-spirited Christian, after application to God, and diligent use of meanes to finde-out truth; might fairely propose, without offense taken, what upon search he findes cause to beleeve; and whereon he will venture his own soule."[17] This (I said) might be converse to mutual edification; and without disturbance to the world: and so I have long thought; and do continue to think so still: and, if herein I be in an errour, I shou'd be glad to be shewn it.

For the point of Reconciliation—I shall write you out a coppy of my notes, in that point: wherby you will easily understand, how you wrong both my wordes and meaning.

> Christ doth not save us; by onely doing for us, *without* us: yea, we come at that, which Christ hath done for us, with God; by what he doth for us, *within* us. For, in order of execution, it is, as the wordes are placed in the text; Repentance, before Forgiveness of sins; Christ is to be acknow-ledged, as a principle of grace *in* us; as well as an advocate *for* us. For the scripture holdes-forth Christ to us, under a double notion; 1. to be felt in us, as the new man; in contradiction to the old man: as a divine nature; in contra-distinction to the degenerate and apostate nature: and as a principle of heavenly life; contrary to the life of sin, and spirit of the world: 2. to be beleeved-on by us, as a sacrifice for the expiation and atonement of sin; as an advocate and meanes of reconciliation between God and Man. And Christ doth not dividedly performe these offices; one,

and not the other.[18] For reconciliation between God and Us, is not wrought, as sometimes it is said and pretended to be in the world, between parties mutually incensed and exasperated one against another: when the urgency of a case makes them to forbear hostility, and acting one against the other; their inward antipathie and enmitie in the mean while rather increased, inflamed: because they take not up the difference fairely, nor come to agree in the cause; but *causa continens odii [an issue involving resentment]* still continues: so that, though an amnestie be consented-to, yet are they not friendes; but in heart enemies. Wherfore our saviour, to distinguish, saith; If ye from your heartes forgive not, &c.[19] But with God there can not be reconciliation; without Our becoming God-like: for God's acts are not false, overly, imperfect; God cannot make a vaine shew; God, being perfectly under the power of goodnesse, can not denie himself: because, if he shou'd, he wou'd depart from goodnesse; which is impossible to God.[20] Therfore *We* must yeelde, be subdued to the rules of goodnesse, receeve stamps and impressions from God; and God can not be farther pleased, than goodnesse takes place. They therfore deceeve and flatter themselves extreamly; who thinke of reconciliation with God, by meanes of a Saviour, acting upon God in their behalfe; and not also working in or upon them, to make them God-like.[21] Nothing is more impossible than this; as being against the nature of God: which is in perfect agreement with goodnesse, and hath an absolute antipathie against iniquity, unrighteousnesse and sin. And we cannot imagine, that God by his Will and Pleasure can go against his Nature and Being.

(The phrase, "Divinity *minted* or *taught* in Hell;" I finde not in my notes: but it was suddainly spoken; upon this abuse of God and cheat of our-selves.)

To put this upon a Saviour to doe; and impotently to flatter our-selves in the conceit of such a thing, which *a parte Dei ponit repugnantiam [he takes up the defense with respect to God]*; were, instead of reconciling Heaven and Earth, to divide God against Himselfe. And this is a demonstration in Divinity; beyond which no demonstration in Astronomie is more certain. If we wou'd be true to our-selves, let our faith have no contradiction from within us; let not our sense give our conceits the lye; let us taste and see, &c.—.

Now, whether there be anie thing in all this, contrary to "free grace, freely justifying the ungodly;" as you seeme to inferr: I leave to your self upon second thoughts to judge. Or whether this whole discourse be not, as was by me intended, wholely pointed against those, that "turn the grace of God into wantonnesse;" and pretend to be reconciled to God, through *Justification*; wheras they continue enemies to God, through want of *Sanctification*; and the renewing of the spirit by Christ.[22]

Sir, You wrong me very much; in misquoting, *oritur e nobis [it arises from us]*; and attributing it to the ground of our acceptance with God. I finde in my notes these wordes, "*Salvatio nascitur e nobis, suscipitur a nobis [Salvation is born from within ourselves, it is assumed by us]*;" in the gloss I had upon the wordes, *viz.* "*the true notion of salvation*: a saviour to give repentance and forgiveness. Some look at salvation, as at a thing at distance from them; the benefit of some convenient place to be in; exemtion from punishment; freedom from enemies abroad: but it is the mending of our natures, and the safety of our persons, our health and strength within our selves," (Nothing in this is intended to leave-out the authour of our salvation; or *a quo salvatio oritur [from which salvation arises]*:) "and our good state and condition with God; the work of grace and favour towards us and upon us; our being restored to righteousnesse, goodnesse and truth; and our being reconciled to God, so as we may truly finde the kingdom of God within us.—" \* \* \*

# Notes

1. Samuel Salter: "Ps. cxli.5" (6 n).
2. SS: "Gal. i.8. See in the preface some account of Dr. Hill and Dr. Arrowsmith" (6 n).
3. *V.* Salter's Preface, 59.
4. Thomas Hill (*d.* 1653), *v.* Salter's Preface, 63.
5. John Arrowsmith (1602-1659), *v.* Salter's Preface, 64-5.
6. Regarding Whichcote's lectures at Trinity, *v.* Salter's Preface, 6.
7. BW: "Man's Observance of God in all Instances of Morality; these are Truths of *first Inscription*, and these have a deeper Foundation, greater Ground for them, than that God gave the Law on Mount *Sinai*, or that he did after ingrave it on Tables of Stone; or that we find the Ten Commandments in the Bible. . . . God made Man to them, and wrought his Law upon Men's Hearts; and, as it were, interwove it into the Principles of our Reason; and the things thereof are the very Sense of Man's Soul, and the Image of his Mind: So that a Man doth undo his own being, departs from himself, and unmakes himself, confounds his own Principles, when he is disobedient and unconformable to them; and must necessarily by self-condemn'd. —The Law externally given was to revive, awaken Man, after his Apostacy and Sin, and to call him to Remembrance, Advertency, and Consideration. And, indeed, had there not been a Law written in the Heart of Man; a Law without him, could be to no Purpose. For had we not Principles that are *Concreated*; did we not know something, no Man could prove any thing" (*SS*, Part I, Sermon I, 5-6).
8. SS: "Articuli Fidei non sunt ad normam humanæ rationis exigendi. Vid. A. T. Præfectionn. &c. part 2. page 1" (9 n).
9. BW: "Men's Apprehensions are often nearer than their *Expressions*: they may *mean* the same thing, when they seem not to say the same thing" (*MRA* §77).
10. SS: "II Cor. v.20" (10 n).
11. Shaftesbury wrote, in his Preface to *Select Discourses* (1698): "The Sermons which are here printed, have been selected out of Numbers of others less perfect, there being not any of the Author's extant, but such as were written after him at Church; he having used no other than very short Notes, not very legible; though these have been of great Use to the Publisher, in whose Hands they have been" (*SS*, xxxii). *Ed.*

12. BW: (1) "The Christian World scattered into particular Ways, and multiplied into Sects and Parties, yet do agree in the great and bright Truths of Reason and Christianity, such as are fixed, and of the greatest Magnitude"; (2) "Serious and considerate Persons *such as* are real, and sincere in their Religion, do not *greatly* differ; to wit, *not in those things wherein the Honour of God, or the Safety of Mens Souls are concerned*: (For, these are the *substantial things* in Religion:) Neither do they see that *that* follows which one that doth dissent from them, doth infer to the Prejudice of either" (*SS*, Part I, Sermon I, 15; Part II, Sermon IV, 240).

13. BW: "You see now, that in Matters of Weight, wherein the Honour of God, and the Safety of Mens Souls are concerned, Scripture is punctual, clear, full, and particular: That our Faith may be better directed, and we ourselves preserved against Cheats and Impostures. But *as to* other Matters, they are left to Christian Prudence, Discretion, and Fidelity.... This is a great Point of Divinity, That God hath left us, in the Christian Religion, as *Free* as we may be, without Loss or Prejudice *to ourselves*: We being only determined to things of Weight, and to such things, wherein if we should fail, we should greatly hurt ourselves" (*SS*, Part II, Sermon III, 222-23).

14. BW: (1) "And Charity hath been wanting, when Men have gone about to make out Scripture further than what hath been plainly declar'd. So that I resolve with myself, that GOD *having* invested Man with *Intellectual Nature*; and given him that high Privilege, and Prerogative of *Reason and Understanding*; doth expect that he should act according to those Principles: And, where HE doth not constitute and appoint, limit and determine; that *there* he doth refer himself to the rational Determination of *that first Principle*, the Principle *of his Creation*. So that, whatsoever is done throughout the Life of Man, that *there is Reason for*; it is warranted by *God*: Provided, still, that a Man doth not vary from any particular and express Institution of God, in Scripture. And, if this were understood; we should have the very Foundation of Differences in the Church of God taken away. It is but a vain Pretence of *Zeal for God*, and *doing him Service*; for US to limit, appoint, constitute and determine, beyond what *HE himself* hath done"; (2) "We are all, whether we dissent or agree one with another in *some Matters*, agreed about *this*; that we all ought to be guided by Scripture. Now *Scripture* is clear, full, and perspicuous, in all Matters of *Life*; and absolutely determining *in* all Matters of *necessary Belief*. But, in other Things; we being removed above Sixteen hundred Years from the Apostles; and, since in the intermediate Ages, many Things have been agitated by the several Parties, and disputed *Pro* and *Con*, and yet not agreed about; and since it doth hardly appear, what was the *Apostle*'s Judgment in those controverted Matters; since they are *what* we cannot certainly determine by their Writings; and no Application to be made to any Person inspired since *that time* in the Succession of Ages; if we do err in these Matters, it is much less than if we had lived in *their* Times. They that are settled in the great Matters of Life and Faith, will out-wear Mistakes in lesser Matters: Or, if they do not; I dare undertake, from the Warrant of Scripture, that if they hold the Head, *Christ Jesus*, such Mistakes shall not hurt them" (*SS*, Part II, Sermon III, 221-22; Part II, Sermon IV, 241).

15. BW: "In Doctrines of super-natural Revelation, we shall do well to direct our Apprehensions, and to regulate our Expressions, by words of *Scripture*"; "Nothing is *of Faith*, that is not in Scripture; nothing is *necessary*, as otherwise expressed; nothing is *certain*, as farther made-out. We may Live in Christian Love and Union; without Consent and Agreement in non-scriptural expressions or forms of words" (*MRA* §578, §1161).

16. SS: "Disputations in the college-chapels of Cambridge are called Problems" (12 n).

17. BW: "Why do I not make the like favourable interpretation of my Brothers miscarriage, which I made for my self ere-while in the like case? If this Rule did but prevail more, there would be much more moderation in the tempers of men" (*SSN*, 83).

18. BW: "The Substance of the Gospel is, Repentance from dead Works, and Faith in the Lord Jesus Christ. These do go together, and encourage each other; in as much as no Man repents, who doth not believe; nor can any believe, who doth not repent" (*SS*, Part I, Sermon II, 34).

19. SS: "Matt. xviii. 35" (14 n).

20. BW: "It is a great saying, *Whosoever is pleased with God, pleaseth God; and God is pleased with him*. It is repugnant, that God should take pleasure in Us; till we do harmonize with Him: which is by our Regeneration, being made like Him and comformable to Him. If we are not God-like, neither is God pleased with Us; nor are We pleased with God" (*MRA* §61).

21. BW: "It is not Faith for righteousness, but righteousness through Faith. Wherefore it is a vain thing to think that Christ came to make a proposition, by believing whereof men should be saved. He came to found acceptance, and to work matter of righteousness" (*SSN*, 62).

22. BW: "At that instant that a mans mind is enlightened from Heaven, a man ceases to walk in lying apprehensions, he is rid of his fond fancies, and can act according to right reason, judgment, and understanding"; "Who will think better of God, than those that have the fullest assurance of their justification. They are most vigorous in all acts of holiness, and in a ready and chearful compliance with his will; so that there is an inseparable conjunction of these two, Acceptation of a mans person in the court of Heaven, and the Sanctification of his person on Earth" (*SSN*, 36-7, 58-9).

# Letter III

## Dr. TUCKNEY's Second Letter.

Sir,

Having now at last this morning, since tenn o'clock, gotten a little free liberty from company, to consider of your large letter; in which your love putt you to so much paines in writing it: I have borrowed two or three houres from my preparation for to-morrowe's sermon; to give you a shorte and suddaine account of my thoughts about itt.

And first, Sir, I cannot but very thankfully acknowledge your favour and love; in that your so earnest care and endeavour for my satisfaction: and your pious ingenuity; in being so desirous, in case you shou'd be out of the way, of better information and direction. For those larger expressions of your greater respects, to the two others you mention, and my selfe; whatever They may be, I, who do or shou'd know my own meanness; do freely and really, without glozing, professe my selfe unworthy of them: and therfore must impute them, to your goodnesse, wholely; and not at all, to anie deserts in my self. What expressions of strangenesse you have of late observed in Them, I must leave to You and Them: for my selfe, this I can very truly say; that as, from my first knowledge of you, I have ever loved you; so, since my returne hither, your great worth in your self, and much kindnesse to me, have obliged me more affectionately to honour you. This indeed, I must confesse, is my— I cannot well say whether, Temper of Weaknesse; it may be both: that I have no skill in court-complements and dissemblings; to hide distastes in the disguise of a counterfeit smile. I have learnt from Sir FRANCIS BACON; that an unreserved openesse and freenesse have bin ever eminent in those, that have bin most manly and generous:[1] I am none of them; butt in this soe farr like them, that I desire to deale plainely with all: especially with those, whom I most respect. And truly, Sir, if there have bin any abatement of intimacy and freedom, either in Them or My-selfe; I think, in your letter you have layd your finger on that sore. I think for Them, I am sure for My-self, that the onely *cordolium [heartfelt grief]* is and hath bin; that we fear, the truth of Christ, much dearer than dearest friendes, hath bin and may be prejudiced; and so young ones in the universitie tainted, and others greeved, by a veine of doctrine; which runnes up and down in manie of Your discourses, and [in those] of some others of verie great worth; whom We verie much honour, and whom You head, as some think; though, for this last particular, I verily think otherwise. A brief *synopsis*, or some fewe particulars of it, I shall present You with by-and-bye.

Sir, you take too much paines, in clearing your-self from reflecting upon me, in your Commencement speech and answers and last Lord's-day's sermon. In my letter I from my heart told you, I heeded it not: I beleeve, it was not *ex intentione operantis [from the intention of the worker]*; whatsoever it were, *operis [of the work]*. If the truth of God be not opposed; I hope, He will quiet my heart; though I be.

For what you say, about your commencement speech and answers; "that the matter of it is a manifest truth, and of great importance; your declared judgement seven yeares before, out of Romans the first and second; in which manie passages, which you cite, seeme to make for it; that you were not offended with my quæstion, but satisfied with my explication; and that your intention in that speech was *de certitudine et dignitate Christianae religionis [on the certainty and goodness of the Christian religion]*; and what was spoken about Reason was accessary, and not primarily intended:"—Give me leave freely and playnely to express my-selfe—That a discourse *de certitudine, &c.* was indeed an argument fitt for such a meeting: but that certainely I beleeve, most of your auditours wou'd have judged, might have bin more satisfactorily and theologically made-out, from the certainty of divine testimonie, and faith in it; than of reason: and wou'd gladly then, and at other times, have *Faith* to have bin advanced; rather than *Reason* cried-up: which is yet so frequently [done], that it is now *cramte [cabbage cooked]*, not *bis [twice]* but *centies cocta [a hundred times]*[2]; and so proves nauseous: and your then so large discourse about it, but the fourth edition of what manie of them had before, in your position, determination, sermons, at Trinity and otherwhere. And for strangers, ministers and others, who had before but sinister thoughts of your judgement in that particular; their prejudice was more confirmed: and so increased, that it hath bin a greefe to divers of your friendes to hear and read what they doe of you in that kinde; and that from all quarters: So that I beleeve, it had bin your wisdom to have forborne: but they apprehended it to be then carried-on with a high hand, both by your selfe and others; so as rendered most of your auditours more disaffected than satisfied: who conceeve, that that saying of "the candle of the Lord, &c."[3] so over-frequently quoted, makes nothing to that purpose; and those instances out of Rom. I and II as little: the first of the places relating to the searching of our owne, or, as PISCATOR[4] conceeveth, of another's heart and actions; not of divine truths: and the latter to what is *Theologiæ Naturalis [Natural Theology]*, in which natural reason is of more use; not to what is purely *super-natural* and evangelical: in which what use yet there is and may be of reason, and the exercise of itt; in my position I endeavoured to expresse. But that our faith shou'd be ultimately resolved *in rationem rei, ex parte objecti [in natural reason, with respect to the object]*; and that *ex parte subjecti, ratio humana [with respect to the subject, human reason]* should be *summus judex [the supreme judge]*; which was expressly asserted by you, in your answer to my argument: as I then said, it was *new*, so now I thinke it very *strange* divinity. And for that you then said, and now in one part of your letter write; that all protestants hold, that *Cuilibet Christiano conceditur judicium discretionis [Freedom of judgment is granted to any Christian whatever]*; it is very true, as you well adde in your letter, against the Pope's usurpation of *Judex infallibilis visibilis in rebus fidei [The Judge is clearly infallible in matters of faith]*: a true beleever shou'd not be a brute, but have something about a Collier's faith;[5] implicitly to beleeve, whatever the Pope and his church saith: nay, he is to be amongst those *eugenesteroi [more noble]*,[6] and it is a part of the ingenuousnesse of his spirit, as he is a man, especiallie as a Christian, *anakrinein [to examine]*, to search, and with the judgement of discretion to judge, whatever the best men suggest. But you will please to observe, what is there said; "they searched the scriptures, whether those things were so": by which it appears, that the scriptures were the rule, by which they judged of the doctrine delivered to them: so that what the scripture or divine testimonie of God held-out, they withoute dispute beleeved: and judged, not itt; but man's doctrine, by itt. And although man's understanding be *subjectum naturaliter receptivum illuminationis supernaturalis [a subject naturally receptive to supernatural illumination]*; and, *eo nomine [specifically for that reason]*, when Faith acts, Reason acts also: yet this is verie farr from resolving Faith into Reason. AU'STINE from the word hath taught me; *quod scimus, debemus rationi; quae credimus, authoritati [what we know, we owe to reason; what we believe, to authority]*.—But I have forgotten my-selfe; in so farr launching into a dispute, which I intended not, about the Commencement buisnesse.—I more briefly touch upon what you write, about your last sermon: in which you say, "you have betaken your-selfe to your notes; which are your rule of speaking": but, I suppose, such a rule, as you doe not strictely tie your-selfe unto; as appeares by your first marginal[7] annotation in your letter. And truly, Sir, were I not so conscious of my owne dulness and unfaythfulness of memorie, I shou'd be very prone to think; that your delivery in the pulpitt and these notes differ: and the rather, because I perceeve others, of better judgements and memories than my-selfe, agree with me in thinking, that you spake to the sense, that in my former letter I expressed.[8] But I am confident, you write; as you apprehend, you spake: and we must beleeve Your notes, rather than Our memories: and therfore I shall followe them; and, as I goe along, compare them with my letter: in which, it may be, I might in some thinges be mistaken.

When you persuade yourself, that "all truly good men among us do substantially agree; in all thinges saving": that word *substantially* is a good salvo; but—those *things saving*—itt may be, we do not agree what is meant by them. What and how manie they are, manie good men differ in; and, it may be, you and I doe: I beleeve, those fundamentall saving thinges are, in some mens' judgements, butt very few; and they leave out of them very many substantial truths; in which if good men shou'd differ, itt wou'd be very uncomfortable: and, as I wrote, itt wou'd be verie unsafe and unsound to say, that they are not certainely determined in the scriptures; butt that they shou'd seeme, in some places or other, to countenance the two contrary parties. Some thinges of lesse consequence, I grant, may not particularly be determined by scripture; but by consequences: and though some other thinges, of greater consequences and higher nature, may be "God's secrets"; yet I beleeve, whatever God reveles or delivers in scripture, they are so farr *huius temporis [of this time]*, I meane *huius vitæ et mundi [of this life and world]*; that, although they be not curiously to be inquired into and judged and measured by our reason and understanding; yet they are, so farr as delivered by God, humblie to be beleeved and submitted-to: and so are by God determined in the scriptures, though we may not easily determine of them. And this perfection I give to the scripture; which, in your next paragraph, you insist upon: for whereas, in your first proposal, I conceeved itt dangerous; that, "in case both parties hold to scripture expressions," though they may differ, and that dangerouslie, in their contrary interpretations of them; "they shou'd agree":—as a manifest syncretism with the worste of hæretiques; who will not denie the wordes of scripture: and therfore in councils and synods they have constantly framed some wordes, to expresse the true meaning of scripture; against heterodoxie: which as You in publique, so divers times in private I have heard others expresse a dislike of insisting-upon, as *fallible*.—

You ask me, "whether on earth there be any power to adde alter or change; and whether it be not the foundation of protestancy, *Scriptura sacra est adaequata regula fidei [Holy scripture is the sufficient standard for the faith]*; and are not scripture-formes sufficient, yea aptest, to convey all saving truths to the mindes and understandings of men"? And afterward, You "think, you shou'd give a great deele too little to the wisdom of God in scripture: if you shou'd not think it sufficient, without any human supplement, to convince popery; and to assert the divinitie of Christ, *&c*; from whatsoever supposed hæresie or blasphemie: and you are persuaded; that good men have light enough from scripture, to inable them to discover and decline such wicked company; *&c*: and that you argued for peace among good Christians; who, tho' differing in their own expressions, yet agree in scripture formes of wordes; *&c*: and therfore shou'd continue friends; and think they rather agree; than not: because they do agree, in what is God's and infallible, though they differ, in what is their own and fallible."—I answer—That I beleeve, there is no power on earth to adde alter or change the scriptures; which are the adæquate rule of faith: but I verilie beleeve too; that true explications and interpretations of the wordes of scripture, though in different wordes from itt, are no such additions or alterations. Nor dare I condemn ancient and modern councils and synods, in the *homoousios, achôristôs, atreplôs, asunchutôs, persona [of one substance, indivisible, immutable, unconfounded, personality]*, *&c*; nor other orthodox commentators, and paraphrasts; as guilty of such a prophane violation: nor, I beleeve, will you yourself; who, it may be, too much affect schoole-expressions: which often rather darken the discourses, than illustrate the truth. These are no human supplements; as though the scripture without them were imperfect: but they onely argue an imperfection in our understandings; which need such helps and glosses, to reade what is written; though in its selfe it be sufficientlie legible. I beleeve alsoe; that scripture formes of wordes are sufficient; and, in a true sense, aptest; to convey to us all saving truth: for in such truths, necessarie to salvation, we truly held; that the scripture, *kata to rhêton* *[according to the letter]*, is playne and evident: but those thinges, which are so saving, You before supposed all good men agreed-in; they were those other thinges, in which you conceeved they differ, which heere you speak-of; and, even in those thinges most saving, though to a cleare and undistorted eye they are cleare enough; yet, if the minde and judgement be weake; it may be, the same truth of scripture, fullie cleare in its selfe, may be spoken in other wordes more playnely to such a weak capacitie: The childe, it may be, will better understande the mother's lisping, than when she speakes more plainelie. All childrens' catechismes are not made-up of the express words of scripture: other wordes, expressing the true sense of them, may more distinctely and particularly discover anie corruption: which was the occasion of orthodox divines in all ages framing of newe wordes and expressions; more punctuallie to holde-out old truths, againste hæretiques' innovations: that as *They*, in their owne wordes, give a false sense of scripture; so *We*, in ours, may give a true. Nor is this, by anie orthodox divines that I knowe of, accounted anie diminution of the wisdom of God in scripture; though some others have accounted it soe: (of whom bye-and-bye;) who are guilty not onely of "supposed hæresies and blasphemies," as your worde is; but of real ones. And although goode men, as you say, have light enough from scripture, to discover and decline such wicked companie; yet truly I must not oppose orthodox explications of scripture to scripture: but thankfullie acknowledge it a great mercie of God; that, by such helps, I may the better understand scripture; and so better discover their depravations of itt: which, whilst I am weake and unwarie, I may be the sooner deluded by; if I must be so charitable as to agree with them, if they adhære to the infallible expressions of scripture; onely differ from man's expressions, which are but fallible.—But you argued thus, "for peace among good Christians; who, agreeing in scripture formes of wordes, shou'd rather think, they do agree; than not: and because they differ onely in their owne expressions, which are fallible."—How I should think that they agree, when they hold contradictory assertions; I cannot think: and for who are good Christians, when every one, that is indeed so, is prone to think another so; and when hæretiques of old, and divers of later times, have bin sober and temperate; *nec sine larva summae pietatis [not even the most pious (heart) is without the worm]* :—I think, that we shou'd look rather to their doctrines, than their persons.

I said, I was sorrie to see you treade, in these proposals, in some bodies footsteppes: to which you answer; "that, if I meane anie late authour, you assure me; that these matters you had in a Probleme, fourteene yeares since; and therfore wonder, that *those* times shou'd beare them; and not *these*: so that you acknowledge, your *heart* is full, and *head* hath bin possessed, of these truths, these manie yeares; and have long since freely reasoned and disputed them with the ancientest, and such as were in chiefe place, in the universitie; &c."—Sir, those, whose footsteppes I observed, were the *Socinians* and *Arminians*; the latter wherof, I conceeve, you have bin everie where reading, in their workes; and most largely, in their *Apologie*:[9] and those very things, which You hint, They dilate. And truly I wou'd not have my good friend come near those mens' tentes: though J.

GOODWIN,[10] like a colonel, can march up in the face of all such imputations. Sir, God knows my heart, that from itt I doe free you in my thoughtes from such aspersions; as having heard you declaring your selfe againste their characteristical tenents: and accordinglie have worde of mouth; when both wayes I have too frequentlie found you in that kind aspersed.

I doe not well understand the latter end of this paragraph of your letter; which I suppose, in your haste, you left imperfect: but if it be, as I thinke it is; that you are not late nor newe in that persuasion of scripture sufficiency, &c; I hope that, more than fourteene years since, you were settled in that persuasion: in which TIMOTHY was, when much younger:[11] but if in your position then you did soe assert scripture sufficiency, as to take-away or diminish the due use of confessions of faith and catechismes, &c; which in other wordes do explaine scripture expressions, and meete-with emergent errours and hæresies; in so doing you trode in the *Arminians'* stepps; who do therfore decrie them; because they finde their heterodoxies mett-with by them. And if it were fourteene years since, you were then but a yonge divine; and might be more subject to mistake: in which, by those reasonings and disputes which you mention, it may seeme; that those ancientest and chief ones of the universitie you disputed with, were not altogether of your minde: and therfore, although, what we suck-in betime, we hardly discharge ourselves of, afterward; yet, be your head and heart never so fullie possessed with such notions, it will be your greater advantage to be the sooner, dispossessed of them.

Your next is about "an ingenuous-spirited Christian's liberty, after application to God, and diligent use of meanes to finde-out truth; fairely to propose, without offense taken, what upon search he findes cause to beleeve; and whereon he will venture his soule: and this conduceth," you think, "to mutual edification; and that, withoute disturbance to the world. And thus, as you have thought, so you continue to think; &c":—I acknowledge the case, as you have written itt, warily proposed: the man must be "ingenuous"; provided he bee so really: "make application to God"; if in sinceritie, a directe way to be guided by Him: "with a diligent use of meanes to finde-out truth"; if with a single heart and eye, not likelie to misse itt: "he fairly and without offense proposeth"; it is not expressed, whether onely in private; or alsoe in publique: and the truth may be so fundamentall, and so established; both by God, in his worde; and by Christian magistrates, in their constitutions and lawes; that the contrarie will verie hardly be so fairelie proposed, as not to fall foule and with offense both on the weake, to their staggering; and the strong, to their greefe: but it is "that, which upon search he findes cause to beleeve; and wheron he will venture his soule": this last clause, of *venturing his soule,* I do not much heede; such efficacie of errour may so seize on a man, that he may with great confidence beleeve a lie:[12] but, as you put the case, he doth not only beleeve; but findes cause to do so: if so, that justifies both God;[13] and man:[14] and therfore God forbidde, that I shoulde condemne him! This conduceth to mutual edification; and is withoute disturbance: and if anie be troubled, it is as some are with Christ himselfe,[15] and his gospell;[16] it is their faulte, not his: though some truthes are not of so great import in themselves, or so necessarie to be knowen; that they shou'd force us upon the disturbance of others contrarily minded, by our unseasonable inforcing them. But, in case the man onely *think*, he findes cause to beleeve;[17] and itt be indeed a *non-causa pro causa [a case based not on prejudice]*: though he shoulde be trulie ingenuous; manie in this kind upon designe personating such a temper: and though he shoulde seek to God for guidance; He often answering some according to their Idol set-up in their heartes:[18] truths may be such, and so fundamentall, and so established; that he shoulde rather stifle his owne first scrupling thoughtes, and check him selfe rather, than speak them out; to the endangering of others.[19] And trulie, such for the moste part are those truths; which now-a-daies They call in quæstion, who plead moste for this liberty: such are Socinians, Arminians, and the *colluvies [rabble]* of all sortes of Sectaries amongst us; who under the protection of this Liberty, which they so crie-up, run-out into all the wildest and foulest extravagances. And therfore whatever an EPISCOPIUS,[20] a —, a J—, or a JUNIUS BRUTUS,[21] might pleade; yett for a lover and assertour of Truth, either to be a full unison with them, or were it butt even —;[22] as, att all times, woulde bee but unsuitable; so, at such a time, in which such a principle hath let Hell break loose; in my poor thoughts, is very unsafe: att leaste, very unseasonable.

For the point of Reconciliation, you give me (I thank you) a coppy of your notes: "whereby," you say,

> I will easily understand; how I have *wronged* both your wordes and meaning: your discourse being both intended and pointed againste them; who pretend to reconciliation with God, in justification; and continue enemies to God, for want of sanctification: in which,

you say,

> Christ doth not save us, by onlie doing for us, without us: yea, we come-att that, which Christ hath done for us, with God; by what he doth for us, within us; for in order of execution, it is as the wordes are placed in the text; Repentance before Forgiveness &c: For the Scripture holdes-forth Christ to us, under a double notion; 1. to be felt in us, as the new-man; &c. 2. to be beleeved-on by us, as a sacrifice and advocate for attonement and reconciliation; &c. God cannot make a vaine shew; God, being perfectlie under the power of goodness, can not denie himself; &c. nor can be farther pleased, than goodness takes place: they therfore deceeve themselves; who think of reconciliation, by meanes of a saviour acting upon God, in their behalfe; and not also working in and upon them, to make them God-like.

Sir, I acknowledge, your notes have helpt my memorie: I did think, you had simply denied Christ's working upon God, in our reconciliation: and had you putt-in the word *onlie*, before the word *acting*; I had not bin so subject to have mistaken:

and yett I was not alone in the mistake; and so, I hope, you will rather say, I was in the wronge; than that I wronged your wordes or meaning: being doubtfull, what you said; and therfore inserted two parentheses in that paragraph of my letter, (if I mistake itt not, and if you meant). And itt seemeth, you did meane, as I there wrote: and therfore, as to that particular, as I have receeved your satisfaction; so I crave your pardon.

Some other things in this there are, in which I crave *your* second thoughts; as you referre me to *mine*: especially about the order of those two notions, under which Christ is held-out to us in the gospell; that he is first felt in us, as the new man; before he is beleeved-on by us, as a sacrifice and advocate: in this I neede a little more light and proofe. If by beleefe you mean, assurance that Christ is our expiation and advocate; I shall not easilie dissent from you: for in ordinarie course, as God workes, so he gives us to feele somthing wrought, in us; before he bring us to that assurance of our peace and pardon: that worke of the spirit, with the witnesse of the spirit, being the matter of our evidence: though I dare not say so universallie; I dare not absolutelie say, that a sinner, converted immediatelie before death, may not have, from the wittness of the spirit, assurance of his peace; though by reason of shortness of time, weakeness of bodie and head, and confusion of spirit in regard of his former sinnfull life, he hath little eyther time or abilitie of list to reflect-upon what God hath now in the instant wrought in him. But if by beleefe you mean, faith's relying or casting himselfe upon God in Christ for mercie; I beleeve, the experience of manie a humble sinner will be a wittness; that hee hath in this sense beleeved in Christ, as a sacrifice and advocate for him; when as yett he could not say, he hath felt anie thing of the newe man in him: I mean, as to his feeling: for, as for the reallitie of the worke; whomsoëver and whensoëver God justifieth, hee also sanctifieth: and, for the order of nature; seeing that faith is before the *apotelesma [fulfillment]* of justification, and faith can not bee withoute a renewall; I was never much against FERINUS[23] his opinion; that sanctification, that is, first sanctification or regeneration or vocation, is in nature before justification: in which sense I admitte what you say, "that wee come-at that which Christ hath done for us with God, by what hee doth for us within us." And for that which you adde; that "in order of execution, repentance is before forgive-ness";—I grante itt; in the full accomplishment of itt: but yett so, as that God, not onlie in his eternall election had before purposed, and by the death of his Son after purchased, our reconciliation: but, even in the execution of that purpose, and appli-cation of that purchase, Hee is before us; and is setting-out first that happie meeting of our fulle reconciliation.[24] Nor in this doth God make a vaine shew; nor is itt contrarie to his goodness, freely to justifie the ungodly, such as are so *immediate antecedenter ad justificationem [immediately before being justified]*, though not *consequenter [afterwards]*; so as to continue such: for so indeed "God cannot be farther pleased, than goodness takes place": and, that hee may bee pleased, hee ever takes order; that sanctification shall ever be joyned with justification.

Sir, in the last passage of your letter you say;

> I *wrong* you *very much*; in misquoting, *oritur e nobis [it arises from us]*; and attributing itt to the ground of our acceptance with God: you onlie said itt of salvation, to express the true notion of it; that, whereas some think, it is a thing at distance from them; freedom from enemies abroad: Itt is the mending of our natures, and the safetie of our persons; the worke of grace within us, and his favour towards us; our being restored to righteousness and goodness, and reconciled to God.

Sir, I am sorry, that I shoulde give you occasion the second time to say, I have wrong'd you again; and this second time very much: it was not my single apprehension, that your wordes, as you delivered them, did seem to look at the ground of our reconciliation. And this *nascitur e nobis [is born from within ourselves]*, in the true and constant acception of that worde, looks suspiciouslie that way. That you said itt of salvation, helpes but little: for that is a large worde: and both in it's sense and I beleeve your's, conteins reconciliation it itt. And trulie, Sir; to say, that eyther salvation or reconciliation *nascitur e nobis*; is, in my poore judgement, a very dangerous expression: sure I am, a stranger to scripture manner of speaking: which, as *all* shoulde much heed; so I expect that *You* will, especiallie: who before, in contradistinction of the fallible expressions and formes of wordes of man's making, judged, and that trulie, scripture expressions to be aptest to conveye all saving truths to our understandings. And I shou'd be glad to knowe, what author you quoted that sentence out of; unless it were your owne: as I have bin apte to think, that both in your sermons and privatt discourse you do often, as it were, quote your-selfe; in uttering latine sentences and axiomes, both in Logick Philosophie Law and Divinitie, which are of your owne making. Butt, whose-so-ëver itt was, and what-ever orthodox exposition you give of itt; in which yett you still sett the worke of God *within* us, before his worke *about* us; yett, that of eyther reconciliation or salvation it shou'd be said, that *nascitur e nobis*; I must ever humbly conceeve, that it is not according to that *hypotypôsis hugiainontôn logôn [form of sound words]*,[25] which wee shou'd hold fast, and not part from.

Sir, by this time I have quite tired-out myselfe; and fear, I shall much more tire you, with these weake lines; that were written as fast as my hande could runne, and that by fittes and startes, as my company and other occasions still calling mee away wou'd give leave: else you had receeved them on saturday; but necessarie occasions prevented mee. It may bee, they will come to you too soone, now; being suddaine raw thoughts, unworthie of your more mature judgement: but, although they will express my weaknesse; yett itt will be enough, if you can read in them my love to you and God's truth: from which double ground itt is, although I have wearied you too much alreadie, that I crave leave yett farther to burden your patience; in making good what I promised, in the beginnyng of my letter, about what hath bin a trouble to some, as concerning some others; and to speake out my whole heart and thoughts, about your-self.

Sir, for yourself; from your first coming to CAMBRIDGE, I trulie said, I loved you: as finding you then studious and pious, and very loving and observant of me.

I remember, I then thought you somwhat cloudie and obscure in your expressions: but I then left you. Since I have heard; that, when you came to be Lecturer in the colledge, you in a great measure for the yeare laid-aside other studies; and betook yourself to Philosophie and Metaphysicks: which, some think, you were then so immersed in; that ever since you have bin cast into that mould, both in your privatt discourse, and preaching; both for wordes and notions: both which, I fear, have rendered your ministry less edifying: as partlie not being well understood, by very manie of your auditours; and less affecting the heart, when so buisying the head to understand both wordes and things. And how richly usefull a spirituall plaine powerfull ministry wou'd bee in the universitie; I need not tell you: but that, in former times, when the quæstion was, why CAMBRIDGE men were account more profitable preachers than OXFORD men; Mr. BAYNES[26] said, the reason was, that God had, from the first reformation, blessed CAMBRIDGE with exemplary plaine and spirituall preachers; and so goodlie pictures hung before the women conceeving, helpt to make the birth more beautifull.[27] When times were *very evil*, God in mercie kept your spirit uprighte; which, with your other worth, brought you as into repute with others, so into the place of the universitie preacher; wherein God hath hitherto preserved you: and may Hee keepe you still, and make you much more fruitefull and serviceable! And I beseeche you, Sir, when God returns you to that taske, that you woulde think much of 1 Cor. xiv.19, affect not to speak in schoole-language; nor to runne-out in schoole-notions: it is farre different from the scripture, both style and matter: it was begot in the depth of anti-christian darkeness; and, very both good and learned men judge, will vanish in darkeness; at the light of brighter day: which wee hope is approching. Some are readie to think; that your great authors, you steere your course by, are Dr. FIELD, Dr. JACKSON, Dr. HAMMOND;[28] all three very learned men; the middle sufficiently obscure; and both hee and the last, I must needs think, too *corrupt*. Whilest you were fellow here, you were cast into the companie of very learned and ingenious men; who, I fear, at least some of them, studyed other authors, more than scriptures; and PLATO and his schollars, above others: in whom, I must needs acknowledge, from the little insight I have into them; I finde manie excellent and divine expressions: and as we are wont more to listen to and wonder at a Parrot, speaking a few wordes; than a Man, that speaks manie more, and more plainlie; and all intelligibly: so whilest wee finde such gemmes in such dunghills, where wee less expected them; and hear some such divine things from them; wee have bin too much drawen-away with admiration of them. And hence in part hath runne a veine of doctrine; which divers very able and worthy men, whom from my heart I much honour, are, I fear, too much knowen by—The power of Nature, in Morals, too much advanced—Reason hath too much given to itt, in the mysteries of Faith.—A *recta ratio* much talkt-of; which I cannot tell, where to finde.—Mind and Understanding is all; Heart and Will little spoken of.—The decrees of God quæstion'd and quarrel'd; because, according to our reason, wee cannot comprehend; how they may stande with His goodness: which, according to your phrase, Hee is *under the power of*.—Those our Philosophers, and other Heathens, made fairer candidates for

Heaven; than the scriptures seeme to allowe of: and They, in their virtues, preferred before Christians, overtaken with weakenesses.—A kinde of a Moral Divinitie minted; onlie with a little tincture of Christ added: nay, a Platonique faith unites to God.—Inherent righteousnesse so preached, as if not with the prejudice of imputed righteousness, which hath sometimes very unseemlie language given it; yett much said of the one, and very little or nothing of the other. This was not PAUL's manner of preaching.—This inherent righteousness may bee perfect in this life. An Estate of Love, in this life, above a life of Faith.—And some broad expressions, as though in this life wee may be above Ordinances:—with divers other principles of religion, by some very doubtfullie spoken of.—And, in case anie cannot so well digest these, I must needs say, I coulde not but wonder to heare some *ingenuous* men complayning, in the pulpitt and elsewhere, of their *rixae et lites [squabbles and disputations]*; and that, about notions and speculations, sects and superstitions; as all opinions are accounted, which a man may hold, and yett bee never the better man for them: and so, that there is a God and a Christ, will thus come to bee but a notion and speculation. Sir, these are some and the moste (if my wearie head coulde remember more, my hand, though wearie, shoulde write them; because I woulde now, once for all, unbosom my-selfe to you:) of the *cordolia [heartfelt grief]*; which I, and other of your friends, have bin affected with: And although, God knowes, wee love you and Them; yet you will not take it ill, if wee love what wee conceeve the truth of God more: and therefore can not desert itt; though wee bee little able to maintain itt. And I hope, that the thoughts of your being reputed a Wise man, and both you and They Learned men; will not stoppe your eares to the weaker suggests of your true friend: and the rather; because, whatever otherwise your worth and abilitie is; yett I knowe you are not ignorant, what verie sinister thoughts are conceived, and reportes scattered, both of your selfe and some others: which from my soule I desire may, by your fulle and plaine appearing for the truth of God, be reallie confuted: and that wee may joyne head and heart and hand, and with one shoulder, in the worke of the Lord; growing up in the truth in love; which was one of the greatest encouragements I had, in my returne to CAMBRIDGE; as hoping to have much helpe in this kinde, by the companie and assistance of such friendes; whom I so much honoured, and so intirely loved: as the contrarie hath bin the trouble of my spirit, in such an unhappie disappointment.—Sir, will you pardon this unreasonable tediousness; and this openhearted and plaine-spoken freeness? itt hath bin from the integrity of the heart of

*Your unworthy Friend;*
ANTH. TUCKNEY.

*Cambridge; Sept.* 15, 1651.

# Notes

1. "Certainly the ablest men that ever were, have had all an openness and frankness of dealing, and a name of certainty and veracity" (Francis Bacon, *Essays* §6, edited with annotations by Richard Whately, 5th ed. [London: John W. Parker and Son, 1860], 81). *Ed.*

2. *crambe non bis sed centies cocta*: a proverbial Latin expression (James Moorwood, *A Dictionary of Latin Words and Phrases* [New York: Oxford University Press, 1998], 37-8; cf. Juvenal, *Satire* VIII.154, *occidit miseros crambe repetita magistros*: "[the student] kills the poor teacher with twice-cooked cabbage [of rhetorical exercises]"). *Trans.*

3. Samuel Salter: "Prov. xx.27" (20 n).

4. Johann Piscator (1546-1625), German Protestant biblical scholar. In January 1596, Lady Margaret Professor Peter Baro preached in St. Mary's, Cambridge, a sermon directed against Piscator and the doctrine of a limited atonement (V. H. H. Green, *Religion at Oxford and Cambridge* [London: SCM Press, 1964], 124). *Ed.*

5. SS: "*Fides carbonaria [The faith of charcoal-burners (colliers)]*, a proverbial phrase, us'd afterwards by Dr. *Whichcote*, lett. 3. and by Dr. *Arrowsmith* in his *Tactica sacra*, printed 1657" (21 n).

6. SS: "Acts xvii.11" (21 n).

7. SS: "P. 15. *N.B.* What the MS. has in the margin, is here every where inserted in the text; but, for distinction sake, put within [hooks]" (22 n). See Editorial Notes. *Ed.*

8. Salter, in the Preface to *Moral and Religious Aphorisms*, states, "It is not unlikely; but I cannot take upon Me to affirm it for truth: that a knowledge of the many copies, taken in short-hand, of Dr. WHICHCOTE's Sermons; and a reasonable apprehension of the injury which his honor'd memory might receive from injudicious publications under his name; engaged the Executors of this great and good man, or rather Mr. BENJAMIN WHICHCOTE merchant in *Bishopsgate* street; (who by particular bequest was instructed with his Uncle's papers;) to put them all into the hands of Dr. JEFFERY" (xix). *Ed.*

9. See below, n. 20, concerning Episcopius.

10. SS: "See the dedication and preface of JOHN GOODWIN's *Redemption redeemed*; which was printed this very year 1651 in Folio, and dedicated to the reverend Dr. BENJAMIN WHICHCOTE Vice-Chancellor, and the other heads of colleges, &c. in the University of CAMBRIDGE. This work is often censured by our author's friend, ARROWSMITH, in his *Tactica sacra*" (27 n). *V.* Salter's Preface, 64-5. *Ed.*

11. SS: "2 Tim. iii.15,16,17" (28 n).

12. SS: "2 Thess. ii.11; John xvi.2; Acts xxvi.9" (30 n).

13. SS: "Ezek. xiv.23" (30 n).

14. SS: "1 Sam. xvii.29" (30 n).

15. SS: "Matt. ii.3" (30 n).

16. SS: "Matt. x.34, 35" (30 n).

17. BW: "Every one, that is Honestly disposed, may find *Direction* for what he is to do; from Right Reason, and Plain Scripture: the only ways, by which Men are taught of God; nor is any other teaching necessary"; "The Truths of God are Connatural to the Soul of Man; and the Soul of man makes no more resistance to them, than the Air does to Light" (*MRA* §35, § 444).

18. SS: "Ezek. xiv.4" (30 n).

19. SS: "Prov. xxx.22" (30 n).

20. Simon Bischop, or Episcopius (1583-1643), was condemned, along with twelve other Remonstants, at the Synod of Dort in 1619. He afterwards systematized the doctrines of Arminianism in a confession of faith popularly referred to as the *Apologia Remonstrantium* (1622). *Ed.*

21. Marcus Junius Brutus (85-42 B.C.), the Roman patriot and philosopher who, in the name of the Republic, was persuaded by Caius Cassius to lead a band of conspirators in the murder of his patron, the dictator Julius Caesar, in 44 B.C. *Ed.*

22. SS: "These three blanks are in the MS; whether Dr. Tuckney wrote so at first, or Dr. Whichcote left them so in his copy, or Dr. Jeffery in the transcript he made from Dr. Whichcote, I cannot say" (31 n).

23. Probably Serinus, either (1) the tenth Bishop of Marseilles (ca. 595-600), (2) the late sixth- and early seventh-century Bishop of Ancona, or (3) the Patriarch of Aquileia (ca. 712-723) (*A Dictionary of Christian Biography, Literature, Sects, and Doctrines, during the First Eight Centuries*, ed. William Smith and Henry Wace, 4 vols. [London: John Murray, 1887], 4:616). *Ed.*

24. SS: "II Cor. v.19. with 20" (34 n).

25. SS: "II Tim. i.13" (35 n).

26. Paul Baynes (*d.* 1617), puritan divine most well known for his commentary on the Epistle of Paul to the Ephesians. Upon refusal to subscribe to the Articles, he was dismissed from his fellowship at Christ's College. *V.* Salter's Preface, 65. *Ed.*

27. "And Jacob tooke him rods of greene poplar, and of the hasel and chesnut tree, and pilled white strakes in them, and made the white appeare which was in the rods. And he set the rods which he had pilled, before the flockes in the gutters in the watering troughes when the flocks came to drinke, that they should conceive when the came to drinke. And the flockes conceived before the rods, and brought forth cattell ring-straked, speckled and spotted" (Gen. 30.37-9). *Ed.*

28. Richard FIELD (1561-1616), Dean of Gloucester, author of the five-volume treatise *Of the Church* (1606-1610). In this work, Field "maintains that 'the whole Church (comprehending all the believers that are and have been since the apostles' time)' is 'freed from error in matters of faith,' and that in matters of faith it is 'impossible also that any error whatsoever should be found in all the pastors and guides of the Church thus generally taken'; but that all might be deceived 'in things that cannot be clearly deduced from the rule of faith and word of divine and heavenly truth' (iv.ii)" (D. Stone, in *A Dictionary of English Church History*, ed. S. L. Ollard, 2nd ed. [London: A. R. Mowbray and Co., 1919], 223). Of the voluminous works of Thomas JACKSON (1579-1640), Dean of Peterborough, published collectively in 1673, John Hunt remarks, "His theology is described sufficiently by the word Arminian. He was not properly a High Churchman, if we compare him with Laud, nor was he a Rationalist, if we compare him with Hales or Chillingworth" (*Religious Thought in England, from the Restoration to the End of Last Century*, 3 vols. [London: Strahan and Co., 1870], 1:466). Henry HAMMOND (1605-1660), chaplain to King Charles I, was at the time of the Restoration appointed to the See of Worcester, but he died before be could be consecrated. During the Interregnum he maintained a controversial presence, writing, in opposition to the puritans, a number of dissertations and defenses of episcopacy and infant baptism (Hunt 1:312-22).

# Letter IV

## Dr. WHICHCOTE's Second Letter.

Sir,

You conceive I said; that Faith is ultimately to be resolved *in rationem rei, ex parte objecti [based on natural reason, with respect to the object]*; and *ratio humana [human reason]* to be *summus judex, ex parte subjecti [the best judge, with respect to the subject]*:—

I shall give you an account, what I have said; and what I do mean. There are *veritates, quae fundantur in rationibus rerum; atque harum est theologia naturalis [truths, which are founded on natural reason; and natural theology is among these]*: as, that *Deus est optimus [God is most good]*, as well as *maximus [greatest]*; that *creatura tenetur Deo obsequi, secundum posse [a created being is required to obey God, as much as possible]*. There are *veritates, quae nituntur revelatione Dei; atque harum est fides divina [truths, which are founded on natural reason; and natural theology is among these]* : [A]1 as *doctrina de Christo expiatore, redemptore, liberatore; revelatio* [B] *de creatione in circumstantiis [the doctrine of Christ the Expiator, Redeemer, Liberator; the revealed truth of the Creation in particulars]*. And *ratio subjecti [subjective reason]* doth *judicare de ratione objecti; et de materia revelationis [discriminate over objective reason; and about the subject matter of revelation]*: but by *judicare*, I mean not an authoritative act; but a perceptive and apprehensive act: as when [D]*visus judicat de coloribus, auditus de sonis [vision discriminates among colors, hearing among sounds]*. For a judging discerning faculty is wholy [D]regulated in its apprehensions *a ratione objecti, sive a qualitate materiae: nam intellectus nullum habet libertatem circa suum objectum; non facit rem aliter se habere, sed percipit rem ut est; et concipit secundum imaginem receptam: hoc est, judicat. Atque veritas, a parte intellectus, consistit in conformitate cum veritate rei [based on objective reason, or on the quality of the subject matter; for the intellect has no freedom with respect to its object; it cannot make a thing seem other than itself, but perceives the thing as it is; and it conceives of it according to the image it receives; this is discrimination. But the truth, pertaining to the intellect, is constituted in conformity with the material fact]*. I have full assurance; that matters of faith are so, as they are reveled; because they are reveled by God: who alone hath power over them, to make them as they are; and is infallibly true, and necessarily good. (I am satisfied, that they are reveled by God; 1. *ab argumentis insitis, sive artificialibus;* [E] *h. e. in artificio rei sitis [from innate or artificial arguments, or those based on an artificial thing]*: et 2. *a ductu divini spiritus [those inspired by the descent of the Holy Spirit]*: for, as St. AUGUST. saith, *si spiritus sanctus mihi non persuaserit, hasce litteras esse a Deo datas; nondun mihi persuasit Christiano esse [if the Holy Spirit did not persuade me, that these letters are dictated by God, he has not yet persuaded me to be a Christian]*.) For those things, which, *quantum ad me [so far as my capacity will allow]*, are matters of faith; as they are reveled by God: *apud Deum sunt materia libertatis et beneplaciti; et ergo, antecedenter ad determinationem Dei, possent aliter esse [they are subjects at the liberty and good-pleasure of God; and therefore, before being determined of God, they may be otherwise]*: and God might otherwise have determined them. But *materia theologiæ naturalis intrinsecam habet necessitatem, aut infallibilem connexionem terminorum [the subject matter of natural theology possesses an intrinsic necessity, and an infallible relationship to its ends]*: In *materia theologiæ naturalis* I do *scire [know]*; because I can demonstrate, *ex principiis certis necessariis et infallibilibus [they are in principle certain, necessary, and infallible]*: in *materia fidei [the matter of faith]* I do *credere [believe]*; because I take things to bee so, as reveled by God: which, if God woulde, might have bin otherwise; because absolutely and of themselves they were in an indifferency. Hence it appears, that *materia fidei* cannot bee [F] *contra rationem rei [contrary to natural reason]*;[2] because *materia fidei est materia voluntatis et libertatis; et ratio rei est materia necessitatis et naturae [the subject matter of faith is matter of free will and liberty; and natural reason is matter of necessity and nature]*: as, it cannot be *de fide, Deum non esse optimum; vel, creaturam non debere Deo subesse [concerning faith, that God is not best; or, that a created being ought not to obey God]*. When therfore wee declare anie thing to be *secundum rationem rei [according to natural reason]*, and therfore necessarilie so; wee do noe prejudice to faith: because *fides versatur in alia materia; scil. in materia, quae cedit sub arbitrio; et necessitatem naturae non habet [belief is concerned with other material facts, such as the subject matter that it concedes under judgment, and which does not possess the necessity of nature]*. (*Credendum est voluntatem Dei, etiam in occultissimis, esse rationabilissimam [We ought to believe that the good will of God is most rational, even in the most obscure matters]*. BONAVENT. Certain it is, that religion is the truest and highest reason; as, on the contrarie, irreligion is sottishness.)[3]

I do withoute scruple beleeve what God hath reveled, and as He hath reveled; because God is infinite in knowledge, infallible in truth, and necessarily good: whence He cannot *deficere [abandon]*, or declare *contra veritatem facti, rationem rei [contrary to the truth of the deed, to natural reason]*; or, in matters of his own voluntary determination, otherwise than as He hath resolved them: And *in omni materia libertatis Deus habet supremam potestatem statuendi [God has supreme powers of establishing every basis.* I do [G] *proxime et immediate [next and imme-*

*diately]* resolve my faith into divine revelation in scripture; and therein rest, with assurance and confidence: as foreknowing, *lumine naturae [by the light of nature]*, that what God reveles is certainly true, and infallible: whom I knowe to be infinite in understanding and knowledge; and in full agreement and necessarie conjunction with goodness and truth. (Neither am I lighte of faith in beleeving:[4] but I knowe, that matters of my faith are matters of divine revelation, as I said before in the margent, *a qualitate materiae, quae est theoprepês, de qua intellectus judicat; et per ductum divini spiritus, a quo intellectus illuminatur et instituitur [from the quality of the subject matter, which is godly, concerning which the intellect discriminates; and through the influence of the Holy Spirit, by which the intellect is illuminated and constituted]*.[5] And when I have before mee a matter of faith, or peece of divine revelation; I do *judicare de sensu [discriminate in regard to the sense]*: not by making what sense I will; but by finding out God's meaning. For the power I have of judging, is not a matter of will and pleasure; but a matter of spiritual sensation and apprehension: and is as much regulated and determined *per qualitatem materiae [through the quality of the subject matter]*, as *gustus per gustabile [taste by means of what is tasted]*. And, if I bee fond or partial, or gratifie anie corruption, I am obnoxious to God, and doe it att my peril: God making an accounte, that hee hath spoken plaine enough to be understood; if I am serious.

To give you what I mean together—1. there is, which is necessarie; and cannot be otherwise: as *bonum est amere Deum [that it is good to love God]*. 2. there is, which is in itself contingent; and determinable at the pleasure of Him, who hath power: as, whether man shou'd bee or no. 3. there is, which is declared by Him, who is infallible; [H] as *expiatio peccatorum in sanguine Christi [the expiation of sinners in the blood of Christ]*. The first is *subjectum naturalis scientiae [the subject of natural science]*; and is *in ratione rei [in natural reason]*: the second is, *materia libertatis et beneplaciti Dei [matter of God's freedom and good-pleasure]*: the third is, *materia fidei [matter of faith]*. So *proximum motivum scientiae est ratio objectiva sive ratio rei: at ratio motiva fidei est revelatio Dei [the foundation of science is objective knowledge or natural reason; but the rational foundation of faith is divine revelation*. (So you see, I agree with you in your quotation out of St. Aug: *quod scimus, debemus rationi; quae credimus, authoritati [what we know, we owe to reason; what we believe, we owe to authority]*.) *Religio autem complectitur et naturalem scientiam,* [I] *et fidem divinam [religion encompasses both natural knowledge and divine faith]*: so that there is in religion both *demonstrabile et credibile; credibile, propter authoritatem dicentis; demonstrabile, per necessitatem rei [what is demonstrable and believable: the believable, because of the authority of the speaker; the demonstrable, because of rational necessity]*. And no opposition between them; *quia versantur in alia et alia materia: scil. fides, in contingenti simpliciter et in se; scientia autem, in necessaria [because they switch between one basis and another, simply in the contingent and self-referential; knowledge, however, is based on what is necessary]*. Yett, if anie think fitt to call them of the first kinde matters of faith; as they are declared in scripture: since scripture awakens our incogitancy, because of our apostasie and degeneracy: I lifte not in this respect to contende with him. Onlie lett him then remember; that they are allsoe of themselves knowable: and stand not on the foundation of revelation onlie.⁶ But let him not think, there is anie thing *de fide [concerning faith]*; which is contrarie to natural knowledge. (Mr. PERKINS, CALVINE,⁷ and others, acknowledge; that the doctrine of faith will well consist with the principles of reason: and doth not destroy that knowledge of God, which is *lumine naturae [by the light of nature]*.) *Contra rationem rei, in naturalibus, est impossibile: contra rationem rei, in moralibus, est malum et deforme [that which is contrary to natural reason, in affairs of nature, is impossible; that which is contrary to natural reason, in morality, is evil and ugly]*. When God demands and challenges, [K] "Are not my wayes equal?" doth not hee appeale to man's principles and rules, wherby hee is able to discerne and judge; whereby God shall be justified, and Man convinced? Certainely, natural light and conscience condemnes iniquitie; and gives testimonie to wayes of righteousnesse. If this bee not so, *unde Deus judicabit mundum infidelium negative*; and where *ignorantia scripturarum est omnino invincibilis [on what grounds will God judge harshly the unbelievers of the world]?*⁸

But I fullie persuade my-selfe: that you and I do not disagree herein, in respect of our inward sense and meaning: and if wee differ onlie in expression, I press itt not; but think an other's expressions may be apter and fitter than mine: I am not such an *authadês [stubborn one]*.

The summe of what I said, in my speech, in sermons, and otherwise; amountes to this—that *materia theologiae naturalis [the subject matter of natural theology]* is demonstrable, by reason; and that *materia fidei sacris litteris contenta est summe credibilis [the subject matter of faith restricted to scripture is most credible]*; and satisfactorie to reason: [L] and unbiassed reason, not in a compromise with sense, not ingaged in a worldlie designe, findes no matter of exception againste it.⁹ In the meane while acknowledging, and my reason easily telles mee so; that, if God deign to speak to mee of himself and his owne affaires, actes of his infinite wisdom and power; I shall hear *illustriora et longe majora finito intellectu [things more glorious and far greater than the limited human intellect]*: and which transcend my understanding, far beyond the transcendency of the sunne, not wrapt-up in cloudes, to my sight. But this transcendency lies *in amplitudine et plenitudine objecti; non in contradictione rationis [in the extent and fulness of the object; not in contradiction of reason]*: (*Nos summus Deo et felicitati nostrae omnino impares [We are in no way unequal to God and our blessedness]*:) and in this case I may be most illuminated, in respect of my selfe; when I least comprehend the object. *Quicquid recipitur, ad modum recipientis recipitur [That which he receives, he will receive, according to the ability of the recipient]*:¹⁰ the bucket, most filled in the sea, yett least conteines the ocean.

You say, "it is now *Crambe, non bis sed centies cocta [cabbage cooked not twice but a hundred times]*; &c."[M] —I have, at several times, examined several pointes by the same principle; *sc. per rationem rei [that is, by natural reason]*: as indeed *tota materia theologiae naturalis [the complete subject matter of natural theology]* is so examinable: and certainlie, this is not *ad nauseam recoquere cramben [to recook the cabbage to the point of nausea]*; no more than it is, upon all occasions, in matters of faith, to prove by scripture: for it is a new examination, in an other matter; and *ratio huius et illius rei [reason pertaining to this and that thing]* are two things: though universallie, *secundum rationem rei in materia necessaria judicare [in matters of natural reason to discriminate according to the necessity]*, be the same principle; as also it is, *in omni materia fidei judicare secundum revelationem a Deo factam in scripturis [in every matter of faith to discriminate according to the revelation of God in scripture]*.

You say, "auditours wou'd have bin better satisfied; if I had theologically discoursed *de certitudine et dignitate Christianae religionis [on the certainty and goodness of the Christian religion]*, from divine testimonie and faith in itt; rather than by reason, &c":—Sir, it was *to zêtoumenon [the object of inquiry]*, [N] whether *religio Christiana* did *niti authoritate Dei [shine with the authority of God]*; were indeed from God; and so were *materia fidei [matter of faith]*: so that I was to shewe, that itt was *theoprepês [suited to God]*, and to prove that, *a qualitate materiae [upon the quality of the subject matter]*: and that itt is, beyond all conviction or controule of humane reason. And I endeavoured to make it appeare; that the truth declared by God, concerning our relief by Christ, was amiable, gratefull, acceptable to minde and understanding, and such as spake ittselfe from God; as our Saviour spake himselfe to be Christ, to the inward sense of the Samaritans.[11] And to this purpose reason was made use of, as a receiver, as a discerner, as a principle to be instructed and taught; not as an author or inventer or controuler of what God speakes: Divine truth allwaies carrying it's own light and evidence; so as that the mind receiving itt is illuminated, edified, satisfied. *Sacra scriptura est autotypos est Deo digna, est Fide digna [Holy scripture is authoritative, worthy of God, worthy of faith]*: it speaks for itt selfe, it recommendes itt selfe to its subject, itt satisfies the reason of the minde; procures it's own enterteinment, by it's owne excellencie. I adde allsoe; that the persuasion of the holie spirit contributes to the minde's assurance and satisfaction. I receive the truth of Christian religion, in a way of illumination affection and choice: I my selfe am taken with itt, as understanding and knowing itt; I reteine itt, as a wellcome guest; itt is not forced into mee, but I lett it in; yet soe as taught of God: and I see cause for my continuance to embrace itt. Do I dishonour my faith, or do anie wrong to itt; to tell the worlde, that my minde and understanding are satisfied in itt? I have noe reason against itt; yea, the highest and purest reason is for itt! (What doth God speak to, but my reason? and shoulde not that, which is spoken-to, heare? should itt not judge, discerne, conceeve, what is God's meaning?)

In what is next in your letter, You say and acknowledge, what I contend-for; that wee should *anankazein [force]* &c; that natural reason is "of use, in evangelical matters; but more, in matters *theologiæ naturalis*."[O] In the last place of this section, you fall-off from the quæstion; when you say—"They beleeved without dispute, what the scripture held-out; and judged not itt, but man's doctrine by itt." My businesse was to prove the divine authoritie of scripture; or the truth of Christian religion: after this is done, then we will examine mens doctrine by itt: but, to prove *autopistian scripturæ [scripture trustworthy, believable in and of itself]*, I must consider scripture, *secundum materiam [as it is in fact]*; not produce itt, as a wittness.

When you say; that *"to gnôston tou Theou [knowledge of God]* concernes not truths, but the searching of hearts; our owne, and others": I cannot herein guesse at your meaning. Somewhat following, you say, belongs to matters *theologiae naturalis [of natural theology]*; wherein wee agree: To that purpose I produced those texts, in my letter to you; and I understand *to gnoston [knowledge]* so too; *scil de cognoscibili per lumen naturae [that is, concerning what is knowable by the light of nature]*. (I since guesse, that this might referre to that other place;[12] [P] "Candle of the Lord": a place, I now sent you not; but, you say, over-quoted by mee: I do persuade my self; that is in the wordes, which I have alledged them for. You instance in the *use* of the principle; and I insisted on the *qualitie fittness* and *sufficiencie* of the principle; as from God, and in the hands of God: for a candle is *res illuminata illuminans [an illuminated thing that gives light]*.)

When you say, "that *cuilibet Christiano conceditur judicium discretionis [to any Christian freedom of judgment is given]*, is true; as against "the Pope &c": I conceeve itt universallie true: as *in omni materia [in all subject matters]*, so *contra omnes personas [against all persons]*. And I must either see cause, why I beleeve the scripture; in whole and in part: or my faith must bee *fides implicita [an implicit faith]*; [Q] soe farre as I doe not see cause.[13]

These five protestant principles have ledde mee into all the conclusions I lay-out, about the rule of faith.—1. *Sacra scriptura est autopistos [Holy scripture is* a priori *believable]*. 2. *Sacra scriptura est adaequata regula fidei [Holy scripture is a sufficient rule of faith]*. 3. *Omnia ad salutem necessaria perspicue traduntur in scripturis [All that is necessary is clearly handed down in the scriptures]*. 4. *Cuilibet Christiano conceditur judicium discretionis [To each Christian freedom of judgment is given]*. 5. *Quilibet abundet in suo sensu [Let everyone abide in his own perception]*: and *Fides non est cogenda [Belief cannot be compelled]*.[14] I understand them all, in a real and full sense; according to the import of the wordes, and what necessarilie followes from them: and so, I verilie persuade my-selfe, they will patronize my four next following conclusions.

You say; [R] it may bee, You and I may differ; in the number of things saving: I hope, wee doe not differ, in the enterteining of anie thing saving; because of *Omnia perspicue traduntur*, one of the five principles: and it is not equallie necessarie to determine the number, as to enterteine the saving principles. I do enterteine the whole scripture; and in the sense my understanding telles me, the holie Ghost meant: using all meanes and helpes I hear-of in the worlde, so farre as I have opportunitie; viz. Fathers, Councils, Expositors, Comments, Confessions, Systemes; and what manie convened have agreed, I have considered, wherein they have agreed, with greater reverence: because *ratio plurium hominum [the reason of most men]* is the best in the world; especiallie, if they have bin free from the suspicion of faction and partialitie: which, you knowe, verie manie councils were not.¹⁵ (You mistake me [therfore]; if you think, I mean to lay-aside the endeavours of Fathers, Councils, or any good men, to cleare-up scripture-truth against errour: but I abate of the degree of certaintie, in what is so done, of what I finde in scripture.

Is there not also an imperfection in the understanding of those, who make interpretations? so that, though wee thank them for their good will, and make use of their paines; yett everie one for himselfe is to discerne, *an glosséma corrumpat vel illustret textum [if the translator would corrupt or illustrate the text]*. A laudable endeavour of them I acknowledge; and I am beholden to them for their help; and I will dulie consider what they say: but I am not sure, because They so resolve; I must see with my owne eyes; my own understanding must be satisfied: otherwise I equalize them to the pen-men of scripture.)

And I persuade myselfe, because of *omnia perspicue &c*; that Hee, who with an honest intention of finding-out the will of God, in order to conformity therewith and obedience thereto; seeking to God to teach him; searcheth carefullie holie scripture: will misse of nothing saving. Notwithstanding the greatest difference that ever I hear'd-of; yet I beleeve, no good man leaves-out anie fundamental: yea, I am apte to think; that manie, who have bin exasperated one against another; are farre nearer to one another in sense, than in wordes. In respect of God, who searcheth hearts, they agree; more than in the view of the worlde, which onlie sees outward expressions. (I beleeve, for one *real* difference, in matters of consequence, betwen persons considerable; there are twentie mistakes of meanings: and coulde they see one another's heartes, they woulde thinke better one of another. [But] opposites too often study to represent each other in the worst sense: I perceeve itt, in men alive; therfore suspect itt of the dead. If once disaffected to each other, they never after deele fairely with one another.)¹⁶

In what you next say, for a good while together; either wee do not differ; or itt is not a pointe, wherein I did engage; and I will not multiplie quæstions, or meddle with other matters; since I onlie intend to give you an account of what I delivered: or, if we do differ, I doe not perceeve my-selfe confuted.

(I agree with you, that things reveled in scripture are to be matters of our enquirie; and that wee are not curiouslie to pry into God's secrets: *mê hyperphronein par' ho dei phronein, alla phronein eis to sôphronein [do not think of oneself more highly than one ought, but think soberly in order to be humble]*.¹⁷ but still, I say, fundamentals are so cleare; that there is little danger of good men differing about them.)

For the quæstion about an ingenuous man's libertie; you resolve my case with mee, and as I doe; and then dispute the quæstion about a pretender and deceiver: I follow you not in any newe quæstion; I leave his opposer to take care to distinguish: *my* case was *in actu signato [in the official sense]*, and so determinable; *your*'s is *in actu exercito [in the practical sense], et cum omnibus circumstantiis individuantibus. Singularium non est scientia [and with all the particular circumstances. There is no general theory of particular cases]*. For my own part, I plead not for libertie of proposing; though I wou'd be verie glad not to bee imposed-upon: [S] for I understand our Saviour, "Cast not your pearles &c. lest they rent you; &c."[18] as granting a dispensation for reservation and secrecy; in case persons will bee mis-chievous. (You [T] seeme to argue againste an ingenuous libertie; because Hære-tiques have bin unexceptionable, and of unblameable life: but, on the other side, I finde; scripture-hæretiques are infamous in their life.[19])

What is added of Socinians, Arminians, &c; [V] in respect of mee, is groundless: I have given no cause nor occasion; I rather approve him, who said; *Non sum Christianus alicujus nominis [I am not a Christian under any other name]*: I may as well be called a Papist, or Mahometan; Pagan, or Atheist. And trulie, Sir, you are wholely mistaken, in the whole course of my studies: [W] you say, you finde mee largelie in their *Apologia*; to my knowledge I never sawe, or heard of the booke before: much lesse have I read a tittle of itt. I shou'd lay-open my weakeness, if I shou'd tell you; how little I have read, of the bookes and authours you mention: of tenn yeares past, nothing at all. I know not, who shou'd bee your informer: but trulie, in a thousand guesses, you cou'd not have bin farther off from the truth of the thing. And for schoole-men; I doe not think, I have spent four and twentie houres in them *divisim*, these fourteene yeares. Dr. FIELD on the Church I ree'd over, eight-teene yeares agoe; but have not looked into him, I beleeve, these tenn yeares: JACKSON and HAMMOND I have a little lookt into, here and there, a good while since; but have not read the hundredth parte of either of them: trulie I shame myselfe to tell you, how little I have bin acquainted with bookes; but for your satisfaction I doe: while fellow of EMMANUEL colledge, employment with pupills tooke my time from mee. I have not read manie bookes; but I have studied a fewe: meditation and invention hath bin rather my life, than reading: and trulie I have more read CALVINE, and PERKINS, and BEZA;[20] than all the bookes, authors, or names you mention. I have allwaies expected reason, for what men saye; less valuing persons or authoritie, in the stating and resolving of truth: and therfore have read Them most, where I have founde itt. I have not lookt-at anie thing, as more than an opinion; which hath not bin under-propt by convincing reason, or plaine and satisfactorie scripture. Had I given lesse to Scripture, than I have don; I beleeve, I had better avoyded, than I have don, those offences againste mee; whereof you advertise mee, that manie have taken them. [X] If I know my owne heart; nothing of worldlie designe, or respect to aught less than the honour of God, and the safetie of my soule, rules in mee; to the balancing of my judgement, in the discerning of truth: I keepe my selfe free, to followe reason and scripture; and I am never engaged againste them, whosoëver shewes them mee. I rather affect to speake with them, who differ from mee; than those, who I thinke, agree with mee;[21] (I speake of matter of opinions; for about fundamentalls I am satisfied:) that I may be ridde of my misapprehensions: wherein I daylie suspect my selfe; and see cause to thinke, that I may bee in some errours; as well as I have bin: whereof I have had experience.—But this is vanitie, to use such a *periautologia [discourse about oneself]*. I am ashamed to thinke, what I have don; and cou'd blot itt oute agen: but to satisfie you, wherein you have mee in suspicion; though itt bee folly in mee to do itt, I lett itt go. You seeme in your letter to anatomize my life; but the description doth not characterize mee: you cou'd hardlie have shot farther from the marke. That I mighte not causesslie suffer in your thoughts, I have written you somthing that is true: wherein yett I applaude not my-self; but itt is my necessitie: *bene novi, quam sit mihi curta supellex [I know well, how poorly my house is furnished]*[22].

(You say; because Hæretiques, [Y] in their wordes, say what is false; therefore Wee, in our wordes, what is true; and this, in thinges *ultra citráque scripturam [above and beyond scripture]*: but the quæstion will bee, Who shall bee the judge? shall a forreigne power command my inwarde sense? To speake indeed I will aske leave; but I must thinke, as I see cause. [Z] Unless you say, *some* have a priviledge of infallible interpretation; or that I may safelie repose on that interpretation, which *some* give; I do not conceeve, how you can make good somthing that you say within 14 lines of the bottom of the second page.)

Whereas you suggeste, that "Fundamentalls maye be shaken and endangered; by such a free proposal: *&c.*"—Truely, I thinke, this cannot worthily be conceeved of such truths: *magna est veritas, et praevalebit: veritas non quaerit angulos [the truth is great, and it will prevail: truth does not seek a corner]*: the foundations of truths necessarie to salvation are so immoveablie layd by God; that no power, eyther of the Devil or of the degenerate world, can overturne them:[23] and the lighte of them is so fulle, so cleare, so satisfactorie; that no ingenuous unengaged teachable minde, as everie good man's mind shou'd bee, can bee mistaken about them. *Omnia perspicue traduntur [All things are clearly handed down]*, *&c.*

In the next place you brand those, who have pleaded for such a libertie; "Socinians, Arminians, *colluvies [rabble]* of sectaries, *&c.*" [A2] —(Do wee not agree with Papistes, in what they hold that is true? the world understandes not the point, you and I reason about; when Socinians and Arminians are spoken-of.) May wee temper and qualifie Divinitie with prudential considerations? May wee do God's work for him; taking itt oute of his handes? or is itt not better to leave the case to *Deus providebit [God's care]*? *Cuilibet Christiano est judicium discretionis [To each Christian is freedom of judgment]*, [B2] is the foundation of Protestancy: therfore everie Christian must think and beleeve, as hee findes cause. And shall hee speak in religion, otherwise than he thinkes; or, if hee bee asked, shall hee answer false?[24] (The greate engagement upon men, to hold them to truth; is: that att a man's perill itt is, to runne away with a lie.[25]) Truth is Truth; whosoever hath spoken itt, or howsoëver itt hath bin abused: [C2] butt if this libertie may not bee allowed to the universitie, wherfore do wee study? wee have nothing to do, but to gett good memories; and to learne by heart. Methinkes, in what you say here, you do not sufficientlie consider; *who* principallie standes charged, and is the grand superintendent over truth in the [D2] worlde.[26]

In the point of Justification, what I said and meant was this; that the beginnings of Grace are wrought in us, before God actuallie justifies sinners. [E2] *Dantur praeparatoria ad justificationem [They provide the preparation for justification]*, hath bin frequentlie determined in the schooles by Dr. WARD.[27] A sinner *non omnino in motu conversionis est subjectum incapax [not at all in the process of conversion is an incapable subject]*, i.e. *non susceptibile, justificationis [not susceptible to justification]*: and this you do not onlie acknowledge, but att large explaine and give a farther accounte of, for which I heartilie thanke you.

By first and second, in the double notion of Christ; I considered distinction, rather than order. [F2]

Whereas you continue to take offence at that speech of mine, *de interna nostra salute; nascitur e nobis, suscipitur a nobis [concerning our internal salvation, it will be born from within us, it will be assumed by us]*.—give mee leave to make us of a proverb of SOLOMON; "The wringing of the nose bringeth forth bloud":[28] Where the *sense* is not to be reproved, wee shoulde not make a man offender for a worde.[29]

[G2] 1. I meant itt distinctlie; or in a contra-distinction to those thinges, *quae extra nos sunt vel circa nos; et sic minus nostra: nam quae maxime nostra sunt, nobiscum portamus [that which is outside us or around us; and thus less than us; for that which is greater than us, which we carry within us]*: but not independentlie, in respect of God; *qui intimior nobis est intimo nostro [he who is more familiar to us than we are to ourselves]*.

That precept of wisdom,[30] "Acknowledge Him in all thy wayes;" I am sure, over-rules mee; head, heart, hand: itt is the inward sense of my soule, digested into a temper, complexion, constitution. I never leave God oute; I ever give Him the principal place; *Omnia a Deo, Omnia sub Deo, Omnia cum bono Deo [All things from God, all things under God, all things with God's goodness]*. In the sense of my minde, I was verie farre from taking from God; to give to myselfe: God is reallie all in all to mee; I hold of Him, derive from Him, live by Him, enjoy my self under Him, hope in Him, expect from Him: there is nothing more written in my heart, than the sense of my dependencie upon Him: there is nothing, that I am more free to acknowledge; than His influence, operation and presence: so farre was itt from mee to understand what you fetch out of the wordes; that nothing seemes to mee more horrid, monstrous, violent, contra-natural: my heart riseth with indignation against such a thing; I have a perfecte antipathie in my soule against itt: I shoulde sinne againste all the experience I have of God in my life; if I shoulde say or thinke such a thing. [H2]

2. In conjunction with a passive exegetical; in which case the latter is explicative and restrictive; yea, as it were corrective of the former: and the latter wholelie over-rules and subdues the former; and becomes master of the sense. [I2]

3. Itt was pursued with a comment, which you dislike not: whereto I now referre myselfe.

4. Itt was but as a glosse, upon the wordes of the text; "Repentance and Forgiveness": and I spake itt of Repentance, respectively as in Us; whereas I had before considered Repentance, respectively to Christ; as his gift.

5. The explication of Christ's giving us Repentance, is to give to Us to repent: and repentance is truely our acte, *sub Deo. Deus openratur per modum purae efficientiae: Voluntas creata producit vitalitatem et formalitatem actus [under God. God works through the means of pure efficiency: his good will in creation produces the vitality and form of our deeds]*. God is not properlie said to repente in us, but to work repentance in us: Wee are truely and properlie said to repente, *sub assistentia, motu, ductu, divini spiritus [under the assistances, the motion, the descent, of the Holy Spirit]*; or as in composition with God's grace.—*Causa creata co-operatur ad omnem actum [That which is created cooperates in every action]*—all saye. [K2]

Whereas you adde, that I doe not keepe to *hyptupôsis hugiainontôn logôn [the form of sound words]*—which concernes mee remarkablie; who so plead for scripture-expressions:—1. *tôn heautôn sôtêrian katergazesthe [work out your own salvation]*,[31] I conceeve to be a deeper phrase; as also others I coulde alledge. [L2] 2. I accordinglie submitte that phrase, as also I doe all others that are mine, to the censure and examination of everie hearer; and am farre from imposing of itt: remembring S. AUG: *si quid proponitur contra rationem, aut sacras litteras; meliore authoritate rejicitur, quam asseritur [if something is proposed contrary to reason, or to scriptures, it ought to be rejected with greater authority than affirmed]*.

In the nexte place you advise mee "not to affect schoole-phrases and learning, in preaching; nor the use of Philosophie and Metaphysicks." [M2] Truelie, Sir, understanding that I oughte not to "do the worke of the Lord negligentlie";[32] but to serve Him in the utmoste use and improvement of myself, and what God hath given me: I have, to my best, endeavoured to confirme truth, and convince the understandings of men therein: and to that purpose, as I have bin able, have made use of all those principles; that derive from God, and speak him in the world: thinking, that the efficacie of the application depended upon the solid confirmation of the doctrine. And I am sure, I have all along bin well understood; by persons of honest heartes, but of meane place and education: and I have had the blessing of the soules of such, at their departure out of the world. I thanke God, my conscience telles me; that I have not herein affected worldlie shewe: but the reall service of truth. And I have alwaies found in myself, that such preaching of Others hath most commanded my heart; which hath most illuminated my head.[33] My way hath bin; first to make-out, then to confirme, lastlie to apply: making more use of the principles of God's creation in man, in matters of reason and natural light; than I have don, in matters of faith. [N2]

—The time I have spent in Philosophers, I have no cause to repent-of; and the use I have made of them, I dare not disowne: I heartily thank God, for what I have found in them; neyther have I, upon this occasion, one jot less loved the scriptures. I find the Philosophers that I have read, good; so farre as they go: and it makes me secrettlie blush before God, when I find eyther my head heart of life challenged by them: which, I must confesse, I have often found. I have somtimes publiquelie declared, what points of religion I have found excellentlie held-forthe by them; and I never found them enemies to the faith of the gospel.[34] I think, St. AUG. saith of St.

PAUL; *non destruit verum, quod invenit in latere Paganorum [he did not destroy the truth that he found on the pagans' side]*: and our Savour reproves the Jewes, by TYRE and SIDON. I have thought itt profitable to provoke to jealousie lazie or loose Christians, by Philosophers; as PAUL did the Jewes, by the Gentiles, enterteining the faith of Christ. [O2] —

By what rule you judge; that Hee, who useth a Latine or Greek phrase or sentence in an English discourse, must needs *quote*; I do not understand: much less, upon that account, be thought to quote himselfe. [P2]

Some things I shou'd have said before; which, though out of place, (for I have but broken pieces of time; and I putt things down, as they come into my head:) I crave leave here to adde—That some impute itt to mee, as Socinianism; that I assert the use of reason, *in sacris [within what is holy]*.—If a Socinian thinks, he can by reason convince of falsehood any thing of Christian religion; and I joyne issue with him, on this point; and shew him, that there is nothing of true reason againste anie thing of Christian faith; do answer all his objections; which somtimes I have don: and more-over shewe him, that the substantials of Christian faith; especiallie, *capita de Christo expiatore, redemptore, liberatore [relating to Christ as expiator, redeemer, liberator]*, as reveled in scripture; are the most credible matters in the world: answerable to the desire of a man at a losse in himselfe, satisfactorie to his earnest, longing, awakened expectation from God: I conceeve, in this case, I deserve as little to be called a Socinian as DAVID, for extorting GOLIATH's sword out of his hand, and cutting the master's head off with itt, did deserve to be esteemed a Philistine. [Q2]

For the points you impute to mee and others, or to mee or others, whom I suppose you think I value—some of them I knowe nothing of; others I must denie wholely; and some, I conceeve, are mistaken.

"The power of nature, in morals, too much advanced: too much given to reason, in matters of faith."—Of these I have, in the foregoing part of this discourse, given account; and thereto I referre my selfe: and I think, I have not given too much. [R2] (God is acknowledged principal; Understanding, a discerning power; Principles, received from God, to be employed under Him.)

"A *recta ratio [right reason]* talkt-of; which I cannot tell, where to find"— [S2] Surelie, *a recta ratio* may there be found; where *vera fides [true faith]* is to be found.

"Mind and Understanding is all: Heart and Will little spoken-of."—I beleeve this findes no authour.[35] (In vulgar use, [T2] Mind comprehends Understanding and Will.)

"The decrees of God quæstion'd and quarrell'd, &c."—I do not remember, that I have heard anie one call them in quæstion: and I knowe none, that submits not to them; as they are declared in scripture: finding there no inconsistencie in them with goodnesse, or the *rationes rerum [the scheme of things]*.[36] [V2]

"Philosophers made fairer candidates, &c."—For their eternal state, I have left them to God: I dare not affirm; that God neyther did, nor coulde, revele aught of Christ to them; or accept them, in and through Christ.[37] [W2]

"Philosophers in their virtues, preferred before Christians, over-taken with *weakenesses*"—A great mistake! itt was allowing themselves in *Sin*; envie, spight, malice, fury, *&c*; things, which speak Hell, as it were, broken loose; and come-up upon the world: turners of the grace of God into lasciviousness, whom the Apostle doth more decrie. *Privatio malignitatem ponit, negatio absentiam formæ [Privation gives rise to evil, negation to the absence of form].* [X2]

"A kinde of moral Divinitie minted, *&c.*"—This I understand not. (Our Saviour insists much of moral Divinitie.[38] St. PAUL neglects itt not.[39] St. JAMES is whole in itt; so as to seeme less to mind Faith. St. PETER and St. JOHN abundant in that you call minted moralitie.—Do not, Sir, disserve one truth; to serve another:—*Sunt omnes divinæ veritates amicæ veritates [All divine truth is beloved by truth].*) [Y2]

"Inhærent righteousness so preached, *&c.*" I am a stranger to anie thing; eyther truely, in respect of itselfe; or intentionallie, in respect of the person; spoken to the prejudice of the righteousness by faith.[40]

"Inhærent righteousness, perfect in this life."—I knowe nothing beyonde a sincere endeavour after itt; and a dis-allowing of all iniquitie, so farre as known or suspected, and diligent search without partialitie.[41] [Z2]

"An estate of Love, above a life of Faith." I wish, I had it! O that my heart were enamoured, inflamed with love to God! O that I were united to Him; as by faith, so by love![42] [A3]

"Above Ordinances"—In my apprehension, the person was mistaken by such as so interpreted him; hee onlie meant *Formalities*. [B3]

"Divers other principles of religion by some verie doubtfullie spoken-of."—Wherein I am concerned, I hope to give an account; when they are particularized in. For I am under the power of the Apostle's rule;[43] "Be readie to render a reason"; and I will give to anie an account of my religion: and I will learn the truth of anie.

"Complaints in pulpitts, and elsewhere, of *rixae* and *lites [squabbles* and *disputations]*; about notions and speculations, sects and superstitions, *&c.*"—I cannot guesse, whom this shou'd referre to; neyther knowe I the matter. [C2] But whereas you subjoyne—"that there is a God, may come to bee accounted a notion and speculation:"—I thinke, there is noe danger of that: because *Deum esse, est scibile et demonstrabile [that God exists, is knowable and demonstrable];* [D3] and *Christum esse, est materia fidei [that Christ exists, is matter of faith]* : and I say with St. AUG: as before in the margent; *si spiritus hoc non persuaserit, nondum mihi persuasit Christiano esse [if the Holy Spirit did not persuade me, he has not yet persuaded me to be a Christian].*—I do not conceeve, that they who have endeavoured by their proposalls to prevent differences among good men, or to allay heat; if in all apprehensions they do not meete, and upon this account have given reasons for moderation, in matters of opinion or curiositie of speculation; [E3] I say, I do not think; that they have comprehended anie such points, as you instance in, under the name of *opinion*, or matter of speculation. Neyther is hee to bee thought to undervalue one pointe of religion; who speakes little of itt, when his argument is another: but is rather to bee thought to keepe close to his text. \* \* \* \*

# Notes

1. *V.* Editorial Notes. *Ed.*

2. BW: "We are not to submit our Understanding to the belief of those things, that are *contrary* to our Understanding. We must have a Reason, for that which we believe *above* our Reason" (*MRA* §771).

3. BW: (1) "Reason *discovers*, what is Natural; and Reason *receives*, what is Supernatural"; (2) "The great Things of Reveal'd Truth, tho' they be not of Reason's Invention, yet they are of the prepar'd Mind readily entertain'd and receiv'd: As for Instance: Remission of Sins to them that repent and deprecate God's Displeasure; it is the most credible Thing in the World: For God made us Creatures fallible, at the best. . . . And any probable Narration made in the Name of God, of the Way and Means, and the particular Circumstances whereby God will do it, will fairly induce Belief with sober, serious, and considerate Minds: And what have we to do with others, upon the Account of Religion? If they be not serious and considerate, they are not in a Disposition towards Religion" (*MRA* §99; *SS*, Part I, Sermon I, 7).

4. SS: "Prov. xiv.15" (43 n).

5. BW: (1) "The *Spirit* in us, is the Reason of our Minds Illuminated by the *Written* Word. The Spirit *now* Teaches, by these Writings"; (2) "The direction of the *Spirit* makes not a Rule, distinct from *Reason* and *Scripture*: is not a *third* Rule. The Spirit adds only Assistance; to find-out the Reason of things, and sense of Scripture. For these *two*, Reason and Scripture, are the *whole* Revelation of the Spirit; in respect of the *Matter*" (*MRA* §337, §920).

6. BW: (1) "It is a thing of the greatest Importance; upon what *Authority* we Believe"; (2) "Men know by the Use of their Reason, that there is a God: And then when a Man receives any Proportion from God's Authority; *that*, is *Faith*. Natural Knowledge, you see, is antecedent and fundamental to Faith. . . . If Reason did not apprehend God, Religion could not be learn'd; for there would be nothing in Nature to graft it on. Besides, we know in Reason, that first Principles are self-evident, must be seen in their own Light, and are perceived by an inward Power of Nature" (*MRA* §1070; *SS*, Part I, Sermon II, 58). Although faith rests upon authority, authority itself is determined by reason. *Ed.*

7. Whichcote here refers to the testimony of two authors in whom Tuckney would be predisposed to place his trust: William PERKINS (1558-1602), puritan theologian and fellow of Christ's College, Cambridge (1584-1594), who wrote against Romanism, in support of the doctrine of predestination, and in exposition of the Apostles' Creed; John CALVIN (1509-1564), the French reformer who wrote the vastly influential *Christianae Religionis Institutio* (1st ed., 1536). *Ed.*

8. BW: (1) "This is the Creator's Law; that all Things in Man should be subject to the Government of REASON (which is God's *Deputy*:) And this is our Trial, in this State; *whether* by the Weight of Body, we will suffer ourselves to be depress'd, and sink downward by minding earthly Things; and so take our Portion here; and fall short of God; or, *whether* by the Reason of our Minds, we will mount upwards, mind heavenly Things, converse with God by heavenly Meditation, and make choise of the Things that are most excellent: Whereby we shall naturalize ourselves to the Employment of Eternity"; (2) "It is the violence of Hell itself to live in practice contrary to the Judgement, the Man that thus acts, doth himself more wrong than all the World, yea, than the Powers of Hell can do him; he puts himself on the fearfullest Wrack that ever any Man endured" (*SS*, Part II, Sermon VI, 287 *SSN*, 31).

*Letter IV* 111

9. BW: "Therefore we conclude, that all the Instances of Christian Doctrine, either they are fairly knowable, if we use our Faculties and Understanding (*and these are the great Instances of Morality and Principles of Reason*;) or else, if we do consider those Things that are considerable in the Case; the Things of Reveal'd Truth, are of fair and easy Belief. The former of these, the great Principles of Reason, they are *by* awakened Minds easily and readily found out. The latter are, *by* prepar'd Minds, fairly admitted and entertained" (*SS*, Part I, Sermon I, 12).

10. SS: "This seems to have been a favourite Thought of Dr. WHICHCOTE's. We have it again in his third Letter thus express'd; 'Though the disproportion will be to our advantage, the vessel more certain to be filled, because of the sea's dimensions': and otherwhise, Thus; 'The ocean can *but* fill the vessel; which a much less quantity of water can do.' The like occurs in a Sermon of Dr. TUCKNEY's before the House of Commons, 1643. 'It is our Happinesse; not that our Vessel is so little, but that the Fountain is so full: *&c.*' Balme of Gilead, p. 19/90" (46 n). Tuckney preached *The Balme of Gilead, for the Wounds of England* before the House of Commons on 30 August 1643. *Ed.*

11. SS: "John iv.42" (47 n).

12. SS: "Prov. xx.27" (49 n).

13. BW: "To be opinionative for the persons sake, is to prostrate the Excellency of Heaven to the Dust of the Earth; unbecoming a Man, defacing to Religion. There is no justifiable excuse for any man to compromise with the judgement of any number of Men never so holy, except he plead his impotency. Thus to act is Popery, an implicit Faith, or non-necessity of understanding. This is the greatest servility in respect of a mans own home, and the greatest flattery in respect of abroad; for a man thus to deny all of God in himself, to unmake, to nullifie himself; a worse act than this the Devil did never do, thus to sin against his own Being" (*SSN*, 72-3).

14. SS: "See Dr. WHICHCOTE's third letter, [p. 73]" (50 n).

15. BW: "In Modesty and Humility, we should rather Question our own Opinion; than in self-confidence, be wilful and peremptory" (*Several Discourses*, 3 vols. ed. John Jeffery [1703], Sermon XXX, 3:445; qtd. in Patrides, 82).

16. BW: "I say it again; that by that time we have made a just Allowance for our different Tempers and Constitutions, which are not *subject to our Choice*; for our different Makes, where upon such Variety of Apprehensions depend; since there are Men of such different Makes, that in nothing they think alike (or, at least, they do not express themselves alike, where they mean the same thing;) by that time we have made Allowance for the Error and Mistake of our own Age, and the Ages that have been before us; when we shall have made Allowance for the general Suppositions which oft take place; for pre-conceiv'd Opinions from Education, Company and Converse; for Conceits rooted in Men, and become natural to them, because they have long thought so; by that time we have made a just Allowance for all these Considerations, and Abatement proportionable; we shall find little reason for Anger and Displeasure with one another, upon occasion of these Differences" (*SS*, Part II, Sermon IV, 242-43).

17. SS: "Rom. xii.3" (52 n).

18. SS: "Matth. vii.6" (53 n).

19. SS: "II Pet. ii.1,3; II. Tim. iii.8; Jude 4" (53 n).

20. Theodore BEZA (1519-1605), Swiss reformer, professor of Greek, and biblical scholar. The most complete and authoritative edition of his annotated Latin translation of the Greek New Testament was reprinted at Cambridge in 1642. At Geneva, in 1560, he published a popular exposition of Calvinist beliefs, the *Confessio Christianae Fidei*, and, after the death

of Calvin in 1564, directed the Genevan Academy, an institution for the training of Reformed ministers. Of PERKINS and CALVIN, *v.* n. 7, above. *Ed.*

21. BW: (1) "None are of such modest Spirits as *they* who live in free Communication and Converse. This I subjoin, for the improving of a Man's self in the way of the Gospel, and answering the vigorous Spirit of the Gospel; *be communicative*. And this is the Purpose of all our Meetings: Free Communication, to answer every Man's Doubts; to give every one Satisfaction. It is the highest Service, and greatest Courtesy we can do one another, freely to tell what we have conceiv'd; and we do ourselves most effectual Good, when we carry on others with us, when we do Good unto others"; (2) "It is not worthy that any man should be known by an Opinion, till he hath freely and ingenuously communicated, and that with competent persons hearing and giving reasons; he is Impotent else and a Fool" (*SS*, Part I, Sermon II, 38; *SSN*, 12).

22. This proverbial expression is an alteration of Persius, *Satires* 4.52: *tecum habita: noris quam sit tibi curta supellex [Look to your house, and recognize how poorly it is furnished]*. Trans.

23. BW: "Fundamentals are of this sort, *viz.* things of undoubted foundation in Natural light. As for a Creature to tender homage to the Creator, to be subject to his Law; to comply with his Will, to entertain his Commands, and such things as are of clear Revelation in Scripture" (*SSN*, 66).

24. BW: "It is not to be expected, that *another* man should Think as I would, to please *me*; since I cannot think as I would, to please *myself*: it is neither in His nor My power, to think as we will; but as we see reason, and find cause" (*MRA* §75).

25. BW: "The *imprisoning and controuling of Truth*, is an Action of the highest Injury, and Offence to God, that a Man can commit; beyond what we can easily imagine: For whosoever hath received any thing from God by mental Illumination, if he doth not pursue it, to the Refinement of his Spirit; he doth *counterwork* God. He who stifles, or goes against his Knowledge, doth in effect give a Check to God's working in him. For us thus to do, would be to reject God, where we most find and *feel* him; to strike at *the Image of God in ourselves*" (*SS*, Part I, Sermon II, 87).

26. BW: "I take it to be one of the choicest pieces of truth, and the soundest point of *Philosophy* in the World, to be sensible of Divine Superintendency. The most quick-sighted *Philosophers* (the *Platonists*) that ever were, are full in this point" (*SSN*, 84).

27. Regarding Samuel Ward (*d.* 1643), *v.* Letter V, 131-32 n. 30. *Ed.*

28. SS: "Prov. xxx.33" (57 n).

29. SS: "Isai. xxix.21" (58 n). BW: "By *candid* Construction, you may frustrate an Enemy; but by *sinister* Construction, you may lose a Friend" (*MRA* §63).

30. SS: "Prov. iii.6" (58 n).

31. SS: "Phil. ii.12" (59 n).

32. SS: "Jer. xlviii.10" (60 n).

33. BW: "It is not to *no* purpose; to speak things, that are not *presently* understood. Seed, though it lies in the Ground *a-while* unseen, is not *Lost* or Thrown-away; but *will* bring-forth Fruit. If you confine your *Teacher*, you hinder your *Learning*: if you limit His discourses to your *present* apprehensions; how shall He raise your Understanding? if He accommodates all things to your present weakness: you will *never* be Wiser, than you *now* are: you will be *always* in Swadling-cloths"(*MRA* §307; cf. §393).

34. BW: (1) "If any one scruple, why I introduce so much *Heathen* Philosophers Examples in a *Christian* Congregation? 1. I would have him give me an account of the

Apostles Argument (*Acts* 17.) to the *Athenians*, of our relation to God; namely, that we are *Jupiter*'s Off-spring. 2. This do I the rather, to provoke you to an holy emulation of them, who only by the Principles of Nature, came to know that Man's enjoyment of himself consisted only in conjunction with *God*"; (2) "I find among the Philosophers, that they never had Expectation of any Noble Truth, from any Man that was under the Power of Lust, or under the Command of Fancy and Imagination; or that lived in the common Spirit of the World; they thought that God did not communicate himself to such" (*SSN*, 86; *SS*, Part I, Sermon I, 23).

35. BW: "Religion is a thing setled in the Heart, a sound Judgement. A Mans Heart is ingaged, and possessed with it after long debate and inquiry; wherefore it is the most deliberative and advised action he undertakes in all his life"; "The Assent of the Will, and the consent of the Mind, they are greatest acts, and most consequential that a man can put forth; they are acts in Justification or Condemnation, *quantum in nobis*, as to us they do either Censure or Absolve, Justifie or Condemn" (*SSN*, 32, 9-10).

36. BW: "That which Reason requires, is to find out the Reason of Things, and to comply with it; to move according to the Dictates of Reason; and to observe the Order of the End; to avoid such things as will do us harm; in short, to live according to the Difference of Good and Evil; to do the *one*, and to avoid the *other*" (*SS*, Part I, Sermon II, 43).

37. BW: (1) "*Ignorance* of mere *Institutes* may be invincible: because Institutes must be declared, by some Instrument of God; whereof the party may have no notice: but, in *Morals*, we are *made* to know and judge and determine; and the light of God's Creation is sufficient thereto: So that *here* there is no invincible and consequently inculpable Ignorance"; (2) "There is but *One* Church in all ages. It is *thought*, the World does not grow Old; it is *certain*, the Church does not" (*MRA* §362, §1107).

38. SS: "Matth. chap. v, vi, vii." (63 n).

39. SS: "Phil. iv.8." (63 n).

40. BW: (1) "*Holiness*, in Angels and Men, is their *Dei-formity*; Likeness to God in Goodness, Righteousness, and Truth. Such *real* Holiness sanctifies the Subject by its Presence: and where That is, the person is made Pure, Good, and Righteous"; (2) "*Relative* Holiness, depending upon an Arbitrary act, is of a Mutable nature; and, where it is, alters not the Nature and Quality of the thing; but only the Relation and Use of it"; (3) "Things *Relatively* Holy, have never been Equalized with *Real* Holiness, but have always been Subservient to it" (*MRA*, §262-264).

41. BW: "Now, *Holiness in Angels and Men* doth import their *Deiformity*, that is, *their Conformity to God*, according to their Capacity; *their* being in their Measure, Degree, and Proportion, *what* God is, in his Height, Excellence, and Fulness. And by this Holiness, we bear the Image of God" (*SS*, Part II, Sermon I, 167).

42. SS: "I Cor. xiii.13" (64 n).

43. SS: "I Pet. iii.15" (64 n).

# Letter V

## Dr. TUCKNEY's Third Letter.

Sir,

Itt being Truth, not Victorie, that wee contend-for; *reciprocare serram [to saw back and forth]* wou'd give but a harsh sound to ingenuous eares: and both your time and mine wou'd bee unthriftilie mispent, in such needless contests. I shall therfore contract things, as much as I can.—For your large and learned discourse, in the three first pages of your letter; wherein you give an account of what you have said, and what you do meane:—for the substance of itt, I accord with you: and though I do not affect *leptologein [to speak precisely], et minutias captare [and to fasten upon details]*; yet give mee leave, by way of annotation onlie, and *in transitu [in passing]*, to touch upon a verie fewe things; and then verie succinctlie to speak-to what hath bin the matter of the eyther seeming or real difference.

A True: but so, as that there is *fides divina [divine faith]* of the former sorte of truthes; *quatenus revelantur [as far as they are revealed]*: which, in the second page, you are not unwilling to allow.

B I beleeve, in somthing more than bare circumstances.

C I admit of the distinction of "authoritative and perceptive"; which others expresse by *judicium decisionis et discretionis [judgment of decision and discernment]*. Faith, I acknowledge, is the act of an intelligent or rational creature: so that Understanding and Reason are necessarie; both *ad recipiendam divinam revelationem, et ad eliciendum actum fidei [in order to receive divine revelation, and to produce the act of belief]*: but that so, as that in manie things I must *credere [believe]* much more, than I can *ratione percipere [perceive by reason]*. If in scripture I perceeve, that a Trinity in Unity is reveled, as a divine truth; and so, in the matter of God's decrees: though I cannot fullie perceeve or comprehend them, I will neyther doubt nor quarrell them; but humbly beleeve them: and so Reason's judging of them falls short of the eye's judging of Colours. If, in true proprietie of speech, *visus [vision]* may be said to judge of them; and it doth not rather belong to an inward and higher facultie.

D True; the understanding cannot rightlie judge otherwise, than the thing is: *veritas rei [natural truth]* being *regula veritatis intellectus [the principle of the intellectual understanding of truth]*.¹ But our present dispute is, about the power of Reason to judge of matters of Faith: And as the Apostle² speaks of "a spirit of wisdom and revelation"; so wee conceeve, that to our right understanding such mysteries, *ex parte subjecti [subjectively]*, hee must bee a spirit of wisdom; and so *ratio [reason]* must bee *divinitus illuminata [illuminated by God]*: and, *ex parte objecti [from an objective standpoint]*, a spirit of revelation; and so *objectum [the object]* must bee *revelatum [revealed]*. And this revelation must bee of the formalitie of the object, which is understood and beleeved; and so, by this illumination of the understanding and revelation of the object, the discerning faculties is fully regulated in its apprehensions of these mysteries: and therfore I cannot tell, whether you may say; "it is wholely regulated, *a ratione objecti [based on objective reason], &c.*"

ᴇ From these *argumenta artificialia insita [inherently difficult arguments]*, and this *materia Deo digna [subject worthy of God]*; I beleeve, a man may *affirmativè [affirmatively]* argue to his satisfaction, in matters of faith; as from such arguments Divines rightly argue the Scriptures to bee the worde of God: but I beleeve too, that in arguing *negativè [negatively]*, that such and such particulars are *not* matters of faith; wee had need bee very warie, how wee conclude: for although that, which reallie and indeed is *materia Deo indigna [a subject unworthy of God]*, *cannot* bee matter of faith; yett that, which seemes so to us, *may* bee. And I beleeve, both Arminians and others have bin too bold; to reject that which in Scripture is playne enough reveled: as concerning some of God's decrees: because they eyther *can not* or *will not* apprehend, how themselves may bee *Deo digna [worthy of God]*.

ꜰ Wee fullie yeeld, that *materia fidei [the subject matter of faith]* is not contrarie to reason: butt then wee beleeve, itt is in manie things much above itt: as you afterwards say, that this transcendencie lieth not *in contradictione rationis [in contradiction of reason]*, but *in amplitudine et plenitudine objecti [in the vastness and fullness of the object]*: and that may bee too bigge for our understanding to comprehend; though not for our faith to beleeve. And as that, which you cite out of BONAVENTURE, is true; *Credendum est, voluntatem Dei, etiam in occultissimis, esse rationabilissimam [One must believe that the will of God, even in the most obscure things, is most reasonable]*: so is this allso, which I adde, out of the same authour; *Facit enim ad rationem virtutis, ut fides credat sine ratione [To him who acts according to virtuous reason, faith may believe without reason]*.

ɢ As *proximè et immediatè [next and immediate]*, so I hope you mean *ultimò [finally]* too: so I understand the following wordes, "and therein rest": *my* faith, both first and last, I resolve into God's revelation. But I pray, Sir, look over the notes of one of your late sermons in St. MARIE's; (I do not remember the text:) and towards the latter end of itt, if I do not much forgett, you did, with some confidence, assert the last resolution *in rationem rei [in natural reason]*: as the like was asserted, in the dispute at the Commencement.

ʜ The second and third parts of this distribution, as to the thing in hand, do *coïncidere [coincide]*: they are both *materia fidei [matter of faith]*; as the first is *scientiae [of knowledge]* and *fidei [of faith]* too; *quatenus a Deo revelatur [up to that which is revealed by God]*.

<sup>I</sup> You meane, I suppose; that religion, *quoäd objectum [as far as its object]*, reacheth to such things which may naturallie bee knowen; as well as to what are beleeved from divine revelation: otherwise divine faith, the first part of divinitie, doth *in cognoscendis vel potius credendis [in knowing and even more in believing]* take-up the whole of religion, as religion; especiallie, as Christian.

<sup>K</sup> The justice and righteousness of God is *theologiae naturalis [of natural theology]*: and therfore that which I wou'd say here, is; that *in theologia naturali, Deus ad nos nostraeque rationis judicium provacat;*³ *in rebus fidei supernaturalis, rationem contemnit: nostraéque intelligentiae, cum caecutiens immo caeca sit, nullam rationem habet [In natural theology, God calls us and our reason to judgment; in matters of supernatural faith, he despises reason; he recognizes no reason in our intellect, as when a blind man leads the blind]*.⁴

<sup>L</sup> I am not herewith unsatisfied; if reason will be satisfied and content, that divine revelation shall bee above itt; and that faith may beleeve, what reason cannot comprehend; as you afterwards grant: and if in the speech you had spoken as much of faith, as you did of reason; and had as much asserted the transcendencie of faith above reason, as you did the agreableness of itt with, or the non-contradiction of itt to, reason; you thereby wou'd have don your faith right and honour; as by what you did (as you say in the bottom of this page) you did it no wrong or dishonour. However, I must still think, you had don *your-self* more right; if you had then treated on another argument.

<sup>M</sup> If that *Crambe [Cabbage]* be nauseous, I crave pardon for my incivilitie in that expression.—To what you adde in this paragraph, I onlie say; 1. I wish, that you wou'd please more ordinariely to choose rather such texts and arguments to treat-of, which are *fidei divinae [of divine faith]*; they wou'd bee most apt to begett divine faith in the hearers: and not so much and so often such; as, you say, are examinable by *ratio rei [natural reason]*: and so by the nature of your matter in hand you shou'd not bee, as you think, necessitated so to handle itt. 2. Though the scriptures, which are so full of such truths, may out of themselves abundantly furnish us to cleare you; without being over-much beholden to such kind of rational discourses. 3. I pray, Sir, consider the Prophets' and Apostles' sermons: whether *they* bee generally upon such arguments; and what is *their* manner of handling them: whether knottie and obscure, to buisy and amuse the brain; and not rather plaine and facile, and in the demonstration of the Spirit; rather than of this kind of reason: the more to affect the heart.

<sup>N</sup> When, in the former papers, you said; that the intention of your speech was *de certitudine et dignitate Christianae religionis [on the certainty and goodness of the Christian religion]*: I then did; and now do think; that the *dignitas et certitudo [goodness and certainty]* may more theologicallie bee demonstrated, from the certaintie of divine testimonie; and of faith in itt, by that divine testimonie: I in part meant scripture; which I think, shou'd bee so farre distinguished from that, which is

most properly called Christian religion, as that which conteines itt; and so may bee a full proof of itt: and though it may be not to a Heathen, yett to a Christian auditorie, such as yours was: and, even to the Heathens themselves; though, I freely acknowledge, these arguments, taken from the matter and other particulars that are *insita [innate]* in the scripture, are verie strong and good; and more proper for such an adversarie: yett 1. they of themselves are not sufficient to persuade; for which I referre you to your quotation out of AU'STINE, in the margent of the page.[5] 2. besides, the certainty of divine testimonie; which bears full wittness from heaven to the Christian religion, contained in scripture: as namelie, the foretelling and fulfilling of prophesies concerning Christ, and his Apostles' and others' miracles to confirme itt, are arguments; which not only to a Christian's but a Pagan's understanding and conscience speake God as much, if not more fully and directly, and to as much conviction; as anie of those arguments, which are taken *a ratione rei [by natural reason]*. And therfore, as you knowe; a learned man,[6] who hath latelie written a tract of the reasonableness of Christian religion; 'speciallie useth that argument, as most convincing. There is verie good matter, in manie of the Heathens' writings; and such, as is *theoprepês [godly]*, but they want such miracles, and other divine testimonies, to ratifie them; which the truth of scripture and Christian religion is honoured and confirmed by.

º And therfore I did not, I think, so falle-off from the quæstion: as conceeving, 1. I may prove the truth of Christian religion, which was *to zêtoumenon [the problem (of theological exegesis)]*, by the divine authoritie of the scripture. 2. If that be quæstioned, the proofe of it is not, as your rule is, "I must consider scripture *secundum materiam [according to nature]*": there is no such absolute necessitie of itt, that it cannot be proved otherwise—itt may, by the certaintie of the testimonie, both of God in prophesies and miracles; and of the beleevers faith: in which there are manie things, which give more than a humane testimonie to itt.

ᵖ For what you say, to that of Prov. xx.27; that, "I instance in the *use* of the principle; and You insiste-on the qualitie fittness and sufficiencie of itt, as from God and in His hand; as *res illuminata illuminans [an illuminated thing which gives light]*: and so you persuade yourself; that is in the wordes, which you have alledged them for:"—I answer; 1. that I indeed instance in the use of the principle: and that use to which by interpreters, and by both the sense and context of the wordes, they are there applied: and itt is *rimari res hominum, non Dei [to inquire into human affairs, not God's]*:[7] and no more can from the place bee inforced. And when hee saith, it is "the candle of the Lord," for this use; we can no more inferre thence, that itt is so for farther use; in the things of God and mysteries of faith: than hee, that saith such a man is the King's searcher in the Custom-house, to finde-out merchants' conceled goods; can thence inferre, that hee is so to search-out the King's Council: or, because a candle can helpe to search-out a dark corner in the house; that therfore itt can in a dark night help mee to see the heavens. 2. Though some interpreters adde; not onlie man's secrets, but God's councils; yett they explaine themselves to meane that Grace, which out of his love hee reveleth by his worde; and infuseth by his spirit:

and so "the spirit of a man" is, as itt were, *naturaliter capax divinae illuminationis [by nature capable of divine illumination]*; so being by the spirit illuminated, wee denie not but it can perceeve the things of God; which otherwise it cannot:[8] In these things especiallie, however there is a spirit in a man; yett the inspiration of the Almightie giveth understanding.

Q I meant not, onlie Papistes; though this *judicium discretionis [faculty of discernment]* is by our divines asserted against them: but, as you say, *contra omnes personas [against all persons]*: the quæstion is; whether, as you adde, *in omni materia [in every occasion]*? nor will I in that gainsay you; if wee agree in the right meaning of *judicium discretionis [faculty of discernment]*. I take itt, as DAVENANT[9] and our other divines do; who, though they do truely assert such a *judicium [faculty]*; yett you knowe, in what sense: they denie itt to bee *iudex [judge]*, so I am sure they will not allowe itt to bee *summus judex, in rebus fidei [chief judge, in matters of faith]*; which in the Commencement-house was asserted: but of that perceptive judgement, which you speak-of before, I have also before said somthing; and therfore no more now. And as for those protestant principles, which you mention; the *Quilibet abundet in suo sensu [Let him abide in his own perception]*, is but the Vulgar's bad translation of the Apostle's *plêrophoreisthô [let him be fully persuaded]*,[10] and may be of dangerous consequence: and therfore rejected by our divines. *Neque haec sententia Christiana esse potest [Nor can this position be Christian]*, is BEZA's judgement of itt. The Apostle's *plêrophoria [full persuasion]* requires our own *certioratio [appraisal]*; but not from our own conceptions, but from the revelation of the spirit and word of God. For the other, *Fides non est cogenda [Belief cannot be compelled]*; in a true sense I admitt itt: but how farre the reall and full sense of itt and the former principle will intrude, and the necessairie consequents of them; I cannot tell: and therfore, till I knowe that, I must *epechein [hold back]*. And, before I goe farther, to close-up all about the power of *ratio, in rebus fidei [reason, in matters of faith]*; I have in publique[11] given as much to it, in *theologia*, both *naturali* and *supernaturali*; as I think you in reason can require: but in these supernatural mysteries of faith, I beleeve, as you well express it, itt is not to be accounted either authour, inventer, or controller. 1. itt was never able to finde them out at firste. 2. when reveled, not able fullie to comprehend them; must not bee such a judge of them, as to arraigne them att it's barre: so as, if they be eyther reallie about itt, yea or seeme to bee contrarie to itt, to reject them; as, in the matter of God's decrees, is too frequent with Arminians and others: or so as lastlie to resolve them eyther *in rationem rei, ex parte objecti [in natural reason, from an objective standpoint]*; or *in rationem nostram, tanquam, summum judicem, ex parte subjecti [in our own reason, as if the supreme judge, based on our subjective understanding]*. If those, and some other such particulars, which I expressed in my position, be granted; there will reallie be little controversie: and if they were clearlie and plainlie in publique declared; itt wou'd take-away manie men's suspicions and misprisions. And if withall you and others wou'd please so farre to denie you selves; as to forbeare the insisting-on these arguments, of the power of nature and reason, in your discourses; which in scripture are rather abased, than exalted: it wou'd prevente heats and oppositions, which att all times are uncomfortable; and especiallie, in these crasie times, may prove of verie ill consequence to the Universitie. And I beseeche you, Sir, not to bee offended att my faithfull playnness with you: your and others' so much going in another strayne, hath not onlie much offended and opened the mouths of verie manie considerable men of another judgement; but allso made some others applaude themselves in their corrupte judgement: as conceeving and concluding, though I beleeve falselie, that they have their abetters amongste Us.

<sup>R</sup> Sir, what followes of the fourth page, so farre as I can well read and understand itt, I do not dissent from itt. As for the hopefulness of good men's less differing in things saving; and that through siding and passion, differences betwen them appear, and seem to bee, more than they are; I denied neyther of these: but I then said, and yett thinke; that they may not onlie differ, in the number of Fundamentals; but also in their resolved judgements, about verie material truths; and that, without mistaking one another's mindes, or making one another's judgements other and worse than they are; and yett on both handes agree in scripture-expressions: in which case, as better to forme their judgements, and to discover worse men's errours, great use was of other than scripture wordes and expressions; and this, without anie alteration of, or addition to, or derogation from, the holie scriptures: which was the thing I spake-to in my former paper.

<sup>S</sup> For matter of *imposing-upon*, I am not guiltie. In the Assemblie, I gave my vote with others; that the Confession of Faith, putt-out by Authoritie, shoulde not bee required to bee eyther sworne or subscribed-too; wee having bin burnt in the hand in that kind before: but so as not to be publickly preached or written against; which indeede is contrarie to that "libertie of prophesying";[12] which some so call-for; but, you say, you plead not for; though your second advice in your sermon seemed, in mine and other men's eyes, to look fullie that way: but I beleeve, what you now write; and onlie adde, that as you plead not for that libertie; so what hath bin said by others, hath not bin to impose of you; but onlie as freelie to assert, what they think is truth; as what you did assert was so, in your judgement: and therfore were not culpable of maintaining *rixas et lites [quarrels and disputations]*; as hath bin charged. Though I heartilie and humblie desire of God; that wee may either so inwardlie agree, or outwardlie not express disagreement; that we may not give occasion of advantage, to more sortes of men than one; that watch for our halting.

<sup>T</sup> That which I spake of Hæretiques' being sober and temperate &c; was not to your second proposal, about liberty of proposing, &c; but to your first, of agreeing with them that agree in scripture expressions: And whereas it was pleaded, that such agreement was desired amongst good men; I replied, that it was not so easie to know, who they were: seeing Hæretiques were not *sine larva pietatis [without the worm in their devotions]*, and were somtimes sober and temperate; not—"unexceptionable and of unblameable life"; as your wordes are. Whereas you find Scripture Hæretiques infamous in their life; I easilie grant itt of those *Gnostique Borboritae*,[13]

and verie manie others, which authours speak-of. And yett in scripture I finde false prophets, in sheep's cloathing;[14] and those in TIMOTHY, having a forme of godlinesse;[15] Pharisees, whited sepulchres;[16] which is enough to express that *larva pietatis* I spake-of. ARIUS and NOVATUS[17] and others, at least for a time, speciouslie devout and pious; and all that I read of St. FRANCIS in BONAVENTURE, and of LOYOLA in RIBADENEIRA, and of BELLARMINE in FULLIGATTI, I do not look-at as Legend; what BERTIUS and others say of ARMINIUS, you know;[18] often those, that have bin most pestilent, have bin, in outward demeanour, at least for a time, sober; and some severe: but *sobrii ad evertendum rempublicam [reasonable men may overthrow the state]*: enough to justifie what I said; that wee are rather to look to their doctrines, than their persons.

<sup>V</sup> For that of Socinians and Arminians; seeing I ingenuouslie cleared you, from those imputations; both in my own thoughts, and against other misprisions; I hope, you will cleare mee, from being in that kind injurious to you: nor will you take in ill part my cordiall good wishes which I expressed, that so good a friend might not bee *in confinio [a borderer]* of such men's tentes: and although hee, that hath the name of Christ called upon him, may and ought, in the sense you meane, to say,—*Non sum Christianus ullius nominis [I am not a Christian by any other name]*: yett, when diversities of judgements have unhappilie begotten diversities of denominations; I had rather, by reason of my adhæring to the truth, that CALVINE maintained; men shoulde call mee a Calvinist: than by reason of eyther an indifferencie, or by a propending to somthing that Socinians or Arminians hold; men, though unjustlie and sinfullie, shoulde besmeare mee with their appellation.

<sup>W</sup> As to what followes in this page, concerning your studies; I must intreate your pardon, as of my too greate boldness, in that it may bee unseasonable freeness; so of my mistakes, occasioned by my mis-apprehension, or rather mis-information: and I crave leave onlie to adde; 1. as to that about the Schoole-men; when I spake of them, I understood, not onlie that narrower compass of them; which some make, from ALBENSIS[19] to BIEL; but so as to take-in VASQUEZ, SUAREZ,[20] and other later authours of that kind: your perusing of whom so little in so manie yeares, but that you say itt and I beleeve you, I cannot but wonder: and must conclude; that eyther those fewe houres of your converse with them made a verie deepe impression in you, moulding you much that way; or, as *nascitur non fit Poëta [a Poet is not created by birth]*, that the natural frame of your head was much in that channel: which must keepe us from wondering, or finding faulte; if in your discourses the streames do so much answer the fountain. 2. They, that told mee of FIELD, JACKSON, HAMMOND, added also CHILLINGWORTH, and HOOKER's *Ecclesiastical Politie*:[21] in the first booke whereof, though it bee manie yeares since I redde itt, and I have itt not nowe by mee; if I forgett not, there bee divers things; which divers discourses now-a-dayes much symbolize with. 3. I verilie thought, you had rea'd the *Apologia Remonstrantium*; a booke, which, when it came out, we so greedilie bought and rea'd: as justifying their Confession of Faith before putt-out, againste the *examen* of the *Contra-Remonstrants*: in which they speake out more fullie, than they had don

before; and in both which of their bookes they are large in the argument wee speak-of. 4. What you say of your little reading and more meditating; I impute to your great modestie, in lessening your own due: or if, as I have cause, I must beleeve you; as I cannot but much approve your course of Meditation; so give mee leave to intreat you, to give diligence to Reading. I have thought, that BERNARD was in the right; when hee said, *lectio, sine meditatione, arida est; meditatio, sine lectione, erronea [reading, without contemplation, is dry; contemplation, without reading, is erroneous]*. In our meditations, wee may unawares flip into an errour; which, because our own, of our own selves, we are hardlie restrained from;[22] from which another's hand may easilie helpe mee up. And if, for that and other ends, I would gladlie conferre with the living; the same motive may persuade mee to converse with others, that are dead; in their writings: and the rather, because they use to bee more digested; than others' extemporarie discourses: especiallie, if, as you do, we make choice of those, that are most pious and learned. I look-at it, as a kind of Communion of Saints; in which I may expect a greater blessing: but so, as not resting on their authoritie. And shoulde not their writings bee better than my thoughts, yett with mee I find itt thus; that by reading I have more hints, and better rise, for more and better notions; than otherwise of myself I shou'd have reached unto: hereby I shall bee better acquainted with the true historie, stating, and phrasing, of any point of controversie; which otherwise I shall too often stumble-att.—But, Sir, may you not justlie disdeigne this my follie; in suggesting that to Him, who needes no spurrs to itt; and better knowes itt, than hee who presumes to suggest itt! SCULTETUS' character, which in his *Speculationes Evangelicae [Evangelical Speculations]* hee gives of AND: OSIANDER,[23] of which from my heart I cleare you; makes mee afraid to bee *autodidaktos [self-taught]*. (See Scultet: Lib. II. cap. v. p. 16.)

[x] In the half of this page, Sir, you express so much ingenuity and integrity; and withall so much condescension, for my satisfaction; that, although you say, you are ashamed in the writing of itt; yett I may more blush in receiving itt. I from my soule free you from designe; I beleeve, you love and seeke the truth; and yett think, you may in some things mistake. You say, that I seeme to "anatomize your life": God help mee more to search into my own heart; that I may not bee so much mistaken, in the one; as it seemeth I am, in the other! God knowes, I am not wont to look verie much into others; who have so much to look-after, in my-self. What I did herein, I intreate you to think, and I wou'd no deceeve you, was not from an ill-minded or buisy curiositie; but out of love and faithfullness, having such an occasion, to hint somthing what others said and I somwhat feared: and if you will please to do as much for mee, such "balm shall not break my head."

[y] For this in the margent; I freelie grant imperfection, in the best interpreters; nor did I ever allow them the priviledge of infallible interpretation: and, if my pen wrote itt, my heart never thought itt. And trulie I have, as carefullie as I cou'd in these straits of time, rea'd over the place you mention in my second page; and can neyther there, nor anie where else in my whole paper, finde anie such wordes; or anie other; from which I can think, how anie such inference can bee made. The like I must say

of what followes; where you say, that I suggest; Fundamentalls may bee shaken and endangered, by such a free proposall: Nothing, all the paper over, that I can find; which either saith or suggesteth anie such matter: I spake of the staggering of weake men; no tittle of the shaking of fundamentall truths: and therfore some of your following lines might have bin spared.—Yett this let mee now say; that if such an expression, of the shaking fundamentall truths, had fallen from my penne; it might verie well have been justified: and that, from Scripture. Not as though the truth in itt self coulde bee so shaken, as to weaken itt: but such speeches respect partlie *intentionem operantis, vel operis [the intention of the worker, or the work]*; and partlie the effect, which thereupon followes; in the minds of weak and unstable persons. And so not onlie the Ark may be shaken; but even the foundations may bee destroyed:[24] (and if you consult interpreters upon this place, you will finde; that I do not wrest itt, in applying itt to this purpose:) as the Apostle presumes, they may; in his *mê palin themelion kataballomenoi [not laying again the foundation]*.[25]

[Z] What I said, I think, is verie justifiable; that, when both Hæretiques and the Orthodoxe hold to Scripture expressions; and They, in their wordes, give a false sense of them; the other in theirs may give a true: not to command anie man's inwarde sense; as you wou'd seeme to inferre: but, as in three or foure lines before I had said; by expressing the true sense more particularlie and distinctlie, to discover their corrupt one: which, I added, was the occasion of orthodoxe Divines' framing of newe wordes and expressions; more punctuallie to hold-out old truths, against Hæretiques' innovations. And what is amisse in all this, I can not see; nor have you shewen mee.

[A2] Sir, here 'bate mee a little: I said not; that *All*, that so pleaded, were such; but my wordes were, such *for the most part*: and that, if neede bee, I shall bee able to justifie: namelie, of those that have written of that argument: whom onlie I related to. But I impute this to your haste, and broken pieces of time, which after you speak of; as I do most of what followeth in this page: as that; "May wee temper and qualifie divinitie with prudential considerations?" I see not, how this relates to what immediatelie went before of Socinians and Arminians; who are in this kind as faultie as anie. If you said itt, in reference to interpreters' or synods' framing of wordes for clearing of scripture, against others' false glosses; I think itt a verie harsh censure, and wholelie unjustifiable: if both this and what followes, to the forcing and imposing upon others judgements; you make to yourself an adversarie, where you found none.

[B2] I do not remember, itt is so stiled by our Divines: and, shou'd itt by some, both they and you will give mee leave to think; that there are other foundations of Protestancie, lower and of more importance.

[C2] "Truth is Truth, whosoëver speakes itt: and I will readily agree with Papist, Socinian, or anie; so farre as hee asserts itt: because itt is not His, but God's."—But this *libertas prophetandi [liberty to prophesy]* I take to bee no such Truth: and I do not the more like itt, but rather the more suspect itt; because Socinians and Arminians do so much pleade for itt: and that, as itt is apparent, out of design; that they might not be hindred in diffusing their poison, in their other corrupt tenents;

which they are more commonlie knowen by: though the worlde is not now so ignorant of Socinianism and Arminianism, as to confine the one to the denial of Christ's divinitie and satisfaction &c; or the other to the five controverted articles. This of *libertas prophetandi*, you cannot but knowe, that they are generallie noted for; and this, in the Countrie, as well as in the Universitie; it may be, in the Universitie most: and therfore the proposall of this libertie there, may be most taken notice of in the proposer; as itt may bee of more ill influence unto the yonge auditours: and a student in Divinitie neede not to be confined, as you speak, to "the getting of a good memorie and learning by heart"; his invention and judgement will have buis'ness more than enough, in aright understanding and more full clearing of receeved truths; and finding-out others, that itt may bee, yett lie hid; without such a libertie of opposing, or doubtfullie disputing, *peri tôn peplêrophoroumenôn [concerning those who have received grace]*, much more without a Cartesian *epochê [epoch]* or supposing them for errours, or not established truths; till I coming *de novo [anew]*, withoute anie prepossession of them, shall study and reason my selfe into a beleife of them. And somthing sounding this way, I thought I heard, within this twelve-month, out of the pulpitte.

D2 By this your last expression, I think, I now better understand your meaning before; about which I doubted: and, itt may bee, mistook: that, whereas in my former paper I spake of this libertie, as dangerous to the weake; and because symbolizing with Arminians and Socinians, the asserting of it by a lover of truth was at all times unsuitable; and especiallie, in these so erroneous times, unsafe; at least, very unseasonable.—

> This, you conceeve, was a suggestion; that Fundamentalls may bee shaken and endangered: which cou'd not worthilie be conceeved—that this was to temper and qualifie Divinitie with prudential consider-ations—the taking of God's work out of his handes, &c; and not sufficiently to consider, who principallie standes charged, and is the grand Superintendent of truth in the world."

—If this, Sir, be your meaning; I must professe to you, that I am not convinced; eyther of anie unworthie conception, or inconsiderate expression. Not in saying, if I had said itt, that fundamentall truths mighte be shaken; of which before: And the restraining of such a libertie is no tempering or qualifying Divinitie with prudential considerations: unlesse it can bee proved, that such a Toleration be true Divinitie; or everie thing that by such a sufferance may bee vented. A prudential prevention of the corruption, of what is true Divinitie; will, I hope, bee no fault in him; who is a faithfull and wise servant:[26] And his keeping of the *depositum [deposit]*, which he is betrusted-with by his master,[27] doth not take his master's worke out of his hand; but acknowledgeth Him principallie charged with his own truth; and to bee the grand Superintendent of itt in the world: whilst, as a Steward under his Lord, hee, according to his dutie,[28] is faithfull to his trust; in being carefull, that not onlie his fellow-servant may not be infected; whom hee hath the charge of: but that the truth ittself, though it cannot be in ittself weakened or over-mastered, may not bee corrupted or blemished; which hee is bound earnestlie to contend for.[29]

[E2] Those "beginnings of grace," which you mention, are, I suppose, much-what the same with, or itt may bee less than, that first sanctification, or regeneration; which I spake-of. And that "actuallie justifying," which you adde, the same with what I called *apotelesma [fulfillment]* of justification: so that herein, I hope, wee shall not differ. For those "preparations to justification," which Dr. WARD[30] so frequentlie determined in the schooles; and which Papistes do so much dispute-for: I professe, I coulde never yett so ripen my thoughts about them; as peremptorilie to determine them, one way or other. Sure I am; that manie good Divines determine againste them: and I think, in some cases, when God doth suddainlie come upon some sinners, *flagrante facinore [in the midst of their crime]*; and then presentlie convert them: itt will bee verie hard to discern them. That expression of yours, of "a sinner *non omnino in motu conversionis [not at all in the way toward conversion]*, &c"; I do not well understand: unless your meaning bee; that a sinner, *qua talis [as such]*, without anie movings toward conversion &c—if so; though, as I said, before your *apotelesma [fulfillment]* of justification, *in puncto rationis [at the moment of reason]*, a renovation goeth first; which doth *elicere actum fidei [elicit the act of faith]*, by which we are actuallie justified: yett *in hoc motu [in this process]* God moves first; and so farre as Justification consists in pardon of sinne, itt is verie considerable; whether *immediate antecedenter [immediately preceding]* itt hath for it's object a sinner, as a sinner, under the guilt and in the state of sinne; though it do not so leave him: and so God properlie justifie the ungodlie.

[F2] In your paper, *kata to rhêton [according to what was said]*, order is considered and expressed; and not onlie distinction.

[G2] I think, You pinch too hard; in calling that, "a wringing of the nose"; which was but a wiping-away of that which dropt from itt: and in applying that,[31] which is spoken of scorners, and such as watch for iniquitie, in catching-at and perverting the right wordes of the Prophets; to mee, who in a friendlie way did expresse to you my dissatisfaction with an unjustifiable expression.

[H2] I cordiallie embrace, what you herein so orthodoxlie piouslie and patheticallie express: of your so depending on God: and of his being all in all. And I verilie beleeve, you meane much more by itt; than Papistes and Arminians &c. do, in their large expression of the influence of the first cause into the second; in itt's operations both of nature and grace: who, notwithstanding that, give too too much to man and his free will. A great asserter whereof in our time, in his verses upon his quæstion in the commencement house, had these two for the close—

> SCIRE *tuum nihil est, oculis* GRATIA *praesit*;
> *Ni praesit votis,* VELLE *tuum nihil est.*
> *[Your knowledge is nothing, unless grace is present before your eyes;*
> *And if it does not appear because of your prayers, your wishes are nothing.]*[32]

¹² By that "conjunction with a passive exegetical," I suppose you meane the addition of *recipitur a nobis [it is received by us]*: and so that *recipitur* so "qualifies and corrects" your *nascitur [it is born (from within us)]*; that it prevents anie such sense, as was feared and objected. I would not *lian exetazein [seek too much]* else, I coulde think; if, according to Popish or Arminian doctrine, *gratia oblata per liberum arbitrium recipitur [present grace is received through free judgment]*; this woulde bee a moral *nascitur*.

ᴷ² I acknowledge, *voluntas creata*, or *creatura [created will* or *the creature]*, is the *subjectum* or *principium quod [the subject* or *the beginning that]*, (in subordination to God, the *principium a quo [beginning from which]*) that doth *formaliter producere actum credendi et poenitendi [formally produce the act of belief and penitence]*: but I woulde not willinglie express it, by *producere vitalitatem actus [produces the vital spirit of action]*; though that word may be tolerable, in a school-sense; but dubious, *in sensu theologiae puriori [in a more strictly theological sense]*.

ᴸ² I conceeve; that *kategazesthe [to perform]* is not of so deepe a sense, as *nascitur [it is born]*: for although somtimes in Scripture it expresseth a meritorious efficiencie;³³ (Somtimes *idem quod* katorthô, *ita prospere ago, ut potiar [the same as "I act well," thus I act with good results, as I am able]*: and somtimes *vinco, supero [to outdo, to surpass]*; when I obteine by labour and overcome difficulties:) yett verie often, both in other authours and Scripture, it signifieth anie efficiencie in general; even of a cause *sine qua non [that is essential]*, and a cause *per accidens [that is accidental]*:³⁴ and therfore much more, a *medium administrans [a middle (cause) that acts]*; or a cause, so called *propter solam praesentiae necessitatem [merely on account of its immediate necessity]*: as our Divines commonlie and trulie answer the Papistes; who, in their disputes about good workes in reference to Salvation, bring II Cor. iv.17. and this of Phil. ii.12. and urge the word *kategazesthe [to perform]* against us. A *nasci [to be born]* therfore, in the true importe of itt, doth signifie more than such a *kategazesthe*, and it is a farre different thing to say, a beleever now by faith, and the improvement of grace receeved, doth by *working*, as a means, come to salvation; and to say, that grace or salvation *ab eo nascitur [is that from which he is born]*.

ᴹ² Itt was a supplicatorie advice, that you would not affecte to speake in schoole-language; nor to runne-out in schoole-notions: not—"the use of Philosophie and Metaphysiques."

ᴺ² Your care not to "do the worke of the Lord negligently"; but to improve your utmost in His service, and solidlie to confirm His truth; I both beleeve and approve-of: neyther did I, nor do I think; in what you have done, you have affected wordlie glorie: and what blessings you have had from the soules, eyther of living or dying men, I rejoyce in; and desire, they may be multiplied a thousand fold: and shou'd hope, it wou'd bee so; if you wou'd please to listen to my advice or desire before mentioned: in being more playne and facile in your discourses. For although, as you say, you have bin *all along* well understood; by persons of honest heartes, but of meane place and education: and, as I may adde, you have herein bin more than approved; by diverse schollars, upon diverse grounds: yett itt will not bee amisse for you to hear also, what very many others say. *Vox populi [The voice of the people]*, in this is, *vox Dei [the voice of God]*. And this lett mee say; I know divers, of honest heartes, of several conditions and educations; that have bin verie farre, with all their best attention, from being able all along to understand you. Some of meane place and education may have stronger parts; which meeting with honest heartes, will better be able to go along with you: but JACOB will drive-on *ad pedem puerorum [at the feet of boys]*.³⁵

O² Your both reading and making use of Philosophers; especiallie, in shaming loose and scandalous Christians with their better principles or practices; I do not remember, that eyther in my paper or otherwise, I ever did blame in you: provided it bee onlie to the shaming of profane and loose Gospellers; without giving occasion of casting shame upon the Gospel ittself. What I have bin in this kind so affected with, in the reading of SALVIAN³⁶ and some others; I cannot bee disaffected, in hearing the like from you. Though this you will give me leave to adde; that the Scripture scarce anie-where speaks particularlie of the Philosophers and wise men of the Heathens, with approbation and honour; but generallie with dislike and contempt. And tho' in some fewe places, itt upbraids the children of the church, in their abominations; with the more commendable practises of the heathen: yet far oftener itt speakes of them, as abominable; and of their principles and practises, as of rockes to bee avoyded; than as of fayre patterns to bee imitated. And therfore we shou'd followe Scripture's pattern; if wee shou'd more insist-on their darkness, ignorance, their falling short of and coming cross to Christ; than on the admiring and advancing of their knowledge and virtues: which att best were but dim and dead, whilst not enlighten'd and enliven'd by Christ. I think itt verie strange, that you shou'd say; that "those you have redde, you have found good; so farre as they hav gon:" in those fewe that I have redde, I have found them scattering a great deale of what is bad, with what is good in them; all along in the way—as also, that you adde; "that you never found them enemies to the truth of the Gospell." Primitive Christians found them such; even amongst the chiefest and subtlest enemies they hadde to deale with: and TERTULLIAN³⁷ eyther was of an other mind from you, or rea'd other Philosophers than you do; when he called them *Haeresium Patriarchas [Patriarchs of Heresy]*.

P² It was not so said absolutely; but qualified with a parentheticall—as itt were. And though hereinn I would not præscribe, yett I must needs say; that the ordinarie use of most is, when in English sermons and discourses they make use of Latine or Greek sentences; they intende, that their auditours shou'd take them for quotations from, or expressions of, other men: and not their own. Which course trulie I approve-of; and so do manie better than I: and although I admitted of GROTIUS his excuse, in his præface to his annotations on the Evangelists;³⁸ that hee forbare mentioning of names, in his quotations—*quod ea videam factioso hoc saeculo magis ad oblimandum quam ad defaecandum judicium valere [because I see that these things in this factious century tend rather to muddy than to cleanse the judgment]*; (who yett for the most parte writes his quotations in a distinct character; that wee may know them not to bee his owne:) yett I beginne to bee half of the mind, that itt is the fairest and most satisfactorie way, in such quotations; to express the authour, as well as the sentence: that the reader or auditour may have better meanes to know, whether itt be wholelie Him; and not wholelie or in parte ours.

Q2 The generall purporte of this paragraph I freelie yeeld to. For the Socinian's fallacie is his Reason; againste which I may oppose mine: and I fullie accord with AQUINAS, in this very poynte thus expressing himself—*Cum fides infallibile veritate innitatur, impossibile ut sit de verbo demonstrari contrarium; manifestum est, probationes quae contra fidem inducuntur, non esse demonstrationes; sed solubilia argumenta [Since faith rests upon infallible truth, it is impossible that the contrary might be verbally demonstrated; it is manifest that the proofs which they present against the faith are not demonstrations, but are difficulties that can be answered].*[39]

R2 For this I referre myselfe allso to what is said before.

S2 I meant a *recta ratio [right reason]* in corrupte nature: and there I cannot finde *righte*, but more or lesse distorted and depraved. Where Faith is, there is a renewall of God's image; in knowledge, as well as holiness and righteousness: and there a is in parte renewed, as well as a *recta ratio*; and a beleefe of that, to which reason cannot reach.

T2 I believe, itt doth; as manie can wittness: and although somtimes *mind* in our English use of the worde include the will; as, when we say, wee have no *mind* to such a thing; yett in most ordinarie acception, mind and understanding are synonymous.

V2 As they are declared Rom. ix; and explayned by those Divines, which wee must account orthodoxe; they have bin conceeved inconsistent with that goodness, and those *rationes rerum [reasons of things]*; which some frame for their ideas.

W2 I beleeve; that, as you cannot affirme, that God *did not*; so neyther, that hee *did* revele Christ to them; the Scripture seeming to speak otherwise of them: and therfore itt had bin best, to have left them in silence to their judge.

X2 I suppose, you heere give mee the wordes of your notes: which if you confined your speech to, I must acknowledge a mistake.

Y2 Our saviour did not come to destroye the moral law; and therfore hee could not bee againste moral duties: and, *Gnostique* Libertines in the Apostles' time arising, no wonder that the Apostle that wrote last, spake to Dutie; as PAUL, in laying the foundation, spake much for Faith. God forbidde, Sir, that I shoulde, as you phrase it, "disserve one truth; to serve an other"! And I think, in my preaching, I use to press inward grace and outward obedience; as much as some others. And woulde you, and some others, as fullie and as frequentlie insist on "free justification, by the imputation of Christ's righteousnesse"; as you and they do on inhærent holiness and righteousness: that no disservice may be done to *that*, by pressing of *this*; matter of complaynte wou'd bee prevented: but, when *this* is insisted upon; with the slighting terms of *notions* and *speculations* given to the other, when contended-for;—to mee it is juste matter of offence.

<sup>Z2</sup> Some have expressed a perfection above this.

<sup>A3</sup> Hee, that hath, "Faith, which worketh by Love"; cannot but joyne Love with his Faith: but trulie, Sir, I hope, you do not desire in this life (in which the Apostle saith, "wee walke by faith";[40] and "itt is our life";[41]) to come to such as estate of Love above Faith; that, with some of our high-flowen menne, you might heere bee above Faith: which onlie in an other worlde is swallowed-up into Vision; and so ceaseth, in some respects; though, in some other, itt even there abides to eternitie.

<sup>B3</sup> In the sermon on Matth. v.20. Ordinances spoken-of were more than Formalities.

<sup>C3</sup> Itt hath bin too often said in publique by some: and wee had more than a touch of itt, in this daye's sermon.

<sup>D3</sup> But yett, if that bee but a *notion* and *speculation*; which a man may holde, and not bee the better man for itt: trulie, by this rule, *Deum esse [that God exists]* and *Christum esse [that Christ exists]* may come to bee no better than *notions* and *speculations*.

<sup>E3</sup> They were all such things, as a man may holde and bee never the better man; and they may bee the most substantiall fundamentalls: and disputes about God and Christ were particularlie named.

<sup>F3</sup> I will not take upon mee, to choose other men's texts for them: but yett I shou'd bee glad, that Gospell-preachers wou'd please to think of such; as wou'd leade them to insist "upon Justification by Faith," and imputed Righteousness": and not onlie, or almost onlie, on such; as give them occasion to speak of "inhærent righteousness": of the advancing of Faith above Reason, and of the Impotencie and Weakness of Nature; rather than the Power of itt: that Faith is the condition of the covenant of Grace &c.—But I, that have bin too bold, in this long letter, with your Time, in this particular; may bee conceeved almost impudente in being so over-bold with Your and Others Libertie—But I crave pardon for all: and nowe that I have freelie opened my minde to you; I have don what, in faithfullness to God and you, I thought I might bee bound to. I commend You and the successe of all to God; and rest Your verie playne, but verie true Friende;

*A— T—*.

Oct. 8; 1651.

When you have looked over these papers, if they bee worthe your labour to do so; I desire you wou'd please to returne them: as not having anie coppy of them.

## Notes

1. SS: "*f. Intellectui*" (67 n).
2. SS: "Eph. i.17" (67 n).
3. SS: "Ezek. xviii.25; Isai. i.5; I Cor. xi.13" (69 n).
4. SS: "I Cor. i.20" (69 n).
5. SS: "Page 42" (71 n).
6. SS: "Dr. Hammond" (71 n).
7. SS: "Zeph. i.12" (72 n).
8. SS: "I Cor. ii.4" (73 n).
9. SS: "JOHN DAVENANT, D.D. Master of *Queen*'s College, and Lady *Margaret*'s Professor of Divinity at *Cambridge*: He was sent by King *James* to the synod of *Dort*; and at his Return from thence made Bishop of *Salisbury*. Some of his Lectures and Determinations are in print; and He had great Reputation, as a Divine" (73 n). In the *Exhortation to Brotherly Communion* (1641), Davenant (1572-1641) argued that, because perfect agreement is impossible, acceptance of the Apostles' Creed should be a sufficient basis for communion. *Ed*.
10. SS: "Rom. xiv.5" (74 n).
11. SS: "*Viz.* when he kept Exercise for his Doctors degree at the public Commencement 1650, on this Thesis; *Articuli Fidei ad normam humanae Rationis non sunt exigendi*: mentioned before" (74 n).
12. Concerning Jeremy Taylor's *Discourse of the Liberty of Prophesying* (1647), v. 9-10. *Ed*.
13. SS: "These were Haeretics, called *Borboritae*; and these joined with the *Gnostics*, as here, are often mentioned in our Author's Latin pieces; and in his friend ARROWSMITH's *Tactica sacra*. Conf. [Greek text] II Pet. ii.22" (77 n). Cf. *kulisma borbore*: to wallow in mud. *Trans*.
14. SS: "Matt. vii.15" (78 n).
15. SS: "II Tim. iii.5" (78 n).
16. SS: "Matt. xxiii.27" (78 n).
17. ARIUS (256-336) "denied the eternity and essential divinity of Christ; but held that Christ was a secondary God, of a different substance, created by the Father before the world, by a free act and out of nothing, and that he created the world and became incarnate from the Virgin Mary." Epiphanius, in *Haereses* §68-69, describes Arius as a man of "popular manners, considerable learning, serious, even austere character and ascetic habits, but unyielding pride and quarrelsome disposition" (*A Dictionary of Christian Biography, Literature, Sects, and Doctrines*, ed. William Smith and Henry Wace, 4 vols. [London: John Murray, 1877], 1:162-63). NOVATUS, third century presbyter of Carthage, who broke from the authority of the Church of Rome on the issue of the treatment of the lapsed, and ordained bishops and deacons who supported his puritan views. *Ed*.
18. The literary references here are to (1) the *Legenda Major*, the official life of St. FRANCIS of Assisi by St. BONAVENTURE, approved by the Franciscan order in 1263, (2) the *Vita Ignatii Loiolae* by Pedro de RIBADENEYRA, a life of St. Ignatius LOYOLA, first printed in English in 1616, (3) the *Vita Roberti Bellarmini*, a life of St. BELLARMINE by Giacomo FULIGATTI, published in 1624, and (4) the *Oratio in Obitum Reverendi and Clarissimi Veri D. Iacobi Arminij*, a life of Jacobus ARMINIUS by Petrus BERTIUS, first published in 1609, afterwards translated into English and republished, along with a short life of Episcopius by Etienne de Courcelles, as *The Life and Death of James Arminius and Simon Episcopius,*

*Professors of Divinity in the University of Leyden in Holland; Both of Them Famous Defenders of the Doctrine of God's Universal Grace, and Sufferers for It* (London: Printed by Thomas Ratcliff and Nathaniel Thompson for Francis Smith, 1672). *Ed.*

19. SS: "For *Albensis*, a learned friend conjectures, shou'd be rea'd *Alensis*, or *Al. Alensis*, i.e. *Alexander Hales*. And I find him so called by our author's great friend Dr. ARROWSMITH, in his second oration, at the end of *Tactica sacra*: p. 14: as also by Dr. TUCKNEY himself in his Latin works; where he often quotes him. We might also read *Albertus*: and the same Dr. ARROWSMITH observes, that after *Alensis* and *Antesiodorensis* had conducted *Aristotle* to the door of the Church; *Albertus* and *Thomas* carried him into the inmost recesses of it. *Hottinger* divides the schoolmen into three ages; which he calls *Vetus Aetos*, *Media*, and *Nova [the Ancient, Middle,* and *Modern Ages]*: the first beginning with *Lanfranc* of *Pavia*, about A.D. 1020; the second with *Albertus*, about 200 years later; the last with *Durandus de St. Porciano*, about 1330; and extending to the Reformation. The first age, he says, was *pudentior [more modest]*; and towards the end of it lived ALEX. HALES; the second was *impudens & temeraria [shameless and rash]*; in it flourish'd *Albertus*, *T. Aquinas*, *Durandus*, *Duns Scotus*, *Bonaventure*, *Occam*, &c: the last was *longè impudentissima [by far the most shameless]*; in it liv'd and wrote *Biel*, *Eekius*, &c." (79 n).

20. Gabriel BIEL (ca. 1420-1495) was the scholastic theologian who followed the nominalist thought of William of Ockham and is largely credited with founding the University of Tübingen. Gabriel VÁZQUEZ (1549-1604) and Francisco de SUAREZ (1548-1617) were Spanish Jesuit professors of theology who lectured on Thomas Aquinas's *Summa* and wrote in opposition to one another in regard to the doctrine of Congruism. *Ed.*

21. Of Richard Hooker (ca. 1554-1600), *v.* 5-7. William CHILLINGWORTH (1602-1644), in *The Religion of Protestants a Safe Way to Salvation* (1638), argued that the Bible is the only authority for Protestants and defended the rights of reason and free inquiry in matters of doctrine. During the Civil War, he served as a chaplain in the Royalist army, was captured in 1643, and died in captivity. *Ed.*

22. SS: "Eccles. iv.9,10" (81 n).

23. Abraham SCULTETUS (1566-1624) was a professor of theology at the Heidelberg who represented that city's university at the Synod of Dort (1616), and afterwards was Frederick of Bohemia's Calvinist court preacher and adviser, a zealous promoter of iconoclast activity. Andreas OSIANDER (1498-1552) was a Lutheran reformer, who played a major role in bringing about the Reformation of Nuremberg. He interpreted the justification of Christ as an infusion of essential righteousness or of the divine nature rather than as an imputation. His character was notorious, principally due to the coarseness and arrogance of his manner during argumentation. *Ed.*

24. SS: "Ps. xi.3" (83 n).

25. SS: "Hebr. vi.1" (83 n).

26. SS: "Matt. xxiv.45" (87 n).

27. SS: "I Tim. vi.20" (87 n).

28. SS: "Matt. xxiv.45; I Cor. iv.2" (87 n).

29. SS: "Jude iii" (87 n).

30. SS: "Samuel Ward DD. Scholar of *Christ*'s College, Fellow of *Emmanuel*, and at last Master of *Sidney*; was very eminent as a Disputant and Determiner of Theological Questions, in Lady *Margaret*'s Chair: which he filled after *Davenant*; and being turn'd-out and very severely handled in 1643, (which he survived a very little while) was then succeeded by Dr. *Holdsworth*, Master of *Emmanuel*; who was never admitted: being himself harass'd and persecuted, and at last turn'd-out of all his Preferments. Our Dr. *Tuckney* had his Mastership

of *Emmanuel* College, Dr. *Love*, Master of *Bennet*, his Professorship &c. Dr. *Ward* was sent with Bishop *Carlton, Dean Hall*, and Dr. *Davenant*, to the synod of Dort; and died of the ill usage he met with, by Imprisonment and otherwise, in 1643" (88 n).

31. SS: "Isai. xxix.21" (89 n).

32. The beginning of the first line, *scire tuum nihil est*, derives from Persius, *Satires* 1.27. *Trans*.

33. SS: "Rom. i.27, vii.8; I Cor. v.3" (90 n).

34. SS: "Rom. v.3, iv.15; Jam. i.3" (90 n).

35. SS: "Gen. xxxiii.14., i.e. softly, as the Children are able to bear" (92 n). For typographical reasons, I have taken an exceptional liberty with the text, replacing Tuckney's Hebrew script with Salter's Latin translation. *Ed.*

36. SALVIAN (ca. 400-480), in *De Gubernatione Dei*, contrasted the vices of native Roman with the virtues of the barbarian invaders in order to argue that the fall of Rome was a witness of God against the decadence of civilization and in order to motivate Christians in their pursuit of virtue. *Ed.*

37. TERTULLIAN (ca. 160-225) was a patriarch of the church in Carthage and vigorous apologist for Christianity against the pagans. *Ed.*

38. Hugo GROTIUS (1583-1645) was the Dutch Arminian theologian who wrote the *Annotationes in Vetus et Novum Testamentum* (1642), in which he adopted a method of philological criticism. *Ed.*

39. Thomas Aquinas, *Summa Theologia* 1.1., *De sacra doctrina*, Art.8. *Ed.*

40. SS: "II Cor. v.7" (96 n).

41. SS: "Gal. ii.10" (96 n).

# Letter VI

## Dr. WHICHCOTE's Third Letter.

Sir,

I have observed; that replies upon replies prove more troublesom, than profitable: and the farther they go-on, still the less of matter; but exceptions, on one side and other, against wordes and phrases: also *omnis ingenii acies post primum impetum hebescit [the sharpness of every mind is blunted after its first attack]*. Yett, since I preferre to give You satisfaction, before anie other buisness; somthing I shall farther adde: leaving manie things to discourse.

<sup>A B</sup> *Creatio est cognoscibilis, lumine naturae; et scriptura insuper attestatur: quo respectu dici potest esse de fide. Modus autem et circumstantiae creationis unice innotescunt per revelationem a Deo; ideóque non nisi materia fidei [Creation is understandable according to natural reason; and Scripture above all attests this: to the extent that it is able to witness concerning faith. The means and circumstances of the creation are wholly made known by divine revelation; and therefore it requires a basis of faith]*.

<sup>C</sup> "You say, in manie things wee must *credere [believe]* much more than wee can *ratione percipere [perceive by reason]*," in your <sup>F</sup> you quoted mee, that the transcendencie lies *in amplitudine et plenitudine objecti; non in contradictione rationis [in the vastness and fullness of the object (of thought), not in contradiction of reason]*: and were therwith satisfied.[1]

*Credere includit Cognoscere; aliter fides est implicita [Belief includes reasoning; otherwise faith is implicit]*: and I do not so much reach the thing, as beleeve in general, what God means is true.

I call in quæstion non of God's counsils or decrees; anie where reveled in scripture: (Mr. PERKINS and CALVINE and best interpreters give for a rule, in finding-out the sense of scripture; never a sense contrarie to the common principles of reason and natural light.) my reason hath nothing againste them; but admires and adores: yett I much doubt, notwithstanding what you said before of orthodox explications, to help our imperfections; whether anie fallible creature can adde anie thing to them, or make them farther out: and whether itt bee not presumption to attempte itt; without speciall commission.—Verie proper and ordinarie to say, that *facultates singulae judicant de rationibus suorum objectorum [the individual faculties discriminate concerning the reasons of their own objects].—*

As *non semper significat aequalitatem, sed similitudinem exempli gratia, illustrationis ergo: simile non est idem, nec per omnia simile: similitudo non currit quatuor pedibus. Aliquod luminosum transcendenter se habet ad vim visivae facultatis; sicut aliquod credibile ad intellectum [likeness is not always significant, but similarity; for example, this illustration: the similar is not the same, nor is it similar in all respects; the semblance does not run on four legs. But it retains the transcendent luminosity, giving force to the visual faculty; just as something is believable to the intellect].*

D "But our present dispute is about the power of Reason to judge of matters of Faith:" so after in [Q]—Did you ever find mee leaving God out, or not acknowledging Him principal, original; and the creature mere vanitie, dividedlie from him; a lye, in contradiction to him? I have declared the qualitie and fittness of the principle, as from God, in the hand of God; "the candle of the Lord": *Res illuminata illuminans [An illuminated thing which gives light]*.[2]—With all my heart and soule I acknowledge and assert (and wholelie depend thereon,) the holie Spirit's superintendencie, conduct, presence, influence, guidance, government of man's mind, in the discerning of the things of God.[3] There is nothing, that I have more insisted upon; and more carefullie endeavoured to demonstrate *de industria [out of labor]*, upon texts purposelie chosen; occasionallie still interposing clauses to this purpose. Yea, itt had a large place in my speech; att which, you say, so much offence was taken. I am not clearer, fuller, in anie-point: I experimentallie know itt, I thank God, to be true; I have wittness of itt within mee; itt is my sufficiencie, itt is my strength, itt is my securitie: God with mee is All in All.—God forgive them the palpable breach of the ninth commandment;[4] who have defamed mee in this kind! Nothing is less true of mee: I might rather have bin accused of anie eville in the world.—

Do not you yourself in your H2 say; "I cordiallie embrace what herein you so orthodoxlie, piouslie and patheticallie express?"—I allwayes consider, and so express, the mind of man in conjunction with the good spirit of God. I abhorre and destest from my soule all creature-magnifying self-sufficiencie. I coulde be abundant herein: for my hearte is full of indignation againste this supposition. The most secrette sense of my soule echoes to that text by you quoted, Eph. i.17; and all other of that nature. I know them to bee all true.

"I cannot tell, whether wholelie regulated *a ratione objecti [based on objective reason]*."—Yes; *tanquam a regula [as if upon a rule]*; which was that I spake to: but *a Dei spiritu, tanquam ab illuminante et dirigente [by the Holy Spirit, as if by a luminous and guiding power]*. So reason is not empowered *contra Deum, aut sine Deo [in opposition to God, or without God]*: but *sub Deo [under God]* is implied.

I acknowledged to you before, that *formale motivum fidei est revelatio fidei [the formal cause of faith is the revelation of faith]*: and you must allwayes remember; that there is in Religion, (I here understand Religion *materialiter [materially]*) *scibile, per necessitatem materiae [that which is knowable, by means of material necessity]*; as well as *credibile, propter authoritatem dicentis [believable, on account of scriptural authority]*: and *ratio objecti rei [objective reason]* never over-ruled, contradicted; and *ratio subjecti [subjective reason]* allwayes directed, determined. In that, which is onlie matter of faith, revelation is all in all: so *ratio objectiva [objective reason]* is never againste itt: (you fullie grant with mee in your ᶠ, that *materia fidei [the subject matter of faith]* cannot bee contrarie to reason:) for that (I mean, *ratio objectiva*) is necessarie, infallible, immutable, *positis terminis [when boundaries are set]*; as, *supposita creatura capaci, eam debere Deo subesse [in a created being there is the capacity, that it ought to obey God]*: but in that, which is *materia theologiae naturalis ex se [the subject matter of natural theology in itself]*, there is *partim scientia, partim fides; sc. scientia rei in se et rationis objectivae; fides autem, quatenus revelatae [in part knowledge, in part faith; that is, knowledge is based on nature in itself and on objective reason; however faith consists of what is revealed]*.

ᴱ I do not think, that to ingenuitie and indifferencie, tempers, which qualifie to a reception from God; as carnalitie and designing do indispose: anie article of Christian faith *seems* to bee *materia Deo indigna [a subject matter unworthy of God]*: and shoulde itt, itt woulde not bee in a man's power to beleeve itt as from God, while itt so *seems*; though a man shou'd struggle with himself never so much. A man can not think againste the reason of his mind: that of necessitie must be satisfied.—But, I think, a man may trulie say of the grand articles of Christian faith; expiation, remission of sinnes: that to one acquainted with his own state and condition, and considerative of God's goodness, the matter of those articles reveled is rather a matter expected, as becoming God, Godlike; than eyther contrarie to reason, or unworthie of God. I beleeve, in the true use of understanding, a serious and considerative mind wou'd bee apte to think; that eyther God wou'd pardon sinne, to penitents who reform, *absolutelie*; or else wou'd propose a way, in which—and termes and conditions, on which hee wou'd forgive and bee reconciled: God being dulie looked upon, as the fountaine and original of goodness. So that, when the revelation of faith comes; the inward sense, awakened to the entertainment thereof, saith; "*eurêka [I have found it]*⁵, itt is, as I imagined; the thing expected proves"; Christ, the desire of all nations: *sc.* the desire of their state: at least, the necessitie of their state.⁶

So far am I from quarrelling with anie of the revelations of God; my reason is no where so satisfied, as in matter of Christian Faith.

ᴳ If I did say, the last resolution was *in rationem rei [based on natural reason]*; it was *in materia necessaria; in objecto theolgiae naturalis [based on material necessity, with the object of natural theology]*. Are not *rationes boni et mali, aeternae et indispensabiles [reasons good and bad, eternal and indispensable]* of this sorte? and have not you granted, that *materia fidei [matter of faith]* cannot bee *contra rationem rei [contrary to natural reason]*? and, if so; put the case, this is evidentlie *secundum rationem rei [according to natural reason]*; as, that wee are to make conscience of eville: The loose Antinomian pretendes the libertie of the

Gospell, against conscience of sinne: may not I confidentlie conclude, that what hee saith cannot bee *de fide [of faith]*; because itt is *contra rationem rei [contrary to natural reason]*?⁷ Is it not dishonourable to Faith at all, to say; that itt doth acknowledge *rationes rerum, tanquam prius natas, fixas et immobiles [the scheme of things as if already in existence, fixed, and immobile]*; makes no attempt upon them, endeavours no alteration in them. All these are necessarilie so, *positis terminis [when boundaries have been set]*: as, *si sit creatura, ut Deo subsit [if a created being exists, it must depend on God]*: since *fides hominum est in materia arbitraria, respectu voluntatis et beneplaciti Dei [human faith has an arbitrary base, with respect to the will and good-pleasure of God]*. ("Godly, soberly, righteously."⁸ *Tria capita doctrinarum quae nituntur rationibus rerum [Three principles of doctrine that shine because of natural reason]*. And these have not onlie acknowledgment, but Countenance protection and confirmation, under and by the grace of the gospell. *Simus Homines, ut simus Christiani [May we be men, so that we may be Christians]*; said one.) For farther satisfaction herein, I referre you back agen to what immediatlie præceded, ᴱ. Sir, I doubt not, but upon farther consideration you will see this, as cleare as the sunne; and not at all derogatorie to faith, nor diminutive of God's power. You have alreadie granted to mee, what is eyther æquipollent to itt, or necessarilie antecedent to itt; *sc. quod materia fidei non potest esse contra rationem rei [that is, that the subject matter of faith cannot be contrary to natural reason]*: if therfore I do prove a thing to bee *contra rationem rei [contrary to natural reason]*, I doe thereby destroy itt, as a matter of faith. I speake of the Truth and Realitie of the thing; not of what may *seeme* to fondness and partialitie. This principle will certainlie over-rule Antinomians; and there is no danger of acknowledging this rule in divinitie: for it will not bee, what may seeme to this or that party, that is carnal; in a worldlie confederacie or designe; but onlie what reallie and in truth is *contra rationem rei*.

ᴴ The distinction is not vayne: because *amplior est materia divinae libertatis, quam revelationis [the basis of divine freedom is vaster than that of revelation]*: in the second place I consider *materiam libertatis; abstrahendo a revelatione [the basis of liberty, considered apart from revelation]*: in the third, *eandem materiam; sub revelatione [the same basis, under revelation]*. You cannot say, that God hath reveled to us all that he hath determined: nothing becomes a matter of our faith, till itt is a matter of divine revelation: for you well say, that *revelatio Dei est de formali objecto fidei. Idem in diverso statu distingui potest a seipso [the revelation of God concerns the formal object of faith. The same can be distinguished from itself in a different condition]*.

ᴵ I acknowledge your distinction betwen religion, and Christian religion: preciselie this latter includes the former, and superaddes a forme.⁹ And I did meane, that religion had *pro objecto et materiam scientiae naturalis, ortam e rationibus rerum; et materiam fidei, nixam authoritate Dei [for its object, also the subject matter of natural knowledge, arisen from natural reason; and the subject matter of faith, resting on the authority of God]*.

ᴷ I wou'd rather say, *non vocat rationem ad consilium [he does not call reason to his council]*; than *contemnit rationis captum [he condemns the man snared by reason]*. God indeed consults not with us; but with his own wisdom and goodness; (wee being patients and under his cure;) for the invention contrivance and provision of remedie: yett God proposeth, with respect to our understandings; viz. what they can receive, what they are able to beare. And indeed, the matter which hee doth propose, viz. expiation of sinne, in the blood of Christ; and our renovation by Him, into his divine spirit; are things gratefull to man's mind: and, in the sense before express'd, as it were, expected.

ᴸ If you had heard equallie and impartialie, and had not too soone conceeved a prejudice; you might have heard, as you desire, as much spoken of Faith as of Reason: also you had not missed of that, of the want of which you now complayne— I meane, the excellencie and transcendencie of matters of faith to finite apprehension; and the happie superintendencie of the holie spirit over man's mind: which two had large place in that Speech—But *Acuit ira animum; ne possit cernere rectum [Anger sharpens the spirit; lest it be able to discern the truth]*.¹⁰ Itt was then exprest, and hath bin since acknowledged, to you; that *magnalia Dei [the great works of God]* are *majora intellectu finito [beyond the finite intellect]*: wee are now but *viatores [pilgrims]*; yea, when *comprehensores in patria, beatitudo objectiva [we return to our homeland, objective blessedness]* will be inadæquate, as too bigg for us; though the disproportion will bee to our advantage; the vessel more certain to bee filled, because of the sea's dimensions. The peace of God, the life and salt of the world, is said to pass all understanding: yett the mind is never more filled, nor better satisfied, than in these things. This transcendencie of the object to the facultie, is not the mind's greevance; but enlargement and happiness; because itt is not in a way of contradiction to the principles of the mind: therfore in this case there is no danger of the mind's being exasperated, and made to quarrel; but a fayre opportunitie of the mind's being absorpt, ingulft in happiness.

Sir, you will pardon mee; upon this third provocation from you, I must not bee wanting to my own innocencie: at least not to God's truth. I think, I did my self right, where I did God service: and in this respect I appeale from you to God. I well know, that the love of Truth ruled in my heart: and I then had, and still have, such evidence and assurance of being in the truth; that I cannot but think, I never spent hour in my life upon a better account. Sir, I had well considered the matter of the speech, before I came there; had resolved my self, upon manie thoughtes, of the certaintie, of the truth, of the importance and usefulness to the auditorie: when I understood your taking offence, and some others; I gave so much to your authoritie and judgement, that I re-examined all over againe: *et tandem confirmatior evado [and at last thoroughly approved, I escape]*; and am fullie settled in my thoughts, that the matter is unexceptionable; and that which must be stood-to: highlie tending to God's honour, and worthie the Gospell: and there is nothing of realitie against itt, but mistakes, misapprehensions, jealousies, and misprisions. Sir, this I woulde not write to you; did I not think the honour of God and Truth engaged, the interest of soules concerned; and were not I my self so assured; as that thereto, if called to itt, I must give attestation with my life. Therefore, Sir, though I deerelie love you, in my relation to you; and highlie honour you, for your owne worth: yett cannot I, out of respect to you, give-up so noble, so choice a truth; so antidotical against temptation, so satisfactorie, so convictive, so quietive; in so full confirmation, to my mind, of the truth of Christian religion. Sir, this knowledge, God being merciful to mee, I will keepe, till I die: not out of worldlie designe, but out of love to my soule. But if I find itt greevous to others, I shall then onlie reserve itt to my selfe; or at most so farre onlie communicate, as I am admitted by superintendents; and desired by those, with whom I maintaine intimate converse: for itt is my judgement in the case, that noble truth is not to bee imposed or prostituted.[11]

M For the present, I confesse, I do extreamlie wonder att your advice; upon divers grounds: and att several things, which you say in this paragraph. But I do so reverence your person; that I shall dulie weigh and consider what you here offer.— "Not so much nor so often to handle such texts, as are examinable by *ratio rei [right reason]*." Are not such truths of high importance, of clearest evidence and assurance, knowable *lumine innato et naturali, quorum non potest esse ignorantia invincibilis [by an innate and natural light, over which ignorance cannot be invincible]*? whereas *de Christo [concerning Christ]* there easilie may bee *ignorantia invincibilis [an ignorance that is invincible]*; which, as necessarie as the knowledge of Christ is to Salvation, *neminem damnat [condemns nobody]*: the neglect and contradiction whereof damnes, where Christ doth not—the knowledge and observance whereof necessarie, where Christ comes to save. I mean, the neglect and contradiction *veritatum, quarum non est invincibilis ignorantia [of truths, over which ignorance is not invincible]*, damnes; whereas *ignorantia invincibilis de Christo [invincible ignorance about Christ]* doth not damne.[12] Such points are, the creature's due observance of God, complyance with His will, surrender of self up to Him, dependence upon Him, acknowledgement of Him, affection settled on Him, reference to Him: good self-government and moderation in worldlie desires and affections; and composure in a still, quiet, calm, serene apprehension of God: the minde discharged of passion undue affection and molestation from sense: justice, righteousness, equall and fair dealing with men; no insolencie, usurpation, arrogancie, oppression: and a multitude of such excellent doctrines; which, if settled in the heartes and lives of men, wou'd make this worlde resemble Heaven; whereas nowe the contrarie speak Hell broken loose. And *too much* and *too often* on these poyntes! The scripture is full of such truths: and I handle them too much and too often! and not discourse of them, rationallie!—Sir, I oppose not rational to spiritual; for spiritual is most rational: But I contradistinguish rational to conceited, impotent, affected CANTING; (as I may call it; when the Ear receeves wordes, which offer no matter to the Understanding; make no impression on the inward sense.)[13] And I think, where the demonstration of the spirit is, there is the highest purest reason; so as to satisfie, convince, command, the minde: things are most thorowlie seen-into, most cleerlie understood; the minde not so much amused with forms of Wordes, as made acquainted with the inwards of things; the reason of them and the necessarie connexion of termes cleerlie layde-open to the mind and discovered. I have no skill at all in the Bible; if the Prophets, and Apostles, and our Saviour himselfe are not frequente in rationall arguments and argumentations.[14] I acknowledge; that, in matters merelie arbitrarie, and of pure revelation; as manie matters they are engaged in are; (as matters of faith, matters *divinæ voluntatis et beneplaciti [matters of divine will and good-pleasure]*; for which no rule but pleasure: for *in gratuitis non sit injura [in good deeds there is no injury]*: as Matt. xx.15.) they say, *Deus dixit [God has spoken]*; and that is enough and most proper, in that case: but they carefullie make appear, that *ratio rei [natural reason]* is not to the contrarie. They do prove, *per rationes rerum, in necessariis ex se; per authorinatem Dei, quoad ea quae determinantur a libera Dei voluntate [through natural reason, in what necessarily derives from it; through the authority of God, from whence things are determined by the free will of God]*. And this I dare undertake to make-out, by a thousand scriptures.

I allways thought; that *that* doth most affect and command the hearte; which doth most fulie satisfie and convince the minde: and what reacheth the minde, but reason; the reason of the thing? *anima apta nata est subesse rationi: generosus animus hominis ducitur [the soul is born and suited to obey reason; a generous soul leads men]*. And the choicest objects and matters admitt of the cleerest highest fullest reason: because they are most lightsom and bright. *Ratio rei plus valet, urget magis, in Deo; quam in creaturis [Natural reason prevails the more, urges more, towards God, than towards created beings]*: in God, *is* allways infallibly, as *shou'd bee*; *Deus [God]* certainlie *optimus [best]*, as well as *maximus [greatest]*: in the creatures, *is* and *ought to be* often divided. Whether I am "knottie and obscure," in the apprehension of others; I am not so competent a judge: I well understand myselfe. *Judicium sit penes Auditores [May judgment rest with the audience]*. I am nothing, but as God enables mee.

[N & O] *Dignitas et certitudo Christianae religionis [The goodness and certainty of the Christian religion]* are not proveable, by testimonie of scripture; but subsequentlie to the demonstration of the divine authoritie of scripture: now since, as you well say, Christian religion is contened in scripture, as the principal matter of itt; they both stand and fall together: and are proved or impugned by the same arguments. If I had don, as you præscribe; I shoulde then have removed the quæstion from Christian religion to the scripture: and must, *iisdem argumentis, sc. ex qualitate materiae et per testimonium spiritus [by the same arguments, that is, based on the nature of the subject matter and through the witness of the Holy Spirit]*; have proved the divine authoritie of scripture.

There are but three heads of arguments, wherby to prove the authoritie of scripture: *sc.* 1. *insita argumenta [inherent arguments]*: which I comprehend under *qualitas materiae [the nature of the subject matter]*. 2. *testimonium spiritus divini [the witness of the Holy Spirit]*. 3. tradition. *Qualitas materiae [The nature of the subject matter]* consists of verie manie ingredients; as *de qualitate materiae sunt [pertaining to the nature of the subject matter]*, 1. *antiquitas doctrinae [the antiquity of the doctrine]*. 2. *sanctitas et puritas ejusdem [the holiness and purity of the same]*. 3, *finis; sc. extirpatio mali, et liberatio a reatu [the end; that is, the elimination of evil, and the liberation from culpability]*. 4. *harmonia singularum partium inter se [the harmony between the separate parts (of the doctrine)]*. 5. *continuatio doctrinae successivis temporibus [the continuation of doctrine in successive ages]*. 6. *praedictiones, eventibus comprobatae [predictions, proven by events]*. 7. *explicatio fallaciarum Satanae et improbarum [explanations of the lies of Satan and of sinners]*. 8. *virtus obligativa conscientiarum [the virtue obligatory upon consciences]*. 9. *declaratio poenarum iniquitatum, quas scelerati de facto luunt [the declaration of penances, which the wicked, upon accomplishment, expiate]*. 10. *enarratio invictae fidei, quae ubique in Martyribus triumphans est [narrations of unconquerable faith, such as is everywhere triumphant in the Acts of Martyrs]*. 11. *pietas scriptorum, et candor; in agnoscendis infirmitatibus suis, et in dando gloriam Deo [the piety and frankness of writers, in recognizing their own weaknesses, and in giving glory to God]*. 12. *miracula [miracles]*. These respectively qualifie the severall partes of scripture: wherfore you cannot well contradistinguish, as you do, the foretelling and fulfilling of prophesies and miracles: for these, and all the rest, are *argumenta petita a ratione rei; atque sunt de qualitate materiae [arguments sought from natural reason, and which are also based on the nature of the subject matter]*. Hence it appears; that I, proving the nobleness and truth of Christian religion *per testimonium spiritus, et per qualitatem materiae [through the witness of the spirit, and through the nature of the subject matter]*; omitted no argument, but Tradition.[15] *Testimonium spiritus [The witness of the spirit]*, though itt bee triumphant, where itt *is*; the spirit being his owne wittness, and carrying along his owne evidence: yet itt is but *argumentum singulare [a singular argument]*: nothing to him, that feels itt not; though enough to him that doth: whereas, to assert and declare *theoprepeia, a ratione rei, aut a qualitate materiae [godliness, from natural reason, or from the quality of the subject matter]*; is to use a generall argument, universallie conclusive. But I have you excused in this exception: if you had had my speech before you, this mistake on your part had bin prevented; and indeed, the greatest part of our difference is; that you mistake mee. So, you see, that Your two arguments, prophecies and miracles, are *de materia scripturae [concerning the matter of scripture]*: but why you adde "Faith in itt," I cannot in the leaste imagine. I let itt pass in your former paper; being not able to find-out your meaning: and now you send it mee agen; but without anie comment. For itt is but *humana credulitas [human credulity]*, and not *fides divina [divine faith]*; till I receeve upon divine authoritie: and this I am not negligentlie to suppose or imagine; but to have itt made-out to mee. For hee, that beleeves what God saith; without evidence, that God saith itt; doth not beleeve God, while hee beleeves the thing that is from God: *et eadem ratione, si contigisset, Alcorano Turcico credidisset [and by means of the same reason, if it applied, he would have believed the Turks' Koran]*; and for evidence might have alledged his faith in itt.[16] I must

therfore confess; that, in this paragraph of your's, my mind receeves no satisfaction. My faith cannot bee *argumentum pro scriptura [argument in favor of scripture]*; but *authoritas*[17] *scripturae est fidei pro fundamento et statumine [the authority of Scripture is to faith as a foundation and backbone]*.

P I receeve no satisfaction att all, in your scant and narrow interpretation of Prov. xx.27. whereby you prejudice God's talent, committed to our trust; and so lessen both our charge and work. The use, as you express itt, is inadæquate to the principle: (so farre as you weaken the principle in man, you also lessen man's sinne and guilt; and so make man less accountable to God, and less obnoxious:) "The candle of the Lord" signifies no shallow thing: itt is a principle, which speakes much of God in the worlde; and is of great pregnancie: and, under the super-intendencie of God's spirit, is of great sufficiencie and efficiencie.[18] And, I am sure, itt hath verie manie parallel and con-significant scriptures; in the sense given by mee. For the purpose, for which you quote Job xxxii.8. and I Cor. ii.14. I refer you back agen to D : I will as freelie and fullie acknowledge God, as I can possiblie; and will thankfullie learne of you to do itt more. I count itt true sacriledge, to take from God; to give to the Creature: yett I look att itt, as a dishonouring God, to nullify and make base his workes; and to think Hee made a sorrie worthless peece, fitt for no use; when hee made man. I cannot but think of a noble able creature; when I reade *ad imaginem et in similitudinem Dei [in the image and likeness of God]*: or if, *in statu lapso [in a fallen state]*, it be as nothing; then you vilifie the restitution by Christ: as more hereafter.

Q By *quilibet abundet suo sensu [let everyone abide in his own perception]*, I understand no more; than *cuilibet Christiano judicium discretionis [to every Christian freedom of judgment]*: and I shoulde rather have adjoined itt to that, as equivalent to itt; than to *fides non est cogenda [faith cannot be compelled]*. This the fruite of haste—"So as lastlie to resolve *in rationem rei, ex parte objecti; et in rationem nostram, tanquam summum judicem, ex parte subjecti [in natural reason, based on the object; and in our reason, the final and supreme judge, based on the subject]*."—Sir, I perceeve, you took verie deepe offence: else what your selfe quote heere of mine, wou'd give you satisfaction; viz. "perceptive judgement": "neyther auther, nor inventer, nor controuler; as you well express itt." For the former part— *in rationem rei, ex parte objecti [in natural reason, based on the object]*; I referre you back to G and D : because I woulde not repete. For the latter, *in rationem tanquam judicem, ex parte subjecti [by reason as the final judge]* :—I remember, I then told you; that it was improper to call the scripture *judex [judge]*; which connotes a person; but *regula et norma fidei [a rule and guide to faith]*. (I then exprest myself; that *judex tenetur sententiam ferre secundum legem; non pro suo arbitrio: atque judex est infra legem, et legi subjectus [a judge is held to give sentence according to law, not arbitrarily; and the judge is beneath the law, and subject to the law]*.) If I did say, *summus judex [the supreme judge]*; itt was respectively to persons, severallie considered; in the sense acknowledged by all Protestants.—*Cuilibet Christiano judicium discretionis [To every Christian freedom of judgment]*; as against the Pope, who arrogates to himself to be *judex infallibilis, visibilis; quoad sensum scripturae, et controversias fidei [an infallible and visible judge, in regard to the interpretation of scripture and controversies of faith]*: so exclusively, in respect of fellow-creatures, not assumed by God in special, as His instruments; not indued with infallibilitie, *quoad hoc [as far as that goes]*: but submissively, in respect of God and revelation from Him; both of matter wordes and meaning: all which determine Us; and at our perill bee itt, if we willinglie mistake, or willfullie elude, his sense. God, who is *kardiognôstês [knower of the heart]*, is judge. Wherefore I marvaile, that you shoulde stick att itt so; [19]for the discerning to resolve *in rationem hujus vel illius hominis, tanquam judicem, ex parte subjecti [the reason of this or that man, as if a judge, in the subjective sense]*: in as much as everie Christian must have particular knowledge, must see with his own eyes, must not compromise, must himself bee satisfied: *aliter redibit fides implicita, papistica, carbonaria [otherwise faith is rendered confused, Papistic, that of charcoal-burners]*: and wee must to ROME again.—"Exalting the power of nature"—To mee a strange imputation! I have indeed called upon men; supposing, as I ought, God to bee with them; to use and employ all gifts, both of grace and nature: the neglect of which, I am sure, will prove matter of self-conviction. But for this I referre you back to [D].—"Suspicions and Misprisions—causing Heats and Oppositions—Your and some other's so much going in an other strayne—" Where they are so groundless and causeless, and some take too much upon them; there is no certain remedie applyable: I do not think, while this temper continues, offences can bee avoided.— Sir, permitt me also *animam liberare [to free my soul]*; and to deale freelie and cleerlie: and I pray, itt may bee without offence. Lett the matter of difference bee discovered: in order to a removall and a more inward closing. I cannot returne to that frame of spirit, in the judging and discerning the things of God; you here and there, in my apprehension, seeme to advise mee to. I have had, in the former parte of my life, experience thereof; and having freelie and fullie delivered myself up to God, to bee taught and ledde into truth; my minde is so framed and fashioned by Him, (or else I am greatlie deceeved in my religion;) that I can no more look back, than St. PAUL, after Christ discovered to him, coulde returne into his former strayne.[20] I give much to the spirit of God, breathing in good men; with whom I converse, in the present worlde; in the universitie and other where: and think; that, if I may learne much by the writings of good men, in former ages; which you advise mee to; and, I hope, I do not neglect: that, by the actings of the divine spirit, in the minds of good men now alive, I may learn more: and I must not shutte my eyes against anie manifestations of God, in the times in which I live. The times, wherein I live, are more to mee; than anie else: the workes of God in them, which I am to discerne; direct in mee both principle affection and action. And I dare not blaspheme free and noble spirits in religion, who search after truth with indifference and ingenuitie: lest in so doing I should degenerate into a spirit of *Persecution*, in the reallitie of the thing; though in another guise: For a mistaken spirit may conceit itt self to bee acted by the zeal of God.[21] And I have observed; that, in *former* times, some; whose names and memories I otherwise honour, and value their writings; have bin sharp and censorious, severe and keen: even to the persecution of such, whom I doubte not but God had receeved. And I greatly feare; that some allso, in *our* times, do so too. And I do beleeve; that the destroying this spirit out of the Church, is a peece of the Reformation; which God, in these times of changes, aimes att: and I feare to bee under the power of the anti-character to the worke that God is about; and to stand disaffected to what God is doing in the worlde. (Hereby I give not way to loose wilde phansies in religion; nor to bolde presumptions: but I do acknowledge true worth; and dulie consider what I finde cause to thinke God imprintes on the spirits of truely good men: who with honest heartes seeke to Him, to be ledde into truth.)—Sir, you have now an account of the secret sense of my Soule; and I have told you, what God hath whispered in my eare: or else I am under such a delusion; as I think, God never delivers such up to; as with honest heartes seeke to Him. And I pray you, Sir, so farre as you value mee in religion, consider this thing with freedom; laying aside awhile præ-suppositions and præ-possessions.—They, who differ from mee, in some apprehensions; though I may conceeve the things, as I apprehend them, weightie; and so, in respect of my own person, I am bound: may bee as honest-hearted towards God and as well lovers of Truth; as I my-self am. In this case I must leave Them to runne Their hazard, of being right or wrong; as I must do Mine: everie one stands or falles to his owne master: (Neyther herein do I consider *Men*; as you seeme to understand me: so much as the account they give for what they say. Some rules and principles being certain and infallible; with which no resolution in matters less certain, may in anie wise clash.) And, where I suppose mistakings, in matters of weight; and itt is a hard matter for mee to determine an equall necessitie to several persons of different parts, education, apprehensions, and under various manifestations from God: as in the case of the "other-wise minded"[22] yet I have nothing harder to say, than that "God shall revele even this to them." I persuade myself; if simple mis-apprehension, or ignorance, of some matters in religion for a time, through darker manifestation of them from God; were so extreamlie dangerous, as some imagine: our Saviour, in good affection, had sooner declared them; more fullie awakened the non-consideration of his disciples.—But, to returne to what I was saying before; I am out of doubte, that trulie good men, dear to God, fell under the persecution of the tongue, the pen, the mis-report, of persons of eminencie; whom, save in this, I do not condemne; but think them among the number of the better sort of their times: in causes, wherein they were not onlie honest-hearted and meant well; but were little, if at all, mistaken. And I pray God, our zeale, in these times, may bee so kindled with pure fire from God's altar; that itt may rather warm, than burn; enliven rather, than enflame: and that the spirits of good men may truely be qualified with Gospell-principles, true fruites of the divine spirit. *Gal.* v.22, 23.—And truely, I think; that the members of the Church, if not the leaders; notwithstanding all the perfections of times before us, so much pretended or applauded; in this point have verie much yett to learne. For I am persuaded; that Christian love and affection, among all partakers of the Gospell-grace is a point of such importance, and certain foundation; so pressed upon us by our Saviour, and his Apostles; that itt is not to be prejudiced, by *supposals* of differences, in points of religion anie wayes disputable; though thought weightie, as determined by the parties on eyther side: nor yett by the *trulie* different persuasions of those; who cannot bee satisfied, eyther in our conceited formes of expression; or particular determinations beyond scripture: which, as some have observed, have indeed enlarged Divinitie; but have lessened Charitie, and multiplied Divisions.[23] For the maintenance of truth, is rather God's charge; (*John* xvi.13.) and the continuance of charitie, our's: (*Heb.* xiii.1.) "Let brotherlie love continue."—There is no exception. Let him bee cautious, who limitts; as considering, that the account is to bee given to God. I think, I may suppose, without offence; that the cunning Devill, who is allways vigilant to do mischeefe; may lay a snare, in the notion of Orthodoxie, against Charitie. *In paradiso Dei serpens latet in insidiis [In God's paradise the serpent lurks in ambush]*. And, as I said before, persons valuable for their love and desire of truth, differing from us, generallie meane better; than our prejudice, occasioned upon this difference, admitts us to conceeve of them: for I make account, that scripture is so cleere and satisfactorie, in matters of weighte; (*Omnia necessaria perspicue traduntur [All that is necessary is clearly handed down]*:) that none, but They, who unworthily practise and design upon truth; can bee mistaken: and these in religion are not considerable; as not being under the power of *itt*, but serving ends: but sure enough, where the Love of truth rules in the hearte, the Light of truth will guide the minde. I beleeve, itt is not to bee found, in scripture, *or otherwhere*; that honestie uprightness, integritie, are in conjunction with hæresie: and the scripture way is, to rectifie simple misapprehensions with tenderness.[24] (Indeed that principle, of scripture's perfection sufficiencie and perspicuitie, inclines me to think; that They, who fullie come-up to scripture; and set themselves with ingenuitie to find-out the sense; seeking to God, to guide them; being not under the power of anie lust, or corruption, or worldlie interest; will *not* substantiallie differ, in their resolved judgements about verie materiall things: as you seem to suppose, [R].)

Sir, this I write to you, out of a good mind; and in the fear of God: with greate respect to You, whom I deerlie love and highlie honour: I think, You write your heart to Mee; and so do I to You: ELIJAH despised not, what the *Raven* brought:[25] I *may be* mistaken; but I think, I *am not*. However, this is my judgement; and I am under the power of these apprehensions: and I pray to God, if I bee in the wrong, to revele farther unto mee; and blessed bee the messenger, sent to mee on His errand; the instrument Hee useth, to remove mee from my errour.—Neyther is itt in my mind, by aught of this I write, to countenance anie loose libertie in religion: for I am well resolved concerning such, in the defence of whom I am engaged; that they are under the power of what in religion is most vital and characteristical. You were pleased to contra-distinguish Orthodoxie and Ingenuitie; which I choose rather to reconcile: and think, that they may fayrely stand together.

[R] In things or expressions, only determinable by scripture, *extra ultra citra scripturum [outside of, beyond, and short of scripture]*; how shall I discover more or less orthodox? who hath extarordinarie commission? who hath the priviledge of infallibilitie? who shall judge? by what warrant can we characterize or distinguish, by non-scripture phrase?

<sup>S</sup> For myselfe; I shall take no more libertie, than is allowed to mee: *Impotentis*[26] *est, non posse sibi soli sapere; et filere [He is impotent, who is unable even to know himself; and barren]*. But I shoulde bee glad; that everie other person, that is considerable in religion; shoulde both have and use the libertie, to tell mee; what he findes cause to beleeve or disbeleeve.—"Not outwardlie to express disagreement &c,"—Whatever others have don; I am sure, I am yett to beginne: and herein I shall followe your counsil.

<sup>T</sup> I never meant, that the cause shou'd bee estimated by men's persons; but men's expressions, by the rule of truth; and their pretenses, by the rule of goodness.

<sup>Z</sup> I only say; itt wou'd signifie somthing: if you wou'd first resolve, who shall judge? (Vide <sup>R</sup>.)

<sup>A2</sup> The WALDENSES and ALBIGENSES[27] pleaded for itt: all under oppression have seen itt: *Vexatio dat intellectum [Vexation gives (itself) to intellects]*.

<sup>B2</sup> Itt is cleerlie the foundation of Protestancie; as *Judex infallibilis visibilis [an infallible and visible Judge]* is of Popery.

<sup>C2</sup> You make Socinianism and Arminianism less formidable: but surelie you do not well, *movere terminos [move the boundary stones]*; much less, to multiplie differences.—Is itt enough? the religion of the nation? of one's education?—You say, "in finding-out *new* truth, and cleering the *old*"—Do you in earnest and consideratelie suppose this?—1. A good ground of Moderation, forbearance and tenderness. 2. This may do well, for his own use: but, according to your principles, hee may not propose to others what hee finds.

<sup>D2</sup> A steward's diligence and fidelitie in his truste, is *one* thing; and his usurpation upon his Lord, is *an other*. Let the Lord make rules for his house; and the Steward take care for the observance of them. The trusted must keep within the limits of his commission. *Non amo nimium diligentes, officiosos nimium [I do not like the excessively diligent and officious]*. Let not UZZAH reach-out his hand to the tottering ark: let not SAUL's haste or danger put him on sacrificing.—[28]"Contend-for the faith"—but against whom? [29]"ungodlie, turning the grace of God into lasciviousness, denyers of the Lord Jesus."—Is there heere a check to the spirit of ingenuitie? Yea rather, "woulde to God, that all the Lord's people were Prophets."[30] Speak to my spirituall edification, who can.

<sup>G2</sup> I onlie borrowed the Prophet's phrase; not considering the context: my meaning was inoffensive "—An unjustifiable phrase—*recipitur [it is received]*, a moral *nascitur [born from within]*." I perceeve, itt is verie hard to remove an offence, once by you taken. Herein, I promised my self; I shou'd satisfie you: but you strain and stretch, to the utmoste possibilitie of the worser sense: in your <sup>H2</sup> you are first satisfied, then doubte; but in your <sup>I2</sup> you are quite off againe. Certainly, that "*voluntas creata [created will]* doth *formaliter producere actum credendi et poenitendi [formally produce the act of believing and of penitence]* <sup>K2</sup>—*elicere actum fidei [it draws forth the act of faith]* <sup>C</sup>—and saith the act of an intelligent

rationall creature ᶜ—all which you say; importe as much as *nascitur [born from within]*, in my sense.

 ᴷ² *Formaliter [Formally]* and *Vitaliter [Vitally]* are equivocall, in ordinarie use: *atque usus et communis consensus sunt regula vocabulorum. Verba valent ut Nummi. Loquendum cum Vulgo [But practice and general consensus provide rules for verbal usage. Words prevail as if they were coins. It's necessary to speak with the populace]*.

 ᴸ² "*Ab eo nascitur [From that which is born]*"—Before, you did ~~falsif~~[31] torture, to make confess what was not there; heere, give me leave to say, mis-quote: itt was *è* not *à*: and these distinguish causes, matter and efficient, or cause and subject.

 ˢ² Have I not always considered the mind of man, in order to good; as in conjunction with the divine spirit? and is not Christ the foundation of recoverie in the creation? So that a *recta ratio* is to be found.

 ʸ² I think, our Saviour's doctrine needes no apologie; nor that of his Apostles after him.

 ᴰ³ This is eternal life: to know thee, the onlie true God; and Jesus Christ, whom thou hast sent.[32]

 ᶠ³ I have verie much heere to say: but I will reserve myself for another time. Are not the third chapter to the PHILIPPIANS, and the third chapter to the GALATIANS, fulle in the arguments you desire? If so, you have an answer. For those you conjoyne with mee; I think, their excellencie lies in a reall and effectuall participation of Christ and of his spirit. I profess myself as full and cleere, as any one in the worlde; in that grand poynte, of our acceptance with God, in and through Christ:—Yett I confess, I cannot but marvaile; to see you balance matters of knowledge, againste principles of goodness; and seeme to insist-on Christ, less as a principle of divine nature in us; than as a sacrifice for us. I acknowledge, they both speak the rich grace of God in Christ to man: I mean, expiation of sinne, in the bloud of Christ, and true participation of the divine nature, to the making of us trulie Godlike or conform to God, through Christ being formed in us: and I know not well—or rather dare not, compare them: both being the provision of Heaven, to make us capable of happiness; and fundamentallie necessarie to our safetie. But certainlie, if wee consider difficultie or danger, in relation to persons; as the subjects or receevers of these great blessings from Heaven: then one is more easilie understood and readilie pretended; when-as the other, as whollie contrarie to carrnalitie, is stuck-att and greatlie neglected. How easie to say, (many allso continuing to "make provision for the flesh, to fullfill the lustes thereof";[33] while they so say and think;) Christ died for mee—self-flatterie saying itt, as well as faith;—and I do *fiduciam in eo collocare [place trust in it]*—the greatest sinner having least matter of self-confidence:—when-as whole inordinate self riseth-up in rebellion, against self-surrender into divine will; and real transformation of man into the spirit image and nature of Christ! And this latter being the great demonstration of the veritie of the subject's faith of the former; itt may seeme, that the former may bee best secured, by the frequente confirmation of and much insisting-upon the latter: the former being understood once for ever, upon a full declaration and thorowe consideration of it; (for once knowen, and ever: *intellectus post primum actum est in habitu, et transit in memoriam intellectivam; atque fides consolidat, comfortat, simplicem intelligentiam [intelligence, after first acting, becomes habitual, and passes into intellectual memory; but faith reinforces and confirms the simple understanding]*:) but the latter being not otherwise to be knowen, than by being felt: which is not, save as sensualitie is mortified and crucified.

(In the Apostles' times, Justification by Faith in Christ was not knowen; or not beleeved: whereas now it is both knowen, and generallie professed: in which respect itt may be well said to bee *Doctrina illorum*[34] *temporum [the Doctrine of those ages]*. Men are to be both informed satisfied and convinced about itt.)

In the Apostles' times; to relinquish the Mosaicall dispensation, and to entertein the Gospell-frame, and to acknowledge all types, promises, prophesies concerning God's Messiah, fullfilled in this person Jesus Christ; signified in persons some more remarkable work of God: than now to acknowledge Christ, and profess some expectation from him; when-as itt is the religion of the Nation, and the first point of Education; and whosoever sticks at itt, is looked-att as a prodigie and monster. Now that Christ is more knowen and freelie professed, let him allso be inwardlie felt, and secretlie understood; as a principle of divine life within us, as well as a Saviour without us. (Christ is the Leaven of Heaven; sent into the world, and given to us; to leaven us into the nature of God.) And this, I conceeve, is worthie Gospell-preachers (as your phrase is) to do; in this progresse and proficiencie of Gospell knowledge and grace, and farther advance of the kingdom of the Messiah: "'speciallie, when-as wee live in a croud of menne"; who indeed professe some zeale for that happie poynt of "Justification by Faith"; yett are sensiblie degenerated into the devilish nature of malice, spight, furie, envie, revenge: in this case, the justification of faith in the world; as allo the subject's satisfaction, of the truth of itt in himself; is the certain conjunction of sanctification, holiness, and a divine nature, with itt; in the nature and reason of the thing, as allso God's purpose and worke.

But, though I knowe, your jealousie and suspicion is groundless; in respect of mee and others; and that you are wholely mistaken, in your apprehensions: as somtime the tenn tribes were, concerning the two:[35] yett, because I highlie honour your person, and greatlie consider you in religion; and the matter is of high importance and consequence: I shall bee, as the suspected there, (from *v.* 21 to the end of the chapt.) zealous and earneste for your satisfaction: and therfore, to what I have here and there, occasionallie, now and before said, I farther adde—I am verie free to acknowledge Christ, the onlie foundation; since the apostasie and sinne of man: Hee alone gave the stoppe to God's just displeasure; His interposing prevayled with God, not to take the forfeiture; or, if taken, Hee procured the restauration and recoverie. Upon this accounte I acknowledge Christ, in parts of nature, reason and understanding; as well as in gifts of grace: so that Christ is not by mee anie where left-out, nor faith neglected; no, nor not advanced to a superioritie and supereminencie everie-where: for I beleeve, that I hold and enjoy my reason and understanding, by and under Christ. And what I have meant exprest and endeavoured all along, hath bin; to call men to the due and carefull use and employment and improvement of what they hold by and under Christ. You have no cause to suspect mee for scant and narrow apprehensions of free grace, Christ's merittes and divine goodness: yett I confess my shallowness; but that is my greevance and burthen: and I woulde have my apprehensions raised, and my thoughts of the Gospell enlarged. I attribute to the creature, upon itt's own accounte, nothing but unworthiness inabilitie and insufficiencie: and look-at Christ, as the onlie ground of acceptance; and his spirit, as the onlie principle of enablement power and sufficiencie.

Sir, these things being by mee freelie and heartilie written and professed, as the most inward sense of my mind; bee pleased to look-back, and consider with yourself; how unsuitable to the frame and temper of my spirit, that representation hath bin; which you have made of mee to your selfe, in your own thoughts: so that I may say; that none hath less trulie knowen mee.

T2 Give mee leave heere, though out of place, to adde—What is in man more considerable, than that; which declares God's law to him, pleades for the observation, accuseth for the breach, excuseth upon the performance?

V2 —The rule, whereby I must judge Orthodox—Those, who speak conformablie to my inward sense of God and his truth, to my impartial apprehension of the scripture-dictate, and the *rationes rerum [the scheme of things]*.

W2 Who leaves them rather to their judge, than hee; who passeth no sentence upon them, as to their final estate?

A3 "We walk by *faith*," till wee bee comprehensors; till wee bee possessed of all that blessedness, which is promised and expected. A true complacential *love* signifies somthing of fruition, in what degree soëver: and whether, and how farre, a man may enter into this state in this life; let Him determine, who hath acted to the utmost extent permissible, of a trulie divine free and unrestrained faith: which is the *prodromus [forerunner]* thereto.

O2 Sure, itt will not bee a casting shame on the Gospell; to say and shew, that what hath bin most worthie and like to divine, in severall ages of the world; hath held best and fullest conformitie with the Gospell.—

In reading Heathen authours, I have affected to imitate the Bee; rather than the Spider. When I said, "good, as farre as they have gon"; I did not exclude *mixturam mali [mixture of evil]*: but they they have don well in some truths, wherein they have engaged; (not doubting nevertheless of a farther advance, *accedente lumine gratiae [if the light graciously dawns]*:)[36] as, *de fruitione ultimi finis; de tranquillitate animae; de contemptu mundi; de amore veri; de zelo rectitudinis et justitiae [concerning the fulfillment of the end times, the tranquility of the soul, contempt for this world, the love of truth, the passion for rectitude and justice]*: These and other noble truths they have well defended and justified; againste the base practise of the degenerating and apostatizing worlde.[37]—

*Est aliquid prodire tenus; si non datur ultra.*[38]
*[It is something to get this far; if I can get no further.]*

*Fides divina non contemnit regulam boni moralis [Divine faith does not despise the rule of good morality].* Now these things of them, as they are usefull to true beleevers; so they are reprochfull to vayne pretenders, who are not honest. *Non semper causam criminantur, qui personam [They are not always incriminated on the ground of their position, but on their character].*

[B3] *Media ordinem mensuram et amabilitatem sumunt a Fine. Nunquam sistendum est in usu Mediorum: omnia Finibus perficiuntur [They mistake for the end the midpoint of a straight and pleasant road. One must never stop halfway; all things are accomplished at their end].* They, who mistake the Means for the End, may be reproved; without prejudice to the Means.

Sir, I will only superadde my craving your pardon for this tediousness; which I little intended, which I begunne. I perceeve, the matter under examination doth not lessen in our handes. If you can receeve anie satisfaction concerning Mee, by aught I have written; I have enough: Your-self I leave to your owne greater experience, and better thoughts. I shall not the less honour you; though my judgement do not wholelie come-up to you.—When you have perused, I pray, return to mee this paper: for I have no coppy.

# Notes

1. BW: "*The Spirit of a man is the Candle of the Lord,* &c. (Prov. xx.27). Natural light may easily be transcended, but not contradicted or impugn'd. That can't be of the Spirit of God which is contradictory to Natural Light" (*SSN*, 9).

2. BW: "The *Spirit of a Man is the Candle of the Lord*; Lighted *by* God, and Lighting us *to* God. *Res illuminata, illuminans*" (*MRA* §916).

3. BW: "The *Spirit* in us, is the Reason of our Minds Illuminated by the *Written* Word. The Spirit *now* Teaches, by these Writings" (*MRA* §337).

4. "Thou shalt not beare false witnes against thy neighbour" (Ex. 20.16). *Ed.*

5. Allegedly said by the ancient engineer Archimedes. *Trans.*

6. BW: "All that the Gospel requires, is, Repentance from Dead Works, and Faith in the Lord Jesus Christ.... For will not any one acknowledge, that if an Inferior give Offence to a Superior, he ought to humble himself, and ask Forgiveness? Can any Man's Reason in the World be unsatisfied in this?—Then, for Faith in our Lord Jesus Christ; is it not very equal, and fit, that if God will pardon Sin, he shoul'd do it in what way he thinks fitting? that if we go to him for Cure, he should take that way to recover us which he thinks best?... Therefore these *Terms* are not only just and equal in themselves; but tend to the Quiet and Satisfaction of a Man's Mind; *and* are restorative to our Natures.—Now the Representation that is made to us by Divine Truth, either natural, or reveal'd, is that which is satisfactory and consonant to the Reason of our Mind" (*SS*, Part I, Sermon I, 18-19).

7. BW: "For, *Liberty*, as a Perfection, is quite another thing from being licentious, or lawless. *He* is least of all FREE, nay he is the veriest *Slave* in the World, that hath either *Will* or POWER to be licentious, or exorbitant, or to vary from *the Law of Right*" (*SS*, Part II, Sermon II, 201).

8. SS: "Tit. ii.11,12" (103 n).

9. BW: "God's end in Man's Creation, was, *Acts* 17. that we should feel out, and palpitate after himself, though he be not far from us all; for in him we live, move, and subsist: and this was spoken of the first communication of himself to Man, in which sense the Spirit of Man is his Candle, *Prov.* 24. Wherefore I reckon upon a true account, that Religion is the most natural thing to Man's mind in the World. And therefore, with *Plato*, I dare not define a man *Animal rationale*, *i.e.* a rational Creature, (but *Animal religiosum*, a religious Creature) for a very near representation thereof we find in the sagacity of inferiour Creatures. But Man alone (standing higher by the head and shoulders than all his fellow-Creatures) can take cognizance of *God*" (*SSN* 85-6).

10. SS: "Dr. WHICHCOTE seems to have cited the old metrical Saw, by memory; so as not only not to have preserved the words and measure; but even not the sense of it. *Acuit*, in Latin, is from his purpose wholely; though *sharpens*, in English, is proper; in one sense of the word. The verse is, *Impedit ira animum; no possit cernere verum [Anger impedes the soul, so that it is not able to discern the truth]*; if I remember it" (105 n).

11. SS: "Matt. x.11,13" (107 n). BW: "Nothing should *alienate* us from one another; but that which alienates us from God"; "Charity of universal extent, is better than Truth of particular apprehension. If we maintained only such Truth, as is unquestionable; our Religion wou'd be *cool* enough. Defend God's Truth, in God's Way" (*MRA* §206, §1164).

12. BW: "*Ignorance* is no Principle of any Action. No Ignorance can excuse *Immorality*, in any Instance whatsoever: but invincible Ignorance doth excuse *Infidelity*, in the chiefest Point" (*MRA* §361).

13. BW: "*The Way of Reason is the Way most accommodate to human Nature.* Therefore let us lay aside imposing one upon another; or to use any canting in Religion. Let us talk Sense, and Reason; for the Apostle doth here shew, and prove *by Reason*: And God himself, who hath all Privilege, he says, he will draw them *with the Cords of Men*. And what is that, but *Arguments* satisfactory to the Mind of Men?" (*SS*, Part I, Sermon III, 66).

14. BW: "The Scripture-way of Dealing with Men, in Matters of Religion, is always by Evidence of Reason and Argument" (*SS*, Part I, Sermon III, 77).

15. BW: "The Sense of the *Church* is not a *Rule*; but a thing *Ruled*. The Church is bound unto Reason and Scripture, and governed by them, as much as any *particular* Person" (*MRA* §921).

16. BW: (1) "*This* also is to put a Lye upon a Man's self, to perswade one's self in any thing without warrant of Reason or Scripture. *To settle in an Opinion, without warrant of Reason, or credible Testimony*, is *Impotency and Fondness*. CREDULITY is a Stranger to Wisdom, and the very *Nurse of Superstition*" (*SS*, Part II, Sermon I, 150); (2) "It is the greatest Impotency in the World easily to believe. It should be the slowest act that ever a man puts forth, to believe, considering how full the World is of Impostures, of falshood, and of lies. ... Better it is to have knowledge without Opinion, than Opinion without knowledge. For in things that are doubtful, thou mayest know both ways without harm; but thou canst not have an Opinion, but either thou are right, or wrong. Either in an Error or in a Truth" (*SSN*, 8).

17. *Sic*; correct spelling: *auctoritas. Trans.*

18. BW: "So if a Man do but use *Reason*; he must see, and acknowledge *God*. The wise Man tells us, That the *Spirit of a Man is the Candle of the Lord*, Prov. xx.27. A Candle lighted by God, and serving to this Purpose; to discern and discover God. And, truly, were it not thus; where in would consist the Excellency of human Nature, above the inferior Nature" (*SS*, Part II, Sermon VI, 294).

19. SS: "The words 'for the discerning' are extremely obscure, if not absolutely unintelligible; and seem to be out of place here" (114 n).

20. SS: "*Hinc illae lacrymae!*" (115 n).

21. BW: "Men say, it is *Zeal of God, for Truth*; and that they ought to be *zealous for the Truth*; and think they may prosecute their Brother upon that account; because he is not of their Judgment: He is in an Error, they say, and therefore they think they ought to bear him down, upon this account. Therefore, this Pretence must be examin'd. To which end I shall suggest these several Considerations: *First*, it cannot be avoided, but that Men *must think, as they find cause*. For, this is most certain, that no Man is Master of his own Apprehensions; but he must think (and cannot avoid it) *according as he finds cause*. *Secondly*, It is no Offence to another, than any Man hath the Freedom of his own Thoughts. By this, he doth his Neighbour no Wrong" (*SS*, Part II, Sermon IV, 239). Cf. Tuckney's first letter (Letter I, 72). *Ed.*

22. SS: "Phil. iii.15" (117 n).

23. BW: "Determinations, *beyond* Scripture, have indeed *enlarged* Faith; but lessened *Charity*, and multiplied Divisions" (*MRA* §981).

24. BW: "All that in any Scripture are branded for Sinners, they are Men that sin against their Knowledge, imprison the Truth of God, and hold it in Unrighteousness. In the Language of Scripture, none are nominated Sinners, but such as *now* we are representing. The Scripture doth never fasten the Title or Denomination upon them that mean well, but are in something mistaken; who now and then are under an Error, having Failings, Imperfections, and Shortnesses; that miscarry upon a violent Temptation or sudden Surprisal. You never find these Men are called *Sinners*: Neither are the Infirmities of the Regenerate call'd *Sin*; tho' these are Sins that require God's Forgiveness, and are a true Cause for us to be humble, and modest, and to depend upon God: But they do not break our Peace with God; neither do they havock Conscience, or denominate a Person *a Sinner*" (*SS*, Part I, Sermon III, 55-6).

25. After prophesying against King Ahab, the prophet Elijah is commanded by God to flee to the brook Cherith, where "the ravens brought him bread and flesh in the morning, and bread and flesh in the evening: and hee dranke of the brooke" (1 Kngs. 17.2-6). *Ed.*

26. *Sic*; correct spelling: *impotens. Trans.*

27. The WALDENSES—named after Peter Waldo, a merchant of Lyons who gave up his possessions in order to feed the poor and to travel about, preaching the gospel. After refusing a papal order forbidding them to preach, the Waldenses were anathematized in 1183. The ALBIGENSES—named after the town of Albi, where, in the year 1176, a council condemned their teachings—were comprised of a variety of Manichaean sects in southern France and northern Italy during the twelfth and thirteenth centuries (*A Dictionary of Sects, Heresies, Ecclesiastical Parties and Schools of Religious Thought*, ed. J. H. Blunt [London: Rivingtons, 1874]). A popular account of the persecutions of the Waldenses and Albigenses is given by John Foxe, in his *History of the Acts and Monuments of the Church*, printed in Latin at Basle in 1554, translated into English in 1563. *Ed.*

28. SS: "Jude 3" (122 n). The Old Testament passages concerning UZZAH and SAUL are, respectively, 2 Sam. 6.6-7 and 1 Sam. 13.5-14. *Ed.*

29. SS: "Jude 4" (122 n).

30. SS: "Numb. xi.29" (122 n).

31. SS: "Thus written in the MS, with a line drawn through it" (123 n). Although the copy of this letter in Whichcote's possession was made by the hand of Tuckney, this cancelled word is not his error, but was faithfully reproduced and commented on by him in his reply (Letter VII). *Ed.*

32. SS: "*John* xvii.3" (123 n).

33. SS: "Rom. xiii.14" (124 n).

34. SS: "Sic MS: but Q. whether it should not be *horum*" (125 n).

35. SS: "*Josh.* xxii.10-21" (126 n).

36. BW: "The death and passion of Christ, are not of our invention. When we were lost, had not he awakened us, we might have felt our own misery, but not have known that we were plunged into it. The Plylosophers themselves in this necessitated extremity, and sad condition, had some sense of their misery, but no knowledge of recovery" (*SSN*, 61).

37. BW: "In Morals, all those of the Heathens that have attain'd to any Reformation, either to the Improvement of their Intellectuals, or the Refinement of their Morals, they all concur with these immutable and indispensable Verities" (*SS*, Part I, Sermon I, 13).

38. Horace, *Ep.* 1.1.32. *Ed.*

# Letter VII

## Dr. TUCKNEY's Fourth Letter.

Sir,

All the spare time I coulde gaine, since the receit of your last papers, has bin spent in writing-out a coppy of them: which, according to your desire, I return; with thanks for your paines in them, and with craving pardon, if I spare mine at present; (if at all) in replying to them. *Currente rota urceus exit [The nettle escapes the moving wheel]*[1]. Farther to engage, will make the worke long and bulkie; and my spare time is short and little: and I have other things to employ itt in. Your præface, though itt seeminglie shoote att rovers; yett, I guess, is particularlie levelled att my replies: which I desired, might be profitable; butt, itt seemes, are troublesom. If "exceptions againste wordes and phrases," I am content they shall go in the rank of that *Canting*, you afterwarde speak-of. "*Omnis ingenii acies post primum impetum hebescit [the sharpness of every mind is blunted after its first attack]*"—so brittle the metal may bee; and if the assailant hath spent all his powder, and wroughte himselfe out of breath, in his first charge: and then a broom, worne to the stumpes, rather scratcheth, than cleanseth. But some heavie dull menne are awakened and come to themselves, at the second or third encounter—*Bos lassus fortius figit pedem [The tired ox more sturdily plants his feet]*.[2]

In the bodie of your after-discourse, in some things I finde you immovable; you being, as you write, under the power of them: and therfore itt would bee in vayne, as to them, for mee to move anie farther: itt is enough, that I have faithfullie expressed myself to you about them. In some other particulars, you satisfie mee, that your judgement is sound; for the main: though I remayne unsatisfied, in diverse things that you express about them. But that, which most dissuades mee from farther engaging, is; that up and down in those papers, though you express divers times more respect to mee, than I deserve; yett withall there are in divers places scattered some harde wordes: as, suspicions, jealousies, provocations, torturing (and itt was allmost *falsifying*) your wordes; your perceeving itt is harde to remove an offense once by mee taken; and that some take too much upon them, *&c.*—which must needs render mee verie disingenuous in your eyes: and therfore att present, I cannot but think itt best to forbear. However, when I can gaine anie little time, (and I hope itt will not bee long, before I shall;) I may putt down in writing some kind of reply to what in your papers I am not satisfied in: that, although I willinglie forbear your trouble; yett att leaste, when I am dead; some, that shall 'light on my papers, may see; that itt was not because I had nothing to say, that I now say nothing: but onely, that I heartilie and humblie beseech God; that both You and I may bee kept in the Faith, and may followe the Truth in Love.—Which with desire and presents of my due respects, I remaine,

Sir,

*Yours, to love and honour you;*
ANTH. TUCKNEY.

October 31. 1651.

# Notes

1. Horace, *Ars Poetica* (Liber Alter, *Ep.* 3.) 22. *Trans.*
2. Erasmus, *Adages* 1.1.47. *Trans.*

# Letter VIII

## Dr. WHICHCOTE's Fourth Letter.

Sir,

 Since I know, if I know myselfe att all; that, in the discerning of truth, I do not dallie; nor have anie worldlie designe: but with all indifferencie of mind do receeve from God, what I have assurance is from Him: I cannot practice upon my judgement; nor use anie force to command my understanding into other apprehensions, in the matter debated betwixt us; than I have exprest to you. For what sense wordes spoken by God bear, and what the reason of the thing appears to bee, to my understanding, assisted by God's Spirit; themselves give law to mee, and wholely over-rule mee: so that itt is not in my power to fall-off from mine own persuasions conceptions and thoughts so grounded. Wherfore if, in this poynte of discerning, we differ; there is no helpe for it: wee must forbear one another: and nothing is to bee done, unless so farre mutuallie to value each other's judgements; as to think, that from such difference there is occasion given to each of us, to examin our own spirits; whether we reteine that indifferencie and ingenuitie in discerning, wee ought allwayes to bee cloathed withall. I think not the worse of You at all, for aught wherein wee differ; but conceeve, you see most cause to say and apprehend, as you do. My self I submitte to your censure: and will onlie say, that if you conceeve otherwise of mee, than as a lover of and pursuer after truth; you thinke amisse. For those passages, at which you seeme to take offense; and of which you make particular application to your self; I can assure you, that the sense and intention of my mind was innocent and harmless: and I am sure, nothing passed my penne; which signifies, in my sense, dis-respect toward you; or under-valuing your judgement. Some wordes you repete, were primarilie your own; what I said in the præface, I alledged as a principle for *my* action; other things reflected not upon you, as you seeme to express: least of all, ought you to have recalled a worde; blotted-out, before itt passed my handes; and a better putt into itt's roome. Had I not highlie valued your person, and cordiallie affected to have given you satisfaction; I had not alienated myself and time from other occasions; which, being then a publique person,[1] I cou'd verie hardlie do. And coulde I, syllabicallie and to a tittle, have said as you said, *non reclamantibus judicio et conscientia*; I was under a temptation to

do itt, through the respect and honour I bear to your person; and a desire in mee, to keepe all fair. Sir, wherein I fall short of your expectation, I fail for truth's sake; wherto alone I acknowledge my self addicted. So justifying nothing, contrarie to my due respect to your person, whom I honour and shall most readilie serve, I take leave; and rest,
    Sir,

*Your's in all Observance,*
*BENJAMIN WHICHCOTE.*

*Cambridge*: Novem. 3, 1651.

# Notes

1. SS: "Vice-chancellor of the University; which office he had laid-down, the morning this letter was written" (133 n).

# Bibliography

apRoberts, Ruth. "Arnold and the Cambridge Platonists." *CLIO* 17 (1988): 139-50.
Arnold, Matthew. "A Psychological Parallel," in *The Complete Prose Works of Matthew Arnold*. Ed. R. H. Super. 11 vols. Ann Arbor: The University of Michigan Press, 1960-1977. 8:111-47.
Blunt, John H., ed. *A Dictionary of Sects, Heresies, Ecclesiastical Parties and Schools of Religious Thought*. London: Rivingtons, 1874.
Brinkley, Roberta Florence. *Coleridge on the Seventeenth Century*. New York: Duke University Press, 1955.
Bunyon, John. *The Pilgrim's Progress*. 1678. Ed. Roger Sharrock. New York: Penguin Classics, 1986.
Burnet, Thomas, ed. *Bishop Burnet's History of His Own Time: From the Restoration of King Charles II to the Conclusion of the Treaty of Peace at Utrecht, in the Reign of Queen Anne*. Ed. 4 vols. London: Samuel Bagster, 1815.
Calvin, John. *Institutes of the Christian Religion; 1536 Edition*. Trans. Ford Lewis Battles. Grand Rapids: William B. Eerdman's Publishing Co., 1986.
Campagnac, E. T., ed. *The Cambridge Platonists: Being Selections from the Writings of Benjamin Whichcote, John Smith, and Nathaniel Culverwell*. Oxford: Clarendon Press, 1901.
Cassirer, Ernst. *The Platonic Renaissance in England*. Trans. James P. Pettegrove. Austin: University of Texas Press, 1953.
Coleridge, Samuel Taylor. *Biographia Literaria; Or, Biographical Sketches of My Literary Life and Opinions*. 2 vols. Ed. James Engell and W. Jackson Bate. Vol. 7 in *The Collected Works of Samuel Taylor Coleridge*. Princeton: Princeton University Press, 1983.
Cragg, Gerald R., ed. *The Cambridge Platonists*. New York: Oxford University Press, 1968.
Cross, F. L., and E. A. Livingston, eds. *The Oxford Dictionary of the Christian Church*. 2nd ed. New York: Oxford University Press, 1974.
Cudworth, Ralph. *A Sermon Preached to the Honourable Society of Lincolnes-Inne*. London: Printed by J. Fletcher for R. Royston, 1664.
—. *A Sermon Preached before the Honourable House of Commons at Westminster, March 31, 1647*. Cambridge: Printed by Roger Daniel, 1647.
—. *A Treatise Concerning Eternal and Immutable Morality* with *A Treatise of Freewill*. Ed. Sarah Hutton. Cambridge: Cambridge University Press, 1996.
—. *The True Intellectual System of the Universe*. 2 vols. 1678. Facsimile ed. New York: Garland Publishing, 1978.
Culverwell, Nathaniel. *An Elegant and Learned Discourse of the Light of Nature*. 1646. Ed. Robert A. Greene and Hugh MacCalium. Toronto: University of Toronto Press, 1971.
De Pauley, William Cecil. *The Candle of the Lord: Studies in the Cambridge Platonists*. London: SPCK, 1937.

Dryden, John. Dedication to *Virgil's Aeneid*. Harvard Classics. Ed. Charles W. Eliot. Danbury, Conn.: Grolier Press, 1909.

Eadmer. *The Life of St. Anselm, Archbishop of Canterbury*. Trans. R. W. Southern. Oxford: Clarendon Press, 1962.

*Fox's Book of Martyrs*. 1554. Ed. William Byron Forbush. Grand Rapids: Zondervan Publishing House, 1967.

Fuller, Thomas. *The History of the University of Cambridge, from the Conquest to the Year 1634*. 1655. Ed. Marmaduke Prickett and Thomas Wright. Cambridge: Cambridge University Press, 1840.

George, Edward Augustus. *Seventeenth Century Men of Latitude: Forerunners of the New Theology*. New York: Charles Scribner's Sons, 1908.

Glanvill, Joseph. *Essays on Several Important Subjects in Philosophy and Religion*. 1676. Facsimile ed. Stuttgart-Bad Cannstatt: Friedrich Frommann Verlag, 1970.

—. *Scepsis Scientifica: Or, Confest Ignorance, the Way to Science; in an Essay on the Vanity of Dogmatizing, and Confident Opinion*. 1665. Facsimile ed. New York: Garland Publishing, 1978.

—. *The Vanity of Dogmatizing: Or, Confidence in Opinions; Manifested in a Discourse of the Shortness and Uncertainty of Our Knowledge, and Its Causes*. 1661. Facsimile ed. New York: Columbia University Press, 1931.

Green, V. H. H. *Religion at Oxford and Cambridge*. London: SCM Press, 1964.

Hall, Joseph. *Christ Mystical: Or, the Blessed Union of Christ and His Members*. Ed. H. Carruthers Wilson. London: Hodder and Stoughton, 1908.

Hooker, Richard. *Of the Laws of Ecclesiastical Polity*. 1593-1662. Rpt. in *The Works of That Learned and Judicious Divine Mr. Richard Hooker*. Ed. John Keeble, 7th ed. Rev. R. W. Church and F. Paget. 3 vols. Oxford: Clarendon Press, 1888.

Hunt, John. *Religious Thought in England, from the Restoration to the End of the Last Century*. 3 vols. London: Strahan and Co., 1870.

Hutton, William Holden. *The English Church, from the Accession of Charles I to the Death of Anne (1625-1714)*. London: Macmillan and Co., 1903.

Inge, W. R. *The Platonic Tradition in English Religious Thought*. London: Longmans, Green, and Co., 1926.

Lewis, C. S. *The Abolition of Man*. New York: Macmillan, 1947.

—. *Studies in Medieval and Renaissance Literature*. New York: Cambridge University Press, 1966.

Lichtenstein, Aharon. *Henry More: The Rational Theology of a Cambridge Platonist*. Cambridge, Mass.: Harvard University Press, 1962.

Martineau, James. *Types of Ethical Theory*. 2 vols. 3rd ed. Oxford: Clarendon Press, 1901.

Maurice, Frederick Denison. *Moral and Metaphysical Philosophy*. 2 vols. London: Macmillan and Co., 1886.

—. *Theological Essays*. 1853. New York: Harper and Brothers, 1957.

More, Henry. *An Antidote Against Atheism; Or, An Appeal to the Naturall Faculties of the Minde of Man*. 1655. Facsimile ed. Bristol: Thoemmes Press, 1997.

—. *The Complete Poems*. Ed. Alexander B. Grosart. Edinburgh: Edinburgh University Press, 1878.

—. *Enchiridion Ethicum*. 1690. Facsimile ed. New York: Facsimile Text Society, 1930.

—. *Enthusiasmus Triumphatus, or a Discourse of the Nature, Causes, Kinds, and Cure of Enthusiasme*. 1662. Los Angeles: The Augustan Reprint Society, 1966.

—. *An Explanation of the Grand Mystery of Godliness*. London: Printed by J. Flesher, 1660.
Nadler, Steven. *Spinoza: A Life*. Cambridge: Cambridge University Press, 1999.
Nicolson, Marjorie Hope. *Conway Letters: The Correspondence of Anne, Viscountess Conway, Henry More, and Their Friends, 1642-1684*. New Haven: Yale University Press, 1930.
Ollard, S. L., ed. *A Dictionary of English Church History*. 2nd ed. London: A. R. Mowbray and Co., 1919.
Passmore, J. A. *Ralph Cudworth: An Interpretation*. London: Cambridge University Press, 1951.
Patrides, C. A., ed. *The Cambridge Platonists*. The Stratford-upon-Avon Library. Vol. 5. London: Edward Arnold, 1969.
Pawson, G. P. H. *The Cambridge Platonists and Their Place in Religious Thought*. London: SPCK, 1930.
Plotinus. *The Enneads*. Trans. Stephen MacKenna. Burdett, NY: Larson Publications, 1992.
Powicke, Frederick J. *The Cambridge Platonists: A Study*. Cambridge, Mass.: Harvard University Press, 1926.
Rogers, G. A. J., J. M. Vienne, and Y. C. Zarka, eds. *The Cambridge Platonists in Philosophical Context: Politics, Metaphysics, and Religion*. Boston: Kluwer Academic Publishers, 1997.
Roth, Cecil. *A Short History of the Jewish People*. Illustrated ed. London: East and West Library, 1959.
Salter, Samuel, ed. *Eight Letters of Dr. Antony Tuckney and Dr. Benjamin Whichcote*. Appended to the *Moral and Religious Aphorisms* by Benjamin Whichcote. London: Printed for J. Payne, 1753.
Shaftesbury, Anthony Ashley Cooper, 7th Earl of. *Characteristics of Men, Manners, Opinions, Times*. 1711. Ed. Lawrence E. Klein. New York: Cambridge University Press, 1999.
Smith, H. Maynard. *Pre-Reformation England*. London: Macmillan & Co., 1963.
Smith, John. *Select Discourses*. 1660. Facsimile ed. Delmar, NY: Scholar's Facsimiles and Reprints, 1979.
Smith, William, and Henry Wace. *A Dictionary of Christian Biography, Literature, Sects, and Doctrines*. 4 vols. London: John Murray, 1877.
Stokes, H. P. *A Short History of the Jews in England*. London: SPCK, 1921.
Strauss, Leo. *Spinoza's Critique of Religion*. 1930. Trans. E. M. Sinclair. New York: Schocken, 1965.
Swift, Jonathan. *Gulliver's Travels*. 1726. New York: Penguin Classics, 1985.
Taylor, Jeremy. *A Discourse on the Liberty of Prophesying*. 1647. Facsimile ed. Menston, Yorkshire: Scolar Press, 1971.
*Theologia Germanica*. Trans. Susanna Winkworth. 2nd ed. London: Longman, Brown, Green, and Longmans, 1854.
Tillotson, John. *A Sermon Preached at the Funeral of the Reverend Benjamin Whichcot, D.D., and Minister of S. Lawrence Jewry, London, May 24th, 1683*. London: Printed by M. Flesher for Brabazon Aylmer, 1683.
Tulloch, John. *English Puritanism and Its Leaders*. London: William Blackwood and Sons, 1861.
—. *Rational Theology and Christian Philosophy in England in the 17th Century*. 2nd ed. 2 vols. Edinburgh: William Blackwood and Sons, 1874.

Walton, Izaak. "The Life of Mr. Richard Hooker: The Author of Those Learned Books of the Laws of Ecclesiastical Polity." 1665. Rpt. in *The Lives of Dr. John Donne, Sir Henry Wotton, Mr. Richard Hooker, Mr. George Herbert, and Dr. Robert Sanderson.* London: Henry Washbourne, 1840. 161-254.

Whichcote, Benjamin. *Moral and Religious Aphorisms.* Ed. Samuel Salter. 1753. Rpt. with an Introduction by W. R. Inge. London: Matthews & Marrot, 1930.

—. *Several Discourses, Concerning the Shortness of Humane Charity, and the Perfection of the Mercy of God, by the Reverend and Learned Benjamin Whichcote.* 3 vols. Ed. John Jeffery. London: Printed for J. Knapton, 1702-1707.

—. *Select Sermons of Dr. Whichcot; in Two Parts.* Ed. Shaftesbury. 1698. Rpt. with a new Preface by William Wishart. 1742. Facsimile ed. Delmar, NY: Scholar's Facsimiles and Reprints, 1977.

—. *Some Select Notions.* 1685. Facsimile ed. Menston, Yorkshire: Scolar Press, 1971.

Willey, Basil. *The English Moralists.* London: Methuen and Co., 1965.

—. *The Seventeenth-Century Background: Studies in the Thought of the Age in Relation to Poetry and Religion.* New York: Columbia University Press, 1967.

# Index

Albigenses, 145, 151n. 27
Anselm, St., 33
Aquinas, St. Thomas, 128
Arius, 121, 130n. 17
Arminianism, 8-10, 15, 17, 87-8, 89, 95n. 28, 104, 105, 121, 123-24
Arminius, Jacobus, 121, 130-31n. 18
Arnold, Matthew, 18, 31, 50n. 150
Arrowsmith, John, 16, 56, 58, 60, 61, 64-5, 75, 131n. 19
Augustine, St., 9, 85, 98, 107-08, 118

Bacon, Francis, 7, 8, 19, 83, 94n. 1
Barrow, Isaac, 62
Baynes, Paul, 65, 92, 95n. 26
Bellarmine, St., 121, 130n. 18
Bergson, Henri, 38
Bernard, St., 122
Beza, Theodore, 104, 111-12n. 20, 119
Biel, Gabriel, 121, 131n. 20
Bischop, Simon. *See* Episcopius
Bonaventure, St., 98, 116, 121
Boyle, Robert, 28
Broad Church, 40-1
Brownrig, Ralph, 44n. 27
Brutus, Junius, 89, 95n. 21
Bunyan, John, 37-8
Burnet, Gilbert, 3, 13
Butler, Joseph, 40

Calamy, Edmund, 59, 67n. 6
Calvin, John, 4, 9, 21, 100, 104, 110n. 7, 133
Calvinism, 23, 38, 48n. 97
Cartwright, Thomas, 5-6, 7
Cassirer, Ernst, 20, 32
Chaderton, Laurence, 9, 18
Charles I, 9-10
Chillingworth, William, 121, 131n. 21

Coleridge, Samuel Taylor, 18, 29, 40, 48n. 97
Colet, John, 3-4
Collins, Samuel, 15-16, 60, 61, 62, 64
Conway, Anne, 18
Cooper, Anthony Ashley. *See* Shaftesbury
Cotton, John, 55, 63, 66n. 2
Coverdale, Miles, 5
Cradock, Samuel, 60, 67n. 7, 71, 73n. 1
Cromwell, Oliver, 10-11, 16, 48n. 100
Cudworth, Ralph, 17, 18, 19, 20-3, 38-9, 46n. 62, 50n. 147, 61, 68n. 13
Culverwell, Nathaniel, 18-19, 20, 33-5, 49n. 134

Davenant, John, 119, 130n. 9, 132n. 30
Descartes, René, 8, 18, 19, 22, 35, 38, 45n. 49
Dillingham, William, 19, 33, 58, 65
Dort, Synod of, 8, 21, 95n. 20, 131n. 23, 132n. 30
Dryden, John, 38

Elizabeth I, 9
Episcopius, 8, 89, 95n. 20, 121, 130-31n. 18
Erasmus, 3-4, 25, 29, 43n. 1, 43n. 4, 154n. 2

Ferinus. *See* Serinus
Ficino, Marsilio, 4
Field, Richard, 92, 95n. 28, 104
Fisher, John, 3, 4, 43n. 1
Fleetwood, James, 62
Fowler, Edward, 37-8
Francis, St., 121, 130n. 18
Fuller, Thomas, 17, 62

Gale, Theophilus, 31
Glanvill, Joseph, 22, 35, 49n. 116

Goodwin, John, 63, 64, 87-8, 94n. 10
Grocyn, William, 3
Grotius, Hugo, 127, 132n. 38
Gulliver, Lemuel, 38

Hales, Alexander, 131n. 19
Hales, John, 8-9
Hall, Joseph, 21, 132n. 30
Hammond, Henry, 92, 95n. 28, 104
Hampden, Renn Dickson, 40
Hazlitt, William, 19
Herbert, Edward, 39
Hill, Thomas, 15, 59, 61, 63, 64, 75
Hobbes, Thomas, 19, 26-7
Holdesworth, Richard, 10, 15, 16, 44n. 27, 56, 131n. 30
Hooker, Richard, 5-7, 12, 121
Horace, 54, 149, 153

How(e), John, 56
Humanism, 7-8
Inge, William R., 30

Jackson, Thomas, 92, 95n. 28, 104
James I, 8, 9
Jansen, Otto, 44n. 23
Jeffery, John, 62-3, 65, 69n. 16, 94n. 8
Jewel, John, 5
Jews in England, 11, 27, 44n. 29, 48n. 100

Kant, Immanuel, 17
Knox, John, 5

Laud, William, 9-10, 11, 67n. 8
Lightfoot, John, 61, 64
Linacre, Thomas, 3
Locke, John, 17, 39-40
Loyola, St. Ignatius, 121, 130n. 18
Luther, Martin, 4

Marlowe, Christopher, 7, 32-3
Maurice, Frederick Denison, 18, 32, 49n. 118
Mildmay, Walter, 9
Milton, John, 8, 10-11, 32, 59
More, Henry, 9, 17-18, 19, 20-33, 38

Norris, John, 35
Novatus, 121, 130n. 17

Oldenburg, Heinrich, 28
Origen, 4, 24
Osiander, Andreas, 122, 131n. 23

Patrick, Simon, 17
Perkins, William, 100, 104, 110n. 7, 133
Persius, 112n. 22, 132n. 32
Piscator, Johann, 84, 94n. 4
Plotinus, 4, 18, 22, 23-5, 92-3
Preston, John, 9

Quakers, 11, 44n. 30

Royal Society, 28, 63

Salvian, 127, 132n. 36
Sandcroft, William, 9, 15
Sandys, Edwin, 5
Schopenhauer, Arthur, 33
Scultetus, Abraham, 122, 131n. 23
Serinus, 90n. 23
Shaftesbury, 7th Earl of, 16, 40, 50n. 142, 63
Smith, John, 17, 18, 20-33
Spenser, Edmund, 4-5, 43n. 5
Spinoza, Baruch, 26-8, 31, 48n. 97, 48n. 102
Sterry, Peter, 16
Suarez, Francisco de, 34, 121, 131n. 20

Tauler, Johann, 24
Taylor, Jeremy, 11-12, 120
Tertullian, 127, 132n. 37
*Theologia Germanica*, 47n. 86
Tillotson, John, 60, 61, 62
Tindal, Matthew, 39-40
Toland, John, 39
Travers, Walter, 5-6, 7
Tschirnhaus, Ehrenfried Walther von, 28
Tuckney, Antony, 10, 15-16, 19, 20-1, 40, 55-9, 111n. 10
Tulloch, 40, 50n. 150

Vasquez, Gabriel, 121, 131n. 20

Waldenses, 145, 151n. 27
Wallis, John, 60, 67n. 7
Walton, Izaac, 5
Ward, Samuel, 106, 125, 131-32n. 30
Westminster Confession and National Covenant, 10, 16, 59, 120
Whichcote, Benjamin, 12, 15-17, 19, 20-33, 59-63, 67-8n. 11, 68-9n. 13
Whitgift, John, 5, 7
Williams, John, 55, 60, 67n. 8
Wordsworth, William, 29-30
Worthington, John, 17, 60, 67n. 7

# About the Author

Tod E. Jones teaches at the University of Maryland, College Park (UMCP), where he is appointed as adjunct faculty in the Department of English and as a special lecturer for User Education Services in the university libraries. His academic interests are in British literature and Anglican theology. He is the author of *The Broad Church: A Biography of a Movement*, published by Lexington in 2003, and articles published in *The Victorian Newsletter*. He holds a PhD in English from UMCP, an MA in English from San Diego State University, and a BA in Biblical Studies from Harding University, Arkansas.